DATE DUE			

EMANUEL FEUERMANN, VIRTUOSO

OTHER BOOKS BY SEYMOUR W. ITZKOFF

EMANUEL FEUERMANN, VIRTUOSO

A BIOGRAPHY

by

SEYMOUR W. ITZKOFF

with

NOTES ON INTERPRETATION

by Emanuel Feuermann

and

A DISCOGRAPHY OF FEUERMANN RECORDINGS

by Fred Calland and Seymour W. Itzkoff

The University of Alabama Press
University, Alabama

For Julie and Gerry

Library of Congress Cataloging in Publication Data

Itzkoff, Seymour W
  Emanuel Feuermann, virtuoso.

  Discography: p.
  Includes index.
  1. Feuermann, Emanuel, 1902-1942. 2. Violinists,
violoncellists, etc.—Biography.
ML418.F4919   787'.3'0924 ₍B₎   78-11827
ISBN 0-8173-6450-1

CONTENTS

ILLUSTRATIONS

PREFACE

Above all others, Emanuel Feuermann admired Fritz Kreisler, Pablo Casals, and Jascha Heifetz. These were his models, his ideals, and his rivals. The first two were of an earlier generation. In a sense, they opened the road to the contemporary standard of string playing. But it was Jascha Heifetz who, Feuermann felt, personified the contemporary art of the violin. And it was this violinist's position in the musical world that Feuermann attempted to reach by exploiting the possibilities of this still-laggard concert instrument, the violoncello.

It is fair to say that if Heifetz had a rival in the person of that mythic nineteenth-century figure, Nicolo Paganini, there is no one who can stand close to what Feuermann achieved for the violoncello in the few years of his life. Casals was Feuermann's inspiration in the sense that the great Catalonian liberated the cello as a truly expressive musical vehicle. He placed the cello before the public. But just as Emanuel Feuermann's violinist brother Sigmund was his first goad, to be equaled and superseded, it was a series of great violin virtuosi—Kreisler, Elman, Wolfsthal, and finally Heifetz—who challenged Feuermann to recreate the nature of cello playing. That standard has not been equaled since, and it has only rarely been approached.

Many will attest to this claim through having been witness to Feuermann's living art. Others, like myself, who unfortunately were too young to have heard him—he died in 1942 at age thirty-nine—can infer it only from the evidence of his few recordings. The musical world was robbed of his maturity. We must remember that when Casals made *his* first recordings in 1916—salon pieces—he was also thirty-nine.

That we are beginning to look more closely at our musical traditions is due, I believe, to our sudden realization that smug assumptions about the progress or evolution of our cultural lives can no longer be maintained. The almost careless spontaneity of discovery in musical creativity, whether in composition or performance, has well nigh disappeared. How different from today was that memorable Sunday in 1919 when over nine thousand people, mostly working class, turned out to hear two violin concerts. The first was by the young Jascha Heifetz in Carnegie Hall. Later that evening, a joint recital by Mischa Elman and Eugene Ysaÿe crowded them in at the Hippodrome. And there were droves of other virtuosi, too. A few years later, the public could hear great cellists—Casals, Piatigorsky, Feuermann. How different the musical scene is today. One hesitates to describe this difference. Listening to the old hands, one knows that the changes are substantial. Thus, we must remember and attempt to recreate this era, at least in words.

Several books have been written about Casals. Piatigorsky produced an engaging autobiography. This book is an attempt to fill the most serious gap, a biography of the greatest cellist of them all.

It has not been a difficult task to find those who feel as I do and to enlist their aid in gathering the necessary material for the biography. This assistance is reflected on every page of the book. Perhaps it was the special character of Feuermann's personality that elicited infectious enthusiasm. I hope that some of his natural charm—his teacher, Julius Klengel, called him that "divinely favored artist and lovable young man"—is reflected in this story of his life. But there was a deeply serious side to Feuermann, often hidden, a dedication to his art, that he did not want the outside world to notice. If he finally gave in to certain "show biz" aspects of his career, he did it reluctantly. Beyond that, he did not want that other world, which he struggled so hard to master, to become a matter for public discourse or, heaven forbid, part of a cult of admiration.

I can mention only a few of the many who have contributed to this book, those who have made major contributions or who have extended unique courtesies for which I am indebted. One cannot overestimate the help of the two who were closest to Feuermann—Eva Feuermann Lehnsen, his widow, and Sophie Feuermann Brown, his youngest sister. His students, Claus Adam, for many years with the Juilliard Quartet, and Mosa Havivi, now a respected authority and dealer in string instruments, have given generously of their knowledge and time.

Olga Heifetz, Hans Lehnsen, the National Orchestral Association for releasing to me the as-yet-unpublished Feuermann performance tapes, Al Hulsen, formerly of WFCR, Amherst, Massachusetts, who started it all with a series of broadcasts on Feuermann that won for us an Armstrong FM Award, Fred Calland, now music director of the Public Broadcasting Service, Washington, D.C., for his important work on the discography— all deserve great thanks for their various forms of assistance. Overseas, Michael Taube and Adolph Hoenigsberg in Israel and Jane Cowan and Nanie Jamieson in England extended special courtesies and information that were extremely helpful.

Finally, I want to thank my own authority on things violinistic, my wife Pat, for her critical commitment to the project. This book is for my daughter and son, Julie and Gerry, now violinists themselves. They have taught me much about the process of learning to play a stringed instrument, knowledge I could not have gained merely by remembering my own travail with the cello. To The University of Alabama Press, John P. Defant, and James Travis, a grateful word for the sponsorship of the project.

Northampton, Massachusetts   S. W. ITZKOFF

EMANUEL FEUERMANN,
VIRTUOSO

Virtuoso should be a title of honor . . . . . the greatest ability, respect for a piece of art and the ability to fit one's personality to the art work. . . . I believe that even among the greatest names on the stage, only a few deserve it.   —Emanuel Feuermann, 1942

1

GALICIAN ORIGINS

Kolomea

Only a few decades before the events of our story, the railroad came to Kolomea. As planned by the entrepreneurs and officials who sponsored the railway line, the roadbed leading to the depot in the center of the town would pass directly through the Jewish section of the city. The Jews were naturally incensed, but relatively powerless in the matter. After all was said and done, it was a small price to pay for progress.

At the gala inaugural, by which time all remembrance of torn-up homes and displaced families had presumably disappeared, it seemed as if the entire town had gathered. The first distant echoes of the train whistle touched off great excitement. And when the great black iron engine first came into view, huffing and puffing, a chorus of exclamations and cheers issued from the platforms. The two main sponsors and planners of the project, gentlemen of dubious honor whose names have unfortunately been lost, were beside themselves with enthusiasm. They jumped down upon the tracks waving and gesticulating as if to urge the engineer on to the culmination of this historic trip.

It is difficult to know for sure whether the cause was confusion on the part of the engineer, what with all the waving and cheering, error due to inexperience, or indeed a malfunction of this malevolent industrial monster, but instead of slowing to a halt, the engine lurched forward and, alas, both gentlemen became victims of their own enterprise.

The grisly retribution exemplified in this story goes a long way towards illustrating the social and psychological milieu of the Jews of the extreme eastern part of the Austro-Hungarian Empire at the close of the nineteenth century. Slowly but surely, the modern world was infiltrating its influence, and new sets of values and expectations were quietly transforming the attitudes of the Jews. The world was indeed in motion; and, for those with the initiative and alertness to seize opportunity, wider horizons were visible and even attainable.

Kolomea was a moderately prosperous trading town, the business center of a large farming area. It was then in the first stages of a modest industrialization, which even included the production of oil. It had 35,000 people, of whom half were Jews. The average Jew would probably have been surprised to learn that Jews made up only half the town. To him, Kolomea was ostensibly a Jewish city, run by a small Gentile colonial elite that represented the great power center far to the west, in Vienna.

Here, on November 22, 1902, Emanuel Feuermann was born, the third child and second son of Rachel (Regina) and Maier (Max) Feuermann. The Feuermanns were one of the musical families of the town and thus the *bris* (circumcision) of Emanuel was the occasion for a celebration attended by the local musical dignitaries. Unfortunately Maier was away with a touring orchestra at the time. However, the venerable Hersch Schechter stood in for him at the ceremony, assisted by the leader of the Judische Musikrat (Jewish musicians association), David Hersch, who predicted a bright musical future for the boy. And when Machty Kleinman, the ever-reliable midwife, held the cradle up so that all could toast the infant with whisky and sponge cake, a murmur of pleasure went through the group. Not only had it been an easier birth for Rachel than Sigmund's, two years earlier, but Munio, as they already called him, was obviously a stronger, more vigorous infant.

Emanuel Feuermann was born into a family with good prospects. In their five years of marriage, the Feuermanns had been blessed with three children (a girl, Gusta, was their first-born), and they had recently purchased a fairly large house from a relative of Maier's who had emigrated to the United States. At the age of 31, Maier was already a highly successful musician of the town, as a performer on the violin and cello, as conductor, and increasingly as one of the best teachers in a music-hungry city. Even the Hoenigsbergs, the musical patricians of Kolomea, who at the time Maier was first wooing their Rachel saw him as a musical upstart with a questionable future, given his completely unaided and independent efforts, had to stand back and admire Maier. His enormous drive and constant hustle to improve himself and his lot had surprised and won universal respect. From a self-centered and vain adolescent, casual about all things educational, musical, or economic, he had matured into a person from whom big things could be expected.

To understand the Feuermanns, the Hoenigsbergs, indeed the entire burst of Jewish musical achievement of this era, one must consider the historical and geographical context. Kolomea was founded on the desolate eastern plain of Galicia by the Polish nobility sometime in the early thirteenth century. It is located on the Pruth River north of the Carpathian Mountains. Yet despite its relatively southern situation in Poland, it is subject to cruel Siberian winds from the east and north, without the mitigating southerlies that dump their moisture on the lovely slopes to the south.

Kolomea probably figured in the late sixteenth- and early seventeenth-century campaigns against the Austrians, Turks, and Cossacks by Poland's most famous warrior, Zolkiew, himself a Ukrainian turned Galician. Close by Kolomea, in Czernelica, a little village on the Dniester, stands a fortified castle built by a later Polish ruler, Jan III (Sobieski), for his own use as part of his erratically successful military career, which he spent mainly waging war against the Turks. In a uniquely fortuitous moment this great Pole turned back the Turk, Kara Mustafa, at the gates of Vienna in 1683, a victory decisive in gaining for him the fame of an immortal.

There is a most-cherished synagogue in Kolomea that was supposedly erected by Sobieski for the Jews of the town to honor his Jewish lieutenant, Jan Samuel Chryanowski. In 1675, at nearby Tremboula, Chryanowski, with only a small Polish force, is said to have held off a massive Turkish army for eleven days, as he waited for the tardy Sobieski to relieve him. The ensuing victory marked an important political turn in Sobieski's career, as one more disaster could have been too much for the Polish nobility to tolerate.

The Jews had arrived in Kolomea from the west, fleeing persecutions and crusades in Germany, not too long after the Poles had settled there. It was a primitive land, polarized between nobility and serf. The Jews were welcomed by the feudal lords because they performed a useful function. Excluded from political power, agriculture, and many craft guilds, they were restricted to money-handling, trade, and scholarly functions, activities too demeaning for the Polish nobility. In time, taxation from the Jews provided an important economic resource for the central authorities. They were a disdained but essential minority.

Too busy with the pomp and ritual of war, status, and land, and concerned with enforcing the feudal yoke on the peasantry, the nobility allowed the Jews to develop their own independent communal structure. Eventually Jewish life became a world within a world. Communities from all parts of Poland were welded together as interdependent *Kahals* that saw to their corporate and individual needs and represented to the Polish aristocracy the rights and responsibilities of all members of the faith.

The Jews flourished far more than just economically and politically. For reasons not known, the Galician Jews, more so than Jews in other parts of Poland, developed an especially rich Talmudic tradition of scholarship, and also supported numerous synagogue musical forms. In later years the Galician Jews of Vienna formed the mainstay of the Jewish religious scholars in the Austrian Empire.

Kolomea entered into Austrian hegemony and history in 1772 when Poland was conquered and subsequently divided by Frederick of Prussia, Catherine of Russia, and Marie Thérèse of the Hapsburgs. With this partition and the active anti-Semitism of Marie Thérèse, the *Kahals* were dissolved. While the Jews of Russian Poland made their way east to new and, they hoped, greater opportunities, the Galicians suffered the vagaries of this female autocrat, as well as those of her somewhat more merciful son Joseph.

Nevertheless, the horizons of these Jews were altered. Inevitably they were being influenced by their new national destiny so that instead of to Lwow (Lemberg) or Wrclow (Cracow) their eyes and ears were focused further to the west, to Budapest, Prague, and, most important, Vienna. Long immersed in a babble of Polish, Russian, Ruthenian (Ukrainian), and even Moldavian, they now listened, in addition, to Hungarian and the western Slavic tongues (Slovakian and Bohemian). But it was German that had its greatest impact. It was more than its closeness to their own Yiddish. German represented to them a new and greater source of power and culture than they had confronted before. The Jews now turned with eager anticipation to the west.

At first they were rigidly forbidden to enter the larger cities; in Vienna the strictures were especially severe. But with the revolutions of 1848 and the accession of the beloved Franz Joseph, a new era was inaugurated for Jews. They began to take advantage of a variety of newly granted civil liberties and political, educational, and economic rights. In increasing waves they began to pour out of the villages and the ghettos of the towns towards the large cities. Even in Kolomea a new tenor to life was noticeable. Their first efforts were aimed at improving their economic state. Jews moved into enterprises and trades that had been denied them and then, tentatively at first, began to exercise some political influence. True, they may have been daunted in the full exercise of their freedom by the persuasiveness of modernity, as illustrated in the railroad incident. But gradually, and in a restrained and apologetic manner, they moved to secure at least a modest measure of protection and self-determination.

A story that the Jews tell about themselves exemplifies their attitudes in this regard. They had strong desires to participate in the modernization that was infiltrating their town. One thing of particular moment was the state of the main thoroughfare in their section of Kolomea. It was alternately a choking and rutted Sahara or a mud-splattered swamp. In short, it was a disgrace and embarrassment. Officialdom finally conceded, after some pressure, that the street was a danger as well as an eyesore. In time the work crews arrived and began to excavate, preparatory to paving. When they had penetrated about a foot below the muddy surface, they discovered (to the chagrin of the Jewish officials) the original medieval paving blocks, about which all had long been forgotten. This last event was supposed to have taken place about the time of Maier Feuermann's birth in 1871.

The years of widening horizons affected the Feuermann family. His father died when Maier was thirteen and left two younger sisters, himself, and his mother. They were left with almost nothing, and, although there was some help from relatives, it soon became necessary for Maier to contribute to the family income. Heretofore Maier had enjoyed the pampered status of eldest son. Now he was expected to assume an entirely unfamiliar role.

His father, who had learned to play the violin for his own amusement, had given Maier some lessons, but Maier was a reluctant student. His association with the Hoenigsberg family provided a wholly new context of musical experience. It was impossible to resist picking up an instrument to practice in their home, for it was all they did. And such a variety of instruments to sample and experiment with! With this kind of motivation Maier was soon capable of playing with the Hoenigsbergs at the various celebrations and affairs for which they were hired to provide the music.

This new environment was intoxicating to Maier. The Hoenigsbergs had been musicians in Kolomea for generations. They breathed music. As Maier chummed around with Shmuel (Samuel) Hoenigsberg, he became absorbed in their self-confident commitment to this way of life. Slowly but inevitably Maier's avocation was transformed into his vocation.

Only in Mendel Hoenigsberg's own lifetime (Mendel was the father of Rachel and Shmuel) had the Jewish musicians of Kolomea begun to move out of the world of the synagogue and from the various ceremonials and *simchas* (celebrations) of Jewish musical life. The Gentile tradition of serious music by contrast was international in nature and infinitely rich in its formal structure. It was as intellectually exciting as it was emotionally satisfying. Once released from the fetters of ghetto life, these musicians plunged into the study of this music with an innocence and enthusiasm that was total. No longer were they *proste klesmers* (common minstrels); rather they were professionals with an artistic obligation that transcended Galicia. Yet they would never deny themselves the opportunity to play at a wedding or a *bar mitzvah*. As the railroad brought a variety of musical ensembles, soloists, opera, and operetta, the vision of new economic and social opportunities widened. Finally, the union of the modern world of culture and the traditions of Galician Talmudic scholarship found a focus in these Jews' own evolving sense of vocation.

After dabbling awhile on various instruments, Maier soon began to concentrate on the violin, on which he had continued to improve, and the cello, for which he felt there was a definite lack of competition. And as he passed into his late teens, he practiced with increasing diligence on both of these instruments. The violin and cello were the solo stringed instruments of the orchestra, both crucial to any ensemble and, very important, rarely wanting for prospective students.

Mendel had placed a double bass in Shmuel's hands to fit him to the Hoenigsbergs' orchestral needs. It is interesting to note that even though Shmuel was destined at an earlier age for a musical career than Maier, it was Maier, the interloper, who went further. Shmuel, it is true, was of a more fragile disposition, being asthmatic. On the other hand, he would rear six healthy sons, all to be musicians.

Unfortunately there were inherent limitations in Maier's career. He began to make large forward steps in his technique comparatively late. And even here, out of touch with the centers of violin playing and teaching, it was primarily an intuitive learning, picked up by watching, listening, and asking. The legendary stories of great virtuosi, whether of the violinists Sarasate or Vieuxtemps, or cellists Davidoff or Popper, were not enough to reveal the secrets of virtuosity. It was brute determination that catapulted Maier to the forefront of the musical scene in Kolomea.

By the time Rachel and Maier were married, in 1897, the Hoenigsbergs had long been won over; in fact they were somewhat in awe of this musical intruder. They now predicted that Maier would go far in the profession. He was even known as the *drövganger* (a person of dauntless ambition). He was included in the Sunday morning concerts in town, as violinist or cellist depending on need. On several occasions he had conducted in a commendably competent manner. He had even acted as leader with a small touring group. Maier was yet only 26.

While it was fine to be versatile, Maier perceived that he did not have a broad or deep enough knowledge of orchestral music to look forward to anything more than an occasional provincial or *Kür-Orchester* conductorship. Also, Galicia was full of violinistic talents. He could never compete with some of the wizards he increasingly encountered. Hence he opted to concentrate on the cello, for which the demand, both performing and teaching, was increasing, and the supply scant. He chose well, for in the years 1897 to 1902 the constant need for a cellist as well as cello teacher found Maier Feuermann available and willing.

He was now traveling out of Kolomea into Lemberg and the towns of Bohemia and Moravia. He had toured as far south as Rumania, once to Constantinople. Maier, still young, thought of his career as open-ended and full of possibilities. His versatility and initiative were widely known and admired. He had students for every conceivable instrument—flute, clarinet, mandolin, *etc.*—as well as for violin and cello. He taught them all.

In all things and in all contexts, eventually, potentialities are fulfilled and inherent limitations revealed. Increasingly, after the birth of Emanuel, his absences on tour were accompanied by disruptions in family life, and by interruptions in his teaching program. It was not as physically easy or economically rewarding to tour. Too often they saw the same towns and same hotels. All in all it was less inviting with each new opportunity.

These circumstances eventually forced him to restrict his playing and to concentrate on teaching. In this, as in everything Maier did, circumstance became the means for new opportunity. One day in the spring of 1904, he returned from his teaching rounds and announced to Rachel that he would begin to teach Sigmund, the elder son, now barely three and a half, to play the violin. As testimony to the intention, he removed from a paper bag in his overcoat pocket a tiny violin. With all the music that permeated the household, the child had naturally evinced an interest in music. In imitation of his father, he had often pretended to play the violin or cello, fingering whatever piece of wood or pot was available.

But this was probably not the source of Maier's motivation. He was literally surrounded by the stories of the great violin masters. He knew of the enormous successes of legendary Jewish virtuosi, Hubay (Huber), Auer, Joachim, and Brodsky. Younger artists—Kreisler, Zimbalist, Huberman, and Flesch—also reflected the increasing number of Jews who had penetrated the inner circles of musical life in the cities to the west.

Already Shmuel had begun teaching his two older boys, and Maier's natural sense of competitiveness stimulated him to act, now that he had more time at home. We have the interesting contrast of a sickly Hoenigsberg father teaching his healthy sons at an early age and a strong, vigorous Feuermann attempting to push a weak and sickly child. Sigmund had developed slowly as an infant and at eight months had suffered severe convulsions as well. Yet at age three and a half, Sigmund did not show any significant effects of his slow beginning. He was active and alert. His thin body and pale face set off his large head and bright eyes that bespoke curiosity and intelligence.

Maier had never taught such a young child and thus his first efforts were tentative. The spring and summer were largely devoted to exploring the various approaches of which he had heard in connection with young prodigies. Then suddenly in late summer the child began to react to his father's suggestions. And in an almost preternatural way, as if making up for all the lost days in which he had been forced to stay indoors, Sigmund was anticipating the father's instructions. The left and right hands began to coordinate, his ear could discern intervals, scales were soon clearly recognizable. Here in a child who was obviously not destined to perform heavy physical tasks, the crucial small muscle controls seemed unusually well-developed.

A new excitement overtook the family. Maier's tentativeness was transformed into determination. Even Rachel, who was skeptical at first, became enthusiastic, and was persuaded to overlook Sigmund's delicate health, to see in the violin a therapy for child as well as family. Now expecting her fourth child, she gave over the supervision of Sigmund to Maier, who was committed to exploiting the gratifying talent of this eldest son.

A regimen that was to continue uninterruptedly for over three years soon took shape. Maier had to leave the house early in the morning to do his teaching and rehearsing, often not returning until evening. The child was thus awakened while it was still dark, the kerosene lamps lit (there was no electricity in Kolomea yet) and, wrapped in his wool robe, was given a short but intensive lesson. The mother was shown what had to be accomplished; Maier's injunctions for their fulfillment were strict. Sigmund passed most of each day in this manner. Fortunately he was allowed to practice in a number of short sequences, just to the limit of his physical capacity. Although Sigmund obeyed docilely, he would take every opportunity, with little Munio (Emanuel) at his side, to break away and play with his few toys.

His progress amazed Maier. With each sprint forward, the father became more indefatigable about pursuing his goal. Within two years, when the boy was barely five, Sigmund played his first recital for the friends of the family, including the members of the Judische Musikrat. The recital was modest, a few solo pieces of no exceptional difficulty but well within the boy's technical and physical capacity.

Inexorably the solo repertoire expanded and within the next two years, most of the violin repertoire began to be presented to him. The child had an enormous capacity to absorb both the technique and the musical content. By 1907 two more daughters, Rosa and Sophie, had been added to, and completed, the family. Rachel, so absorbed in family and household chores, had by this time given Maier free rein with Sigmund, even though she sometimes protested that he was pushing the boy too hard. Maier usually replied excitedly that Sigmund was a genius and that he had no other choice.

During this period, Munio was left pretty much to his own devices. His musical education was absorbed as he watched Sigmund practice, his father teach and play, often imitating both of them. Father and Sigmund constituted his sun and moon, he worshiped them silently while yet all-absorbed in being his mother's child. Physically active and ebullient, he was quite a distinct personality. Possibly it was this difference that allowed Maier to ignore him until Munio on his own initiative expressed his readiness.

Noting Munio's perennial playful, even mischievous imitations of his elders, Maier one day (Munio was not quite five) asked him if he would like to play on Sigmund's little violin. Sigmund, now growing rapidly, had graduated to a slightly larger instrument. Maier taught Munio in the same way as Sigmund but not with anything approaching the same zeal. He simply did not have the time or mental energy. And because of Munio's different qualities and apparent lack of concentration, the father assumed that Munio was not ready and left him largely to his own resources. He tended to neglect the systematic élan that informed his teaching of the older boy. Munio was not dismayed, but played on his violin as if it were the greatest of toys, alternating it between his chin and his knees, whatever his mood happened to be.

One day something took place that because of subsequent events remained in the parents' minds. A local minister had procured a small cello
for his child, a boy about Munio's age. He brought instrument and child to
Maier for instruction. For reasons long forgotten now, the cello was left at
the Feuermann house. The moment Munio spotted the little cello, he
became transfixed, he shrieked with delight, grabbed his new toy, and
demanded that Maier teach him to play this instrument. Much as he loved
to imitate his brother on the violin, the prospect of playing the same
instrument as his father was irresistible.

Maier was unusually patient with this enthusiasm, somewhat amused
and flattered, and thus he indulged the boy. He showed him the rudi-
ments, how to hold the instrument and the bow, the new intervals; in
general he treated Munio's initiation in much the same way as Munio had
approached it, as a lark. Though it was a bit large for him, the cello
provided several months of great fun for the boy. Maier unfortunately
took little note of this, as he was having a difficult time keeping up with
Sigmund.

Then, as suddenly as it had come, the cello was gone. Somewhat
reluctantly Munio went back to the violin. It was better than nothing. Both
parents noted that Munio was drawing a better sound from the instrument and had gained not only in facility, but in stamina. But as the boy was
still largely "fooling around," still playing alternately violin (while he was
being taught) or cello, sometimes even guitar, Maier only made a mental
note to work with him more systematically as time allowed.

Music was the boys' entire life during this period (1907–1908). On
occasion they played in the street with other children. More often the
need to keep at least Sigmund at his practicing, together with the problem
of managing five children, forced Rachel to keep them indoors. This was
especially true for Sigmund. He was stronger, yet there was no need to
take chances. One of the more glorious games the boys played when their
mother's attention was elsewhere was "pull the cart." Only the carts were
their violins and the ropes were the strings of their instruments, which
they tied around the violin scrolls. They dragged their instruments un-
ceremoniously along the floor racing and jostling each other as if they had
discovered the greatest contest in the world. The stomping, giggling, and
occasional quarreling would bring the mother running. Violins would be
restrung, music set before the boys and the father would return home to a
vision of two youthful scholars hard at their appointed tasks.

The fall of 1907 marked a turning point in the lives of the Feuermanns.
Sigmund was developing too rapidly even for Maier's encompassing
guidance. The child could manage chords, changes of position and string,
even bowings, which defied Maier's understanding. At times he did not
know which direction to take. He could always teach Sigmund new or
alternate fingerings, perhaps tell him how to interpret musical markings,

but when it came to certain technical matters—for example, a difficult bowing, an awkward combination of double stops, or a complex pizzicato passage—he now had to depend on Sigmund to progress intuitively. The repertoire itself began to reveal difficulties that Maier could not solve. Unfortunately there was no one else in Kolomea to whom Sigmund could be entrusted.

After much consultation with friends, Maier decided to take Sigmund to Lemberg to play for a Professor Wolfsthal, then the leading violin pedagogue of the capital of Galicia. Wolfsthal had gained some additional fame as the father of the young Max Wolfsthal, then gaining a reputation as one of the better young virtuosi in the Empire.

At this time Lemberg had 160,000 people. It was an important rail and transportation center and was rapidly developing an industrial base. Lemberg was a real city with access to cultural affairs throughout the world. Its 50,000 Jews were able to provide for themselves a completely autonomous cultural and religious life; they participated as well in the wider cultural and political endeavors of the community. Yet in spite of Jewish capitalism and a relatively decent standard of living for all, there were limitations even here. Anti-Semitism in these provincial centers was sometimes even more bitter than in either the great metropolis or the small *shtetl*. Also the geographical isolation and the limits of general prosperity usually necessitated that the young go elsewhere to fulfill their ambitions.

There is an element of mystery in this visit to Lemberg. It has been reported that Sigmund performed the Mendelssohn Concerto with Lemberg's excellent symphony orchestra. Certainly by age seven he was capable of playing the concerto. But the story has not been confirmed. Needless to say, Professor Wolfsthal was deeply impressed. He stated that the boy was indeed a *Wunderkind* of the most extraordinary rarity and that Maier Feuermann was responsible for a serious trust. Wolfsthal confided to Feuermann that he had a second great talent here in Lemberg, his youngest son, Joseph, the same age as Sigmund, who possibly was an even greater talent than Max. For now, Wolfsthal would teach him. But later Joseph would be sent elsewhere.

Wolfsthal strongly advised Feuermann to take Sigmund to Vienna. He would love to teach him; perhaps he would become famous because of the child. But Sigmund's talent was truly exceptional and ought to be nurtured at the center of the musical world. In the back of Wolfsthal's mind and certainly in Maier's were thoughts of the immediate economic possibilities for *Wunderkinder,* given special emphasis in Mischa Elman's extravagant debut in Berlin two years earlier. Elman had left Alexander Fiedemann in Odessa (which was larger than Lemberg) to study with Leopold Auer in St. Petersburg, and even this great Russian capital was insufficient for the full revelation of Elman's talent.

The idea of pulling up the family's roots to move to Vienna, however, troubled Maier. They were well-established in Kolomea and what would Maier be in Vienna? Wolfsthal was persuasive. He recommended a Professor Feist, a student of the great Sevčik and one of the finer violin pedagogues of that city. Feist had recently founded a quartet at the Academy of Music, was well-known, and had contacts in the Jewish community that gave him access to philanthropists. Feist would, on Wolfsthal's recommendation, grant an audition and be able to bestow on the child a complete scholarship and support. This would include all his music lessons, a tutor for his regular schooling, and room and board. Placing him with Feist could, Wolfsthal emphasized, cost the Feuermann family nothing and would insure the realization of the boy's talent.

After much hand-wringing in Kolomea, the family decided that Sigmund should be taken to Vienna and placed with Feist, if the latter consented. In the interval, a letter had been received, noting Wolfsthal's letter of recommendation and indicating that Feist would be most happy to audition the young virtuoso. Kolomea was astir at the impending events. Maier was busier than ever. More engagements to play, as well as new students, betokened the increased stature of the Feuermann name. These were a frenetic few months for all. A formal farewell recital in the largest auditorium in town seemed to be the proper way to mark the occasion and Maier was beside himself with excitement as he made the preparations.

It was a gala affair, with the young, imperturbable prodigy outfitted in black velvet jacket and shorts, a large embroidered white lace collar folded about his shoulders. The program was serious, worthy of a Joachim. Maier insisted on this. The boy played, in addition to the Mendelssohn concerto, works by both Corelli and Schubert, and by moderns such as Goldmark, Wieniawski, and Tschaikowsky.

In January of 1908, father and seven-year-old son set off for Vienna. The audition with Professor Feist went as well as Maier could have hoped. Sigmund went through his repertoire fluently. Even the sight reading, which Maier had anticipated, was executed competently. Feist was apparently moved. "The child is obviously talented," he said judiciously, "but of course there is much to be done." He then launched into a long professorial discussion of the various elements of Sigmund's playing in need of correction and improvement. He was just condescending enough to make Maier uncomfortable. Was this their first taste of Viennese *hoch Kultur* and bigotry, to be addressed as if fresh from the provinces? Finally Feist paused and looked at the child, who was poking around in the music-laden shelves, and then at Maier, and in a softer, yet even firmer tone, he concluded, "Mr. Feuermann, we do not want to exploit this child, he is not for the music halls, but for the concert platform. He will need time, much time, but he may be one of our greatest violinists."

Maier was still both puzzled and troubled. This was a new world for him. Could he leave his child here in Vienna? Feist granted Sigmund everything that Wolfstahl said he might do. If he left him, would the family grow apart from the boy? Ought they move to Vienna? He was almost thirty-seven, too old, he thought, to create a new career for himself. He discussed this nightly with the relatives and *landsleute* from Kolomea with whom he was staying. They were firm in their advice that Sigmund be left with Feist and they assured Maier that they would look after him. Reluctantly he agreed and, after several days, kissed and hugged his precious possession goodbye and began the long trip back to Kolomea.

When he arrived it became obvious that this plan would not do. And though the need to resume and regularize their patterns of life took immediate precedence, Rachel had already made up her mind and Maier accepted the inevitable. As the weeks stretched by and spring approached, Maier accommodated himself to the change of plans. He now persuaded himself that teaching in Kolomea had real limitations and that his energies were certainly not being fulfilled in its daily routines. Also, as a performer, he was well aware that he had reached a plateau and that the most he could ever expect was ordinary orchestral engagements. In retrospect, he concluded that the most exciting aspect of his life had been with Sigmund. Sigmund was his creation. He had nurtured the boy from the beginning. All his intellectual energies had gone into this task. It did not matter that it had only occupied him several hours a day. Without the boy, teaching and playing were flat.

The arguments, recriminations, and punishments that visited the Feuermann home could all be traced, Maier realized in his calmer moments, to the emptiness now existing in their home. Rachel's sad and weary expression, even as she nursed tiny Sophie, was an additional indictment and command, to which he finally acceded.

Once the decision had been made, a new enthusiasm overtook the Feuermanns. Possibilities, unlimited now, churned through Maier's imagination. Even the children sensed the change. Munio, now without his brother, had been the most forlorn. He had nagged incessantly and in turn been berated and chastised by his parents. Now when Munio asked about Sigmund and a cello, instead of a scowl from father, he was met with enthusiasm. "Munio," he once cried, "in Vienna you will have a real cello, just like the parson's boy."

Soon letters were being written, and furniture sold. *Mishpoche* (relatives) were constantly on hand; there were tense greetings and tearful farewells. The family would soon be on its way.

Vienna

One thinks of the great wave of immigrants in the late nineteenth century as going westward for opportunity and freedom. Yet we know that from the thirteenth to the nineteenth century the Jews had drifted eastward until they reached the fastness of the Russian plain. Now the flow reversed. Literally every week emigrants left Kolomea. Far off to the west and across the ocean lay America and its vision of space, jobs, and toleration. For the average Galician Jew without special skills or education, this land of unlimited opportunity became an irresistible magnet. In America, it was claimed, there was not even anti-Semitism. The American government "liked" Jews.

For the Feuermanns, the choice was more complex. The few Feuermann kin in Kolomea had already left for America. On the other hand the Hoenigsberg clan was largely intact, ensconced in its ancestral town. A few had moved to Vienna, the second most popular goal of the emigrants.

There was, in addition, Berlin. The stories that had been brought back to Kolomea indicated that this city was a vast metropolis, perhaps as wealthy as New York, where enormous opportunity existed for both Jew and Gentile. Unlike Vienna, with its somnolent economy, Berlin was a town of the bourgeoisie, hectic and thriving, yet it still retained a deep interest in music. Berlin had Joachim, Busoni, D'Albert, Nikisch, and Strauss. Indeed when one heard the success stories of the young Austrian, Polish, and Russian geniuses now appearing, inevitably it was Berlin that had to be conquered. Berlin was the mark of ultimate social and economic success in the east-European musical world.

However, in the end, it was Vienna the Feuermanns decided upon. America was a tantalizing vision. But would it be good for Sigmund? Was America an incubator of talent or an exploiter? All successful musicians did make their fortunes there. But had anyone heard of a great American violinist? Who would teach their young genius? How would the Americans react to a child prodigy from such a far-off and obscure part of the world?

Berlin, too, shared many of these defects. It was strange and formidable. Without close contacts and friends, life might be too cold and unrewarding and it would lack the compensations already being offered to Sigmund. Vienna was at least a known quantity, still the repository of the richest musical culture in Europe. There they had friends and contacts. In Vienna, following in the footsteps of Gluck, Haydn, Mozart, Beethoven, and Schubert, the Feuermanns would search for success.

It was Vienna in the declining days of the Austrian Empire. But for all the talk of superficiality and philistinism in the populace, its tendency alternately to ignore, ridicule, and excoriate its great musical figures, contemporaries such as Brahms, Bruckner, Wolf, Reger, Mahler, and the young Schönberg (eventually also his disciples, Berg and Webern) found in this city an atmosphere in which they could create.

The scoffers could point to the over 4,000 cafés, where the indolent Viennese leisurely comported themselves, to the 1,500 confectioners who contributed to the general state of satiation and self-indulgence, to the six theatres for operetta, a home for the real heroes of the Viennese public— the Strausses, Lehar, Stolz, Millocker, Kalman, and Oscar Straus.

To counter the detractors, the defenders of Vienna pointed to the literary world of Vienna, to von Hofmannsthal, Zweig, Dehmel, Werfel, and Schnitzler. Berlin certainly did not have such counterparts, nor could it yet create an environment conducive to the productive efforts of such a diverse assortment of intellectuals as Freud, Max Reinhardt, Trotsky, Masaryk, Herzl, Ludwig Wittgenstein, Fritz Brentano, or Ernst Mach. No, when all was said and done, the attraction of Vienna, especially for those interested in music, could not be equaled. The Philharmonic, the Court Opera, notables as Leschetizky, Kreisler, Schnabel, Weingartner, Walter, all added up to a glittering panorama.

The city of their choice was also the residence of a million and a half people in a slowly-dying empire of 53,000,000, the *"Wasserkopf"* (bloated head), as she was fondly known, already bereft of much of the power and glamor of former years. Some said Budapest was much more exciting and fun these days than the pallid waltz city of the Viennese nobility, which still limped along inside the walls of aristocracy. Yes, the situation was desperate, all admitted, but not serious. Vienna was undergoing its second golden age, a new awakening. When one realizes that in but a few years the entire structure of Austrian life would be no more, its cultural renascence is puzzling.

The answer to this enigma lies in our example of the Feuermann pilgrimage to Vienna and its horizons of opportunity. It lies in the manner by which Viennese culture had been first infiltrated and then dominated by the Jews. Until 1848, Vienna was closed to all but three or four thousand legal and extralegal Hebrew inhabitants. By 1900, of the one-and-a-half million of conglomerate nationality who made up its populace, about 10 percent, or 150,000, were Jews. In these fifty years, two generations, the Jews had risen to a leading position in every area of intellectual and cultural life, and this in spite of severe if sporadic anti-Semitic episodes and restrictions. Not only that, though most Jews were relatively poor, a significant group of affluent Jews had taken the lead in promoting this cultural hegemony. They had, in addition, risen to positions of political influence made possible by the democratic reforms forced upon Franz Joseph.

Whereas at the beginning of this late nineteenth-century period Vienna had acclaimed Brahms and Bruckner, now its leading figures were

Mahler and Schönberg. As the old Austrian tradition decayed, the Jews with versatility and energy took on the cause of German culture. This frightened not only the anti-Semites but the orthodox Jews. The desire to succor the synagogue traditions and to retain the barriers to assimilation was desperate. These Jews saw the religious tradition slowly dying on the one hand and their ethnic uniqueness being breached on the other.

In early May of 1908, the Feuermanns arrived in Vienna. An apartment had been obtained for them in the sprawling Jewish quarter of Leopoldstadt. It was a fairly ample one in an old building that had not as yet been converted to electricity. As the family ruefully noted in retrospect about those early months, the apartment had "many other things" lacking. But there was a compensation. Now the ubiquitous and joyful sound of a small violin echoed through the apartment. For both Rachel and Maier the return of Sigmund to the family more than made up for strangeness and inconvenience.

Barely had the belongings been placed, the rudimentary furnishings and other essentials for life obtained, than Maier was out on the street scouring the town for work. There were numerous *landsleute* close at hand who had some connections and Maier immediately took advantage of even the most tenuous possibilities. Unfortunately, the splendor of Vienna, which had awed him on his first visit, was now revealed to gloss over much that was shabby. Yet despite its tawdriness, Vienna provided enough excitement to compensate for its imperfections.

What was more dismaying, Maier's silent fears about the lack of musical opportunity were confirmed. There was a glut of musicians looking for jobs that were extremely scarce. The musicians' union, in reality a branch of the municipal civil service, was a closed guild. Music teachers were plentiful and only the most famous could attract students who could pay for lessons.

Maier felt rebuffed and frustrated. Although he probably did not submit himself to soul-searching, the reasons were evident. He was not young any more, had no record of significant performance, and thus was obviously ordinary, if competent. His teaching in Kolomea was of no interest to anyone. Orchestra and pit jobs were at a premium, as were those with the best café orchestras. He would not stoop to playing in the smaller side-street establishments amidst the kinds of people who patronized them.

Finally, after several weeks, his persistence bore fruit. One of his first leads, a friend from the Marienbad Kürorchester, ran into him on the street and told him of a vacancy in the Marienbad ensemble. If he hurried, he could get the job without having to compete for it by audition. It would mean, however, that he would have to leave Vienna until the fall. There was the problem of abandoning the family while they were just in the earliest stages of adjustment to the new life. However, there could be no second thoughts. He was in touch immediately with the manager and got the position on the basis of his past experience with such groups.

A few things had to be settled before he left, especially with regard to Sigmund. He had already begun to reinvolve himself in the boy's training. He felt that Feist, in his eagerness to inculcate the child in the special method for which he was known, had been somewhat negligent with regard to Sigmund's overall technical advancement. Mother Feuermann was given explicit instructions in this regard and was thus left with the general supervision of the family while Maier attempted to establish some foundation for their future. In addition to promising to keep in close contact with things at home, he alerted his various friends to their responsibilities for his brood.

One of Maier's last acts before he left has given rise to many legends concerning Emanuel. No sooner had they arrived in Vienna than the child started in again about his cello. His pleas were even more poignant, considering the awe in which Sigmund was now bathed and the huzzahs elicited from whoever visited the apartment. Since Maier's old violin was no longer in use for teaching and since he would be gone for some months, he improvised a peg for the violin, tuned it like a cello and handed it to Munio: "Munio, here is your cello, now play. We will get you a real one when I come back." Though discernibly disappointed, Munio was intrigued by the peg. He could muster the imagination to transform reality into possibility and saw his father off with a measure of contentment.

Twice a week mother Feuermann left the children with ten-year-old Gusta and took Sigmund to his lesson with Feist. Her letters dutifully reported the exact events of these lessons. Maier wrote back promptly, asking her to transmit explicit questions to Feist, to give him suggestions for new material for Sigmund, or suggesting technical matters Feist should pursue with the child. Soon his interest not only reflected his steady sense of proprietorship, but also a plan that he was developing in Marienbad.

At the spa he had made the acquaintance of a number of the musicians in the orchestra. They were very curious as to the prodigy's development and Maier was more than eager to supply the superlatives. Soon Maier's stories made their way beyond the musicians to the guests and management. When a tentative invitation was offered, Maier explained the difficulty in regard to Feist's injunction not to exploit the boy. The unanimous opinion of all was that a child now nearly eight would not be exploited by virtue of making such an appearance.

This was a great opportunity, not only for Sigmund and Maier, but for the family itself. These people were for the most part Viennese and would do the Feuermann reputation no harm. The problem lay in Feist—not just in the scholarship he had given Sigmund, but also in the modest allowance he provided the family in lieu of Sigmund's living with him. A series of hasty communications passed between father and mother. First there was some surprised hesitancy and protest, but soon acquiescence, in the name of the immediate and urgent good. The mother was to take Sigmund to Professor Joseph Zimbler, who would prepare Sigmund in repertoire for the recital. This was to take place—and in this Maier was explicit—without any interruption of the routine with Feist.

Zimbler, like Feist, was one of Vienna's more talented violin teachers. Maier had met him when he first began scouting around for a playing job. At that time Zimbler, knowing about Sigmund through the usual music teachers' grapevine, had hinted that if Maier were to transfer Sigmund to him, he might be influential in obtaining a cello job for the father in one of the theatres. But Maier, not yet being that desperate and having the excessive pride of a newcomer, turned him down. He was not yet ready to barter Sigmund for a dubious hope. Indeed, even had he been in a worse financial situation, there were certain things that Rachel would adamantly oppose.

But this was different. Maier knew that Zimbler would be eager to agree even to a temporary apprenticeship in the hope that were something to go wrong with the arrangement with Feist he would inherit Sigmund. Zimbler was also not obligated in any way to the father. In this manner the peculiar regimen began. Zimbler gave Sigmund three lessons a week, making no effort whatsoever to mitigate differences in style and technique. Rachel trembled with each visit to Feist. Because she knew how important the outcome might be for the family, she persevered. Sigmund accepted it all with childlike equanimity. What Feist told him to do with the left hand he did. What Zimbler told him to do with the bow arm, he did. What Feist suggested he try with the right hand. . . . Before each appearance with Feist, the mother would stand with Sigmund on the landing and whisper, "Remember, Sigmund, not a word." Sigmund would nod assent.

Feist was troubled. It was not the prepared lessons that disturbed him, but the sight-reading that gave him pause. Sigmund would occasionally do things that shocked him and do them with an assurance that belied the fact that Feist was his teacher. His suspicions grew as the études and scales he asked Sigmund to audition evinced idiosyncratic stylistic flourishes that more and more outraged his sense of proportion.

"What has happened?" he finally roared in indignation to the mother one day. He knew, yet he dared not admit it to himself. Rachel hesitated for a moment, and then with a tearful sigh of relief, blurted out the entire story to Feist. The teacher was of course completely deflated. Lacking a greater sense of composure, he would have thrown them both out. It would have satisfied his ego but done little else for him. He could not allow Sigmund to pass into Zimbler's hands. In solemn tones, he extracted a promise from the mother that this recital under Zimbler's tutelage would be the last. After this the child would be returned to the cloister of his studies. Rachel quickly agreed and with great relief saw to the completion of the series of lessons with Zimbler, hoping that things would return to normal after the recital.

Maier was naturally shocked when, on his return to Vienna to fetch Sigmund for the important moment, he heard the entire story. However, he was alert in noting Feist's complaisance. The recital in Marienbad was an enormous success. Maier had seen to it that the repertoire would show Sigmund's virtuosity at its best. The audience was duly awed. Sigmund fit all their preconceptions as to what and how a child prodigy should play. Perhaps, Maier hoped, the stories that filtered back to Vienna would create the break he needed.

The letters exchanged during the remaining months were cheery. Maier was lionized in Marienbad, Rachel was content with the relative calm. Sigmund was happy with Feist's more conciliatory, almost deferential attitude. He would often comment that Professor Feist was nicer to him. The only one unhappy was Munio. For a while, his surrogate cello satisfied him and he had much fun in experimenting on it, forever trying to imitate what Sigmund was practicing on the violin. On and off, a few minutes here and there, no badgering or demands, just unadulterated aural pleasure. But as the summer wore on, the letters to Maier inevitably concluded with a postscript: "Munio wants to know when you are going to bring him a cello." When Maier arrived to fetch Sigmund for the Marienbad event, Munio imperiously demanded to know the whereabouts of the cello. The letters continued in this vein into the fall.

In October, unfortunately, no benefactor magically appeared, offering to subsidize the family and relieve them of their cares. The Marienbad money was almost gone. True, Sigmund was asked to play in several resplendent homes and the honoraria were deeply appreciated. There was so much talent in Vienna that a certain lack of concern was inevitable. Maier, however, was an inveterate optimist. He could see possibilities in the worst of situations. Sigmund was developing so rapidly now under Feist's less dictatorial yet highly capable tutelage that eventually success would be theirs. Maier was especially hopeful since, in his opinion, none of the young violinists that he had heard could compare with his Sigmund.

In November, one of his summer associates told Maier about a cello opening in the Tonkünstler Orchester. Maier was not a member of the union and he knew how nepotism usually predetermined the outcome of the auditions. Nevertheless, since the job was civil service and since the

Tonkünstler, while not the equal of the Philharmonic or the Court Opera, was one of the best musical groups in the city, he would audition before the orchestra committee. He had trepidations, because while he felt he was competent for the quality of playing required, most of these instrumentalists were a notch above him in polish and élan. They, however, were lackadaisical Viennese and he was a determined and intrepid Kolomean. What he had to do was to get by the audition.

The day of the audition he set forth with not only his cello, but also with Sigmund, violin in hand, in tow. At the hall, it seemed that half the cellists in Vienna had also applied for the position. The auditions went quickly, and though he had to undergo a few taunts from the other waiting cellists: "Mister, the little boy needs a job too?" he eventually found himself next in line. The whole affair seemed perfunctory and deflating, judging from the faces of those who left the audition room.

As he entered the large bare room with Sigmund, one of the three judges looked up and called sharply, "Leave the boy outside." Maier practically ran forward and in a most deferential and confidentially obsequious manner implored them to listen to his son, stating that the boy was an undiscovered genius and that, as the father, he deeply desired their opinion, since they were distinguished musicians of a distinguished orchestra.

They were both amazed and angry. Either the father had fantastic *chutzpa* (arrogance) and had something further up his sleeve or else he was a crackpot and ought to be thrown out forthwith. Yet, as the father unabashedly persisted and since they were tired and bored, they hesitated. It might be amusing indeed to hear the last movement of the Mendelssohn played by the child. The concertmaster of the orchestra was one of the three judges and was especially curious. To silence the father and his nonstop torrent of words, they finally agreed to let the boy play.

Sigmund; not having said a word during all this time, scurried to his violin case. "Can you really play the Mendelssohn Concerto, little boy?" the concertmaster inquired as he examined Sigmund's new three-quarter-size violin, which Feist had provided. "Oh, yes, sir," the boy replied, "I can play all three movements." Maier quickly interrupted, "and he's hardly seven years old." (He was eight.)

Sigmund started to play with a striking burst of energy. The musicians were silent except to exchange quick glances with each other. When Sigmund finished the movement one of them arose and went to the door, telling the waiting cellists to enter the room quietly and listen. He ran back to his seat and called out, "Play it again, little boy." Sigmund looked at Maier hesitantly and began to play once more.

Maier had not said a word. He stood stiffly against the wall, the only sign of emotion his darting eyes as he watched the listeners while his son played. In a few moments, to murmurs of amzement, it was over. The audition for the cello position was over, too. It could not be allowed that the trustee of such a rare jewel should go without a job. Feuermann henceforth was cellist with the Tonkünstler, without ever having had to open his cello case.

2

PRODIGIES

In the fall of 1909 Otakar Sevčik arrived in Vienna to assume the position of professor of violin at the Vienna Akademie für Musik. One of his prime responsibilities was to initiate a master class for young, talented students at an advanced level. This news effected an immediate rise of tension in the Feuermann family, for Sevčik was one of the two or three greatest violin pedagogues in the world at that time and the leading teacher in the Austrian Empire. Anticipation was only heightened by the additional report that in his first master class, Sevčik would restrict enrollment to ten students.

Papa Feuermann's intentions could never have been in doubt from the first announcements. These were initially indicated by his careful and systematic investigation into the time, place, and circumstances under which the auditions would be given. Mama Feuermann had reservations about this new idea. Suppose Feist learned about the audition, especially if it did not go well. Had there not been enough subterfuge with regard to Sigmund's studies in the past year? In addition, had not Sigmund made enormous progress in this time, progress not only in surface matters of facility and repertoire, but in greater understanding of what he was doing, and in interpretation and musical literacy as well? And finally, there was their life. Had it not taken a sharp turn for the better?

The latter had to be conceded. Life had improved. Often the family was treated to a display in full regalia by Maier in his official civil service uniform, symbolic of his membership in the Tonkünstler Orchester. This was more than a surface holiday show. Maier was deeply proud of his new musical responsibilities and to live up to them, he practiced his cello literally day and night. And his playing did improve significantly. In addition to his salary, there was a small extra income from a few young cello students who had been attracted to this musical home. There was also one nonpaying student. Munio, finally equipped with his own half-sized cello, was now regularly instructed by his father and was thriving under this belated attention.

Sigmund was being gradually liberated from Feist's musical cocoon. The father was encountering an increasing number of invitations to private functions for his young violinist. Feist rarely disapproved. The invitations were too innocuous to refuse and they contributed a small income and some additional notoriety. A niche was being carved in the structure of the vast, harsh city. At this point, the family could have been called bourgeois, in material if not psychological terms. Rachel argued that, with such good beginnings, events should be allowed to evolve naturally. Now should be the time in their lives to stop struggling frenetically.

But Maier was firm. Certainly life in Kolomea meant struggle to find a living. Eventually there came some success and stability. But that was Kolomea. They came to Vienna to find a new life, which meant struggle once more. They were now somewhat successful, but only in terms of life as they encountered it in their first year. Did that mean they should reject the needs of today? Could they give up the opportunity for an audition with Sevčik and, if accepted, refuse to enroll Sigmund? No. If Sevčik would take Sigmund, they would take their leave of Feist, albeit with much thanks, and await ensuing developments.

As Maier had anticipated, the small, bald-headed, half-blind Bohemian was deeply impressed with Sigmund. After all, had not Feist himself been a student of Sevčik in Prague? Innumerable times he had reiterated to the skeptical Maier his own improvements in the treatment of the bow arm as compared with Sevčik's handling of this problem. When Feist was finally informed of the transfer of his star pupil, he said little but to wish the family good luck. His one comment was to the effect that he doubted whether Sevčik would have another student to compare with Sigmund.

With news of acceptance came congratulations, first from neighbors and friends in Vienna, then from as far away as Lemberg and Kolomea. It was now official, a great prodigy would soon be unveiled. In the imagination, indeed in the words of the intimates, there were visions of Sigmund amidst the contemporary pantheon of violinists—Ysaÿe, Zimbalist, Huberman, Kreisler, and perhaps the most famous and successful of Sevčik's students, Jan Kubelik.

The coming of Sevčik to this great capital of music was perhaps inevitable. He would now take his place along with that magnetic pedagogue of the piano, Theodor Leschetizky. This had become an era of great teachers. The significance of these teachers lay in the importance that performance had acquired for the musical public, a phenomenon of only the last several decades. While earlier virtuosi—Mozart, Tartini, Czerny, Paganini, Liszt—had caught the fancy of the public, their genius had been recognized for reasons other than just their performing. These older virtuosi were also great composers, unique romantic personalities, or both.

The virtuoso at the end of the nineteenth century and the beginning of the twentieth was increasingly at the service of the composer—now approaching the peak technical exploitation of the various media, whether voice, piano, strings, or symphony orchestra. Responding to this stimulus, in what began to approach a deluge, the gifted poured forth from all over the civilized world, from Australia, from Russia, from the Americas.

In the case of the violin they came to the important instrumental centers in Europe. The violin school in Berlin had been created by Joachim and Wilhelmji and was now represented by Carl Flesch, Willy Hess, and Willy Burmeister. The historically important Belgian school of violin playing boasted such great teachers and performers as Marsick, Leonard, De Beriot, Vieuxtemps, and now Ysaÿe; its French affiliate could add Alard and now Jacques Thibaud.

In St. Petersburg, the Hungarian Leopold Auer had discovered a vast reservoir of talent. Each year a tide of prodigies passed into his classes. In effect they created his reputation. In Budapest, Jeno Hubay flourished through the always-abundant violinistic resources of the Hungarians. In sum, all over Europe, young violin virtuosi were being trained to reach peaks of technical as well as interpretive competence never before attempted. A demand had been created. The talent merely awaited exploitation.

Sevčik, a kindly, fatherly man of 57, endowed with enormous energy that awed both students and colleagues, was born near Prague. In 1909, when he arrived in Vienna, he was at the height of his powers and reputation. A gifted violin student of Bennewitz in Prague, he had been a concertmaster in Salzburg and in Vienna until 1875, when he accepted an appointment to teach violin at the Kiev Imperial Music School.

Sevčik's extraordinary versatility, typical of the nineteenth-century musician, is illustrated in a story about his early years of touring. He had teamed up with a cellist friend. Since both played acceptable piano in addition to their stringed instruments, they accompanied each other in sonatas. In addition, since they both loved and were trained in the *Lieder* repertoire, they would intersperse their concerts with selections of Schubert songs, taking their vocal turn as each accompanied the other on piano.

In Kiev, Sevčik's naturally analytical mind served him well. As soon as he had arrived, he set to work revising the violin course of study. His success was such that Czar Alexander II awarded him the Order of St. Stanislaus in 1886 for his pedagogic services. His work in Kiev was crucial to the establishment of the Russian school of violin playing. Many Russian violinists, including Fiedemann, later Mischa Elman's teacher in Odessa, got their start with him.

In Prague, Anton Bennewitz had become director of the conservatory. He asked Sevčik to return to Prague as his successor as head of the violin department. Subsequently, from 1892 to 1906 in this accessible and beautiful baroque cultural center, Sevčik became an established authority in violin pedagogics. However, during these years his health had begun to decline. An operation that resulted in the loss of an eye (the wound originally caused by the breaking of a violin string), as well as respiratory surgery, had by 1898 made it necessary that he abandon performance. Henceforth he devoted himself entirely to teaching and the perfection of his violin method. And the students came: Kubelik, Kocian, Sametini, Marie Hall, Sascha Culbertson and Daisy Kennedy; the children of such greats as Wieniawski, Wilhelmji, and Hugo Heerman. In Vienna, along with Sigmund Feuermann, the American David Hochstein (later, tragically, killed in World War I) and Erica Morini were attracted to his classes.

The trip downtown to the impressive Musik Akademie that fall morning in 1909 marked a new beginning for the Feuermanns. On the surface the classes held at the music school were merry affairs. The children, of whom Sigmund was the youngest, were, like all youngsters, prankish, playful, and uninhibited. But Sevčik seemed to have had no difficulty in managing them. He demonstrated with his own violin rarely, and then sketchily. But he would take much time showing the students how to finger, bow, and in general manage and solve particular difficult passages. Every technical problem was a challenge to his ingenuity; he delighted in solving each in the most precise and logical manner possible.

Often Maier would bring Emanuel to the lessons. The boy was progressing nicely on the cello. The father taught him with much less intensity than he had Sigmund; he was content with the pace the boy set for himself in his typical, playful way. When the exercises were absorbed, several new ones were assigned, and perhaps a simple piece. Maier's acuity and energy went elsewhere. He probably took Munio along as much for duty as for the positive results he might have hoped from having him observe a Sevčik lesson. Maier sat him down unobtrusively in a corner and told him to watch and listen. Munio as usual focused on Sigmund.

Sevčik's regimen was an intensive one. He had developed his method of violin pedagogics to meet the most rigorous demands of the contemporary repertoire. He created a half-tone system of fingering to help accomplish this end. This system helped the player regularize his fingering so that no unequal intervals would be encountered on any string, as would be the case in the diatonic scale. The result was not only to improve awareness of pitch and intonation, but to put under the fingers of the player routines that would make him infinitely more flexible. To this end, Sevčik had created a multi-volumed series of exercises that constituted his magnum opus for violin pedagogics. But in his teaching he also utilized the traditional violin repertoire. There was no piece of music, therefore, that did not lend itself to this form of technical intellectualization.

Whenever difficulties occurred, whether fingered octaves, left hand pizzicato, or moving double-stopped trills, Sevčik would add additional complications. He would greatly increase tempi or change the direction of the passage, whether ascending or descending, in order to make it that much more difficult. His philosophy was that the technical problems of a passage could be solved by doubling the complexities and difficulties, always adhering to the same canons of articulation, intonation, and rhythm prescribed in the original passage. In this manner, even Paganini caprices might be made to seem elementary.

The total atmosphere generated by the Sevčik approach, while genial and informal, was intensely competitive. There was a standard of technical excellence by which each student was judged. Thus individuality of expression or personal idiosyncracy was regarded dubiously. Everyone was reaching for the same mark. Perhaps the most competitive was Sevčik himself. He was consumed with a vision of instrumental accomplishment he could now bring to fruition only through his students. Summers he would go home to Pisek, near Prague. Even here he would not allow himself a real vacation but would always teach a few selected students.

One story describes how Sevčik would rise early in the morning in Pisek and make his rounds of the peasant houses where his students boarded. The students, who started practicing with the first rays of the sun, were at first unaware of their unseen listener, standing outside their windows. Each of the houses was visited until Sevčik had made his complete tour. Later in the day at their lessons Sevčik would point out either their errors or their strong points. None of them could afford the luxury of a moment's relaxation during the long internship. The master might be listening.

This approach met completely with Maier's own intellectual and personal inclinations. When Sevčik stated that a student should practice eight to ten hours a day, Maier promptly returned home to have Rachel enforce the injunction on Sigmund. And as solicitous a mother as she was—even stubborn at times—she could not object to the voice of authority. Before her eyes the results of this regimen on little, compliant Sigmund were evident.

Not all agreed with the Sevčik method. Vienna was a meeting ground for musicians from all over the world. Discussion of the merits of the various schools of playing had gone on for decades. It was an enthusiastic, yet harmless, avocation of musicians. Resident alumni of the formerly regnant Franco-Belgian school, now going into partial eclipse, were particularly vociferous opponents of Sevčik. Concerned with nuance, phrase, and elegance, if not sensuosity of sound, they railed against Sevčik's technical approach. "He is turning his students into a group of mechanical idiots," was one current accusation. The respondent usually focused on the casual sloppiness of the Belgian approach to technique, and its proverbial insecurity in the vicissitudes of performance.

The most intriguing competitor was Leopold Auer. And a young violinist such as Efrem Zimbalist, who had studied with both Auer and Sevčik, commanded the interest of all appreciators of the art. Auer, like Sevčik, had long ago given up performance. He was a good violinist for his own day and later on founded the St. Petersburg Quartet. During his younger days he had studied for a time with Joachim. Yet when Tschaikowsky had asked him to give the first performance of the latter's violin concerto, Auer had refused. He laid the music down and pronounced it unplayable. The honor and resulting fame in introducing the famous concerto fell to Joseph Brodsky, who had felt he had the requisite technique to cope with it.

Auer was less cerebral than Sevčik with regard to technique. Usually he left it to his assistants to bring the student along technically until he was ready for repertoire. His classes were a combination of interpretive coaching sessions and psychological conferences. He assumed that the students were capable of solving their own technical problems on the instrument if they were only made aware of the musical ends for which the problems existed. For each question put to him about a special difficulty, Auer would throw the question back to the student. "How would you solve it?" Even in the realm of interpretation, where his views were revered, he often cajoled his students to discover for themselves the most lyric and beautiful effect consonant with their own unique equipment and capacity.

It is difficult to say whether this heuristic device was a conscious methodological and psychological approach to the instrument or was improvised, with increasing effectiveness, to make up for his own technical deficiencies. No matter what the case, his knowledge of the instrument was complete. Auer had an idiomatic sensitivity to the possibilities of the violin—with the possible exception of the infamous Tschaikowsky misjudgment. This gained for him and his classes a respect, at times reverence, that worked its own peculiar pedagogical charm.

The Auer method was a magnet that drew literally dozens of the most phenomenally talented students from every part of the world. The names are familiar: Heifetz, Mischa Elman, Efrem Zimbalist, Kathleen Parlow, Michel Piastro, Mischa Fishberg (Mishakoff), Tosha Seidel, Max Rosen, Eddy Brown, Nathan Milstein, among others. There is no doubt that the times influenced the number and quality. But the individual and varied approaches to the instrument, amidst a universally high quality of playing, can only be attributed to the competitive yet independent environment provied by Auer himself.

Through a quite different methodological approach the students in the master class at the Vienna Academy also thrived. The combination of a strong and decisive teacher and a completely committed set of parents was a crucial factor in the flourishing of little Sigmund. While the lessons in Sevčik's studio were uniformly successful, Sigmund enjoyed the regularly scheduled classes more. Lessons were irregularly timed. Sevčik taught as early as six in the morning, reserving the afternoon hours for working on his violin method and then continuing to teach until well into the evening. While the boy idolized his teacher, the private lessons always ended with Sigmund protesting to Maier about the perpetual smell of Limburger cheese on Sevčik's breath. The master had a passion for this morsel. It constituted his only known weakness.

Sigmund spent slightly over a year doing little but studying with Sevčik. He pushed rapidly into all ranges of the violin literature. He was, at age nine, playing the Beethoven, Brahms, and Paganini concerti, and the modern repertoire, classical sonata literature, every variety of étude and even difficult sections of the orchestral and operatic repertoire. Maier was amazed at the way the boy sopped up everything that was put before him. The supposed efficiency of the respected Feist was eclipsed by the ease with which Sevčik handled each step in the child's progress. Everything had its place and proper sequence. Sevčik perceived intuitively both what should be done and what Sigmund was capable of doing. To the Feuermanns, Sevčik was a deity; had he demanded twelve hours of practice a day, Maier would have been tempted to try to push Rachel and Sigmund toward that goal.

Sevčik was obviously taken with Sigmund, but expressed it in the indirect manner of a judicious teacher. He would inquire solicitously about various members of the Feuermann family, of Munio's musical interests, during the master classes as he hovered from student to student. When told that Maier was teaching the young cellist, he expressed some surprise. He implied that every music student needed a "teacher."

Just as his students, Sevčik flourished in his role. There were no favorites. All were precious jewels to him. David Hochstein recalled that Sevčik, in signing a photograph of himself to Hochstein, had inadvertently written "to my best student." When he realized what he had written, he quickly lifted his pen and glanced around the room at the youngsters as they packed their instruments away and wrote over the word *"besten"*--*"liebsten"* (most loved). This typified his attitude towards his students and was in turn unanimously reciprocated.

In the fall of 1910, after barely a year of intensive study, the master informed Maier Feuermann that in his opinion Sigmund had graduated with honors from the master class. Sigmund would of course need more schooling, both lessons and occasional coaching in his master classes. But the intensive phase was concluded.

Most important was the change of roles both father and son were about

Sigmund Feuermann, budding prodigy, 1910

Emanuel Feuermann with his father's cello, 1910. Note machine head pegs.

to undergo. Sevčik had agreed that they could now accept the concert engagements that were being constantly proffered. In fact a debut recital was being arranged by the teacher for the Akademie itself. Quickly Maier obtained a leave from the Tonkünstler Orchester. He would continue to play only between his son's engagements. Maier could almost savor the tang of success. Everything was progressing with amazing smoothness.

An important element in what had turned out to be a crucial as well as fruitful year in the Feuermanns' lives was their involvement with Wilhelm Kux. Kux was a wealthy Jewish banker from Czechoslovakia who, although still in his early fifties, was already semiretired. He was a well-known patron of the arts. Kux had taken it upon himself to search out the most promising young string players in Vienna and to provide whatever assistance was necessary in furthering their careers. He was especially interested in that unique assemblage in Sevčik's classes at the Akademie. It was Sevčik who told him of the Feuermanns. When Kux came to them and announced his interest in Sigmund's talent, the Feuermanns were dumbstruck. It was too good to believe—their own *mitzayin*.* A person such as Kux acted as a personal foundation and was hardly thought of as a giver of charity, so it was not considered demeaning to receive this kind of help. They were what they were and there was no point in denying it. Too many other Austrians were as poor. It was not a unique condition. But with a talent like Sigmund's it could be remedied.

Kux proposed that he would obligate himself for that portion of the family expenses which could be attributed to Sigmund's needs, and that in addition all funds needed for his education would be provided for. While there was no need for payment to the Akademie for Sevčik's lessons, as these were on scholarship, a private tutor would be needed for the boy's academic studies. In addition, a good piano was purchased with Kux's help and a teacher provided for all the children for piano and theory lessons. Eventually the family was able to afford a woman to help mother Feuermann in the care of the household.

Kux also made another, prescient suggestion to Maier. This occurred at about the time the arrangements were being made for Sigmund's first tour. Since it was difficult for Maier to pay the requisite attention to the young cellist of the house, perhaps it would be wise to engage an outside teacher. The boy seemed to confirm his father's boasts. He was alert and interested in both the cello and music in general.

Munio, who was just starting municipal school, still considered the cello a plaything. But he was gradually perceiving and becoming sensitive to the social importance of music and performance. His playing on the instrument was now tempered with an awareness of what achievement

---

*This is a word with an interesting etymology. It comes from the Roman Maecenas (Gaius Cilnius d. 8 B.C.) meaning sponsor or patron.

Wilhelm Kux, benefactor and violin collector, left, with friends, 1910.

signified. But this came to him not from his father as it had in Sigmund's case, but from Munio's recognition of the various social roles that others had in life on the basis of their musical standing.

It was a typical Kux recommendation, always aim for the best. Kux's choice for Munio was Friederich Buxbaum, a musician in his early forties, who was considered to be the premier cellist of Vienna. Not only was he first cellist in the Philharmonic and the Court Opera (later the State Opera), but he was the cellist of the Rosé Quartet, at that time among the top two or three ensembles of the genre in Europe.

The leader of the quartet, Arnold Rosé, was the brother-in-law of Gustav Mahler and one of the most beloved musicians in Vienna. He was considered to be a complete musician. Not only was he superb in the quartet literature, but also as soloist and concertmaster of the Opera Orchestra. (Ultimately he was rewarded for his services to Viennese culture by being seized, at age seventy-five, and abused by the Nazis. Rosé was finally rescued and aided by his friends and hosts in England, there, like Freud, to live out his last years.)

Buxbaum eagerly accepted the young boy, more especially so as Munio was being supported by Kux. But, in addition, the boy did seem to display a flair for the instrument. In this move, as in everything else that Kux did, there was an uncanny sense of appropriateness. Perhaps this is why he was so successful in the launching of talent. He was selfless, and thus he was able to appraise each situation with discernment and complete objectivity. The goal was clear—to further his young geniuses. After all, it was quite likely that behind each talent were some very idiosyncratic and strong-minded parents and their precarious economic state did not make them any less difficult.

He perceived the dynamics of the Feuermann family and adjusted his actions to the possibilities inherent in their situation. He would have to stay in the background in the case of Sigmund. Maier was too strong an individualist to brook much interference with his own plans. The most that Kux could do with regard to the guidance of the young violinist's career would be to provide a background environment that might inspire emulation and trust in both young and elder Feuermanns. The very fact that he paid some of their bills would necessitate their consulting him on occasion. Subtlety would have to be the *modus operandi.*

On Sunday afternoons the boys would be delivered to Kux's home for a long session of chamber music. He himself played a modest cello. The house was usually filled with young musicians. The boys found the sixteen-year-old violinist Rudolph Kolisch the oldest in the group. As the years wore on, little Erica Morini became one of the additions to their circle. There was always an abundance of hot cocoa, pastries, and choco-lates to fatten them up. They would return home full of enthusiasm for their Director Kux, joking good-naturedly about his scratchy cello playing, and bursting into convulsions of laughter about his grotesque red hairpiece. A bachelor to the end (at age 102 in Chur, Switzerland) he remained a counselor and devoted friend of the family. Later, he became especially attached to Munio and considered him his own son.

Sigmund's inaugural recital at the Akademie was a sensation. Oscar Nedbal, the conductor of the Tonkünstler Orchester and a former violinist of the Bohemian Quartet, urged Maier to allow the boy an appearance with the orchestra. The reputation of Sigmund had spread throughout the orchestra and there was much persuasion. Maier, however, had other ideas. He wanted Sigmund's first appearance with orchestra to be with Weingartner and the Philharmonic. And as a matter of fact the pianist Moritz Rosenthal had been enlisted to persuade Weingartner to introduce the boy. It was a touchy issue, however.

The manager of the Philharmonic felt that the Viennese public was satiated with prodigies. Literally every week a new one appeared, each bearing a prophecy of fantastic success. Ultimately most of these turned out to be comets and rapidly disappeared. The cumulative public response was one of disenchantment and deception as one youthful "promise" after another turned to naught. Weingartner had become hostile to the whole idea of child prodigies. "Let them wait a few years," was his typical comment.

Thus the orchestral debut was with the Tonkünstler. Sigmund played the first movement of the Brahms, as well as pieces by Paganini, Corelli, and Tschaikowsky. The ovation was immense. Even Maier, from his seat in the rear of the cello section, took bows.

The critical reception was also good. It was enough to persuade Weingartner that Sigmund was more than the usual prodigy. The resulting announcement that a ten-year-old child would play the entire Brahms Concerto with the Philharmonic caused a sensation. The newspapers noted that it had been almost seventy years since a child of that age had been invited to solo with the orchestra. The earlier Vienna Philharmonic soloist was a young Hungarian prodigy named Joseph Joachim.

Thereafter Maier delighted in the competition among concert managers for Sigmund's services. He played one off against the other to get good fees and to obtain the best possible locales and concert halls. He was partially successful. Sigmund was not yet really well-known. He was a phenomenon, yes. But it was hard to predict how often people would come to hear a ten-year-old. Thus there were still certain limitations inherent in his immaturity; even Maier had to concede that. In the end Maier was able to obtain not only the usual run of provincial towns, but also Budapest and Berlin. The latter was especially satisfying to the family. For it symbolized wealth, power, and fame.

At about the time the final arrangements had been completed for their inaugural tour, an important switch in cello teachers occurred for Munio.

The boy had been with Buxbaum less than a year. During this period, the young cellist Anton Walter had made the acquaintance of the elder Feuermann and hearing the latter's typical superlatives about the boy's progress under Buxbaum, attempted to persuade the father to transfer Munio to him. Walter, then only twenty-nine years old, was the cellist of the Fitzner Quartet, the ensemble Buxbaum had left to join the Rosé Quartet. He was not yet well-known. Later, in 1922, he was to join the Rosé Quartet and continue with it until its dissolution. After 1938, when the Nazis took over, he is said to have become a power in Viennese musical circles, occupying a role similar, perhaps, to the one held earlier by Arnold Rosé.

Maier decided to make the change to Walter. We can venture a guess as to why this switch was made. Buxbaum, a large, austere man with a glass eye, an awesome beard, and a fierce temper, brooked few deviations from his opinions, musical or otherwise. Buxbaum was not even daunted by the standing of his esteemed colleague Arnold Rosé. On more than one occasion members of the audience were treated to the spectacle of cellist Buxbaum pounding his feet during performance in an attempt to keep colleagues to his own tempo. This clash of temperaments eventually led to Buxbaum's resignation from the quartet and the accession of Walter.

He was notorious even among his advanced students for his inhospitable attitude to them at their impending entrance into the profession. His favorite comment was that Vienna was dead musically, and that students should go elsewhere. Obviously, he wanted little competition, especially from his own creations. Unfortunately, after 1918, his comments about Vienna became true, as the city was divested of its vast hinterlands.

An incident involving Walter that occurred later is perhaps indicative of the situation that led to Munio's transfer from Buxbaum. Maier was able to appreciate his second son's aptitude only after he had switched him to an outside teacher. At that time he began to assert an interest in the manner in which Munio was being handled that had never been evident when he had taught him at home. Buxbaum was about Maier's age and Maier could very well have seen him as a rival, not so impressive as Sevčik, yet not so malleable as a younger teacher might be. Walter was certainly in awe of the Feuermann name and easily agreed to most of Maier's suggestions, one of which was for him to keep in constant communication with the father when he was off on tour with Sigmund. The incident occurred on one of these occasions when Walter is said to have written Maier, dutifully describing Munio's lesson, noting that there were only five errors. Before allowing mother Feuermann to deposit the note in its envelope, Munio tacked on his own postscript, writing in his tiny, neat hand, "No, there were very many more."

As we have noted, the arrival of Director Kux in their lives coincided with a steady improvement in the material circumstances of the Feuermanns. They had already moved to a larger and more modern apartment in the Leopoldstadt. Later when Sigmund's tour monies and even Munio's first contributions began to be added, the seven Feuermanns obtained a spacious and comfortable apartment at 18, Karl Ludwig Strasse (later Weimar Strasse) near the Turkenschurc Park.

The growth of the children and the perambulatory independence of Sophie, the youngest, gradually liberated Rachel from her immersion in exclusively domestic affairs. Outside help for her became more regular and she began to emerge as a figure in her own right, exerting her personality on the musical development of her children. Maier was forever flitting hither and yon, even when Sigmund was at home. And while there was no question as to who was the dominant figure of the household, Mother Feuermann contributed many subtle influences to the shaping of attitudes and values in music. Her influence was fully appreciated by the children, however, only in later years. Rachel was, in fact, both a critic and a coach, observing and listening to the boys as they practiced, while she went through the household routines. Even Rosa and Sophie, now practicing on the piano, could receive a new kind of attention from their mother.

Rachel certainly made no claim to formal training in music. But having lived in a musical environment her entire life and having been exposed to constant conversation and debate about musical matters, she inevitably developed a sure and intuitive sense of what was appropriate and beautiful and, conversely, what was gauche and distorted. In later years when the family gathered on holidays, each parent would receive plaudits, Rachel as the even, sustaining critic and Maier—partially to his chagrin—as the great promoter and publicist.

This family relationship can be illustrated by an event that occurred when Sigmund was already deeply immersed in his concert career. It happened towards the end of the fall and winter of 1912–13, the second year of the boy's tours. Father and son had returned for a holiday before embarking on the final spring series of that year. There was the usual warm reception on their homecoming. After a sumptuous dinner, Maier picked himself up and in what had become almost a ritual observance, put on his coat preparatory to his departure to his *Landsmann*'s club or the synagogue. Out of the coat he drew a packet of reviews which he proceeded to read aloud to the family in an expansive and congratulatory tone. The reviews were true encomiums. The family was ecstatic; Sigmund received more than his share of embraces and pats on the back of his head.

There were other parents of *Wunderkinder* in their *Schul* (synagogue) and there was a lively competition between elders as to which child was receiving the best reviews. Maier's strongest competitor after the Friday evening services in later years was the elder Morini. Each would carry with him a handful of critical notices concering little Erica or Sigmund or Munio to see whose superlatives were decisive.

On one particular occasion Maier returned home late in the evening to find Rachel quite upset. He had left a number of the reviews on the piano. It was impossible to read ten weeks' worth of concert criticism even to one's best friends and competitors. Rachel held up one of these reviews and asked him sarcastically, yet firmly, whether Maier had read the Berlin critique by Emil Liepe. Maier shrugged and glanced away from her. "Didn't I tell you, Maier, that I did not like the Kreutzer?" . . . and she proceeded to read to him: "A young violinist, Sigmund Feuermann attempted to obscure the fact of his great youth, from his audience. As far as technical talent was concerned, he really succeeded quite well, because what he played was free from error and sure; as far as performance and spirit was concerned, his childlike nature was nevertheless evident at every turn: Beethoven's Kreutzer Sonata! Why drag an immature child onto the stage before he is ready. In spite of youth he has already learned so much and has worked so thoroughly and diligently. Why the impetuosity? Who bears the responsibility for this?"

Rachel paused and then said, "Why should Sigmund play something when he is not yet ready for it? Is it so important that our twelve-year-old play Beethoven's Kreutzer? It is not yet music for him, just notes." "What about the other critics," retorted Maier, "did you read them? Sigmund is an artist, a great natural violinist. Can we deny him the opportunity to play any composer? Do you want him to play only silly exercises? He had a bad night in Berlin. He was probably tired. It *is* possible, you understand!" Mother did not reply. She knew she was right, yet she did not make an issue of it. Maier was too caught up, and was expending himself completely in pursuit of this dream. There was no profit in creating complications at this point.

Maier was not wholly wrong, considering the surface facts. The boy was thriving on the constant public exposure. There were no overt indications that he was being exploited. Sigmund took everything in stride, as if his activities were natural and normal. He was wide-eyed and fascinated with everything to which his travels exposed him. Yet there was a reserve and maturity in his attitude and bearing that impressed Maier and made him deeply proud.

The awe in which Maier held the child's talent was due, perhaps, to their antithetical personalities. In their differences they complemented each other. The father was verbal, assertive, combative, not in the least suave. He was stiff and stubborn. One could be warm toward him only with great effort. If anyone, it was Munio who reflected something of the father's personality. Perhaps that is why he often contradicted Maier in arguments, much to Maier's surprise and inevitably to his rage.

Mother Feuermann often told a story about Munio that epitomized this

Feuermann's mother, Rachel Hoenigsberg Feuermann, 1915.

familial inheritance. Munio had told it to her after having returned from a lesson with Walter. He, of course, was unaware of the significance the elders would draw from the story. It seems that Munio's lesson had gone overtime and there were several students in the anteroom awaiting their turn. Walter was demonstrating a new piece that he had just assigned to the boy. Munio looked at the music over the teacher's shoulder. Suddenly he cried out, directly into the teacher's ear, and apparently with a certain gleeful malice, "Professor Walter, that is not moderato, that is allegro con brio." Walter stopped, turned his head towards the boy, and roared back, "Munio, shush, what do you think, I have no time for moderato." On hearing the story, told in high-pitched excitement, Mother shook her head sadly, but with a smile, at her young cellist, "Ah, just like your father, you have his mouth."

Even if Sigmund and Maier were opposites in personality and, as a result, got on naturally, there must always be a dominating center. And omitting the dimensions of age and maturity, Maier was destined to prevail or at least to attempt to prevail here, as in all his relationships. Maier was the creator, and Sigmund the created.

The results, however, were increasingly phenomenal. At the first concert in Budapest in March of 1911, the reviewer noted that in spite of the frightening parade of ever-more-amazing prodigies, the ten-year-old Sigmund Feuermann displayed a maturity and natural understanding of the music that surpassed amazement. The years 1911–1914 were an unbroken spiral of greater achievements. London was conquered with the Brahms concerto. In Paris in 1913, still only twelve, Sigmund played three concerti with orchestra in one evening, a Mozart, the Beethoven, and the Richard Strauss. Over and over again they returned with success to Berlin.

By 1914, Sigmund had appeared numerous times on the stages of concert halls in all the great cities of Europe, from London to Constantinople. The critics were almost unanimous in their approval of his rare talents. He was the successor to Mischa Elman. The garlands of laurel leaves, which were the trophies artists received in those days (rather than flowers) decorated every wall in the Feuermann apartment in Vienna. When the laurel dried, Rachel frugally ground it up and put it into stews and roasts.

The general critical opinion was that after the young Elman from Odessa (now an adolescent), Sigmund had the most powerful technical equipment of any young virtuoso. (Heifetz had not yet appeared in public outside Russia.) The critics marveled at the way he tossed off the most formidable problems with aplomb and made it appear as if no technical feat were involved. He was now using a small full-sized Andrea Guarneri, lent to him by Director Kux, and he drew from it a tone that was both

Sigmund in England. On tour with the London Philharmonic, conducted by Felix Weingartner, 1914.

sweet and rich. The distinctive Sevčik left hand was matched by an exceptionally controlled and fluid bow arm.

A Berlin reviewer said this about Sigmund as early as March, 1912: "Sigmund Feuermann, a boy of about twelve years of age [he was eleven], played, in addition to a few solo pieces, the Brahms Violin Concerto with the Bluethner Orchestra. Considering only the fact that he was less successful in the solo pieces than in the concerto, one may assume the existence of a quite extraordinary talent. His playing is pure and by all means heart-felt; it offers the most remarkable pleasure since it lays bare, in the most beautiful form, the primordial elements of the soul. This young violinist will give incomparable joy to many people."

Another Berlin reviewer questioned Sigmund's studious approach and wondered at his impassive and controlled demeanor. Perhaps the boy should unbend. In this he was like his father, fulfilling the elder Feuermann's sense of seriousness. Maier would have no external show. His son was an artist, not a vaudevillian.

This attitude caused a nasty scene in London, in 1914, after an appearance with Felix Weingartner. Backstage, amid all the excitement and congratulations, a gentleman with whom Maier had had casual correspondence several months earlier approached him. The gentleman, a theatrical manager, had written of the possibility of Sigmund's touring the British Isles. The success that evening with Weingartner was such that the manager, in his eagerness, blurted out the full implications of the tour. True, it was for 150 appearances. The money, as it now turned out, was to be enormous. The crux of the matter was that Sigmund would be but one act of a variety show. When Maier heard this, his anticipation welled up into boiling outrage and he hurled a furious imprecation at the manager, to the effect that his son was an artist, not a circus clown.

The peak moment of Sigmund's pre-war career came late in the fall of 1913 when Weingartner informed the Feuermanns that he was planning an American tour for 1914–1915. Would they consent to the inclusion of Sigmund on the itinerary? He would be featured at several concerts in various American cities. It was an opportunity that went beyond Maier's wildest dreams. The possibility of seeing America without having to move the family permanently to the new world had never entered Maier's mind. Unfortunately, the war broke out that summer, all plans were scuttled, and the family's musical lives were considerably circumscribed.

The years that took Papa Feuermann away on tour with Sigmund coincided with Munio's apprenticeship under Anton Walter. In spite of the fact that there was no father to drive him incessantly onward, nor a Sevčik to stipulate eight to ten hours of practice each day, the boy's progress was rapid. Walter was more involved with his own playing career and did not have the commitment to teaching of Sevčik, or even Feist.

Thus he allowed Munio a significant amount of freedom, only seeing to it that everything he assigned came back adequately mastered. Munio's playful antics on the cello were only partially amusing to the teacher; but since they proved no handicap in his lessons, Walter, in the main, overlooked them. Besides, Walter was appreciative of the fact that Munio was a second son in the home of a Jewish family whose first boy was a genius. He did not push things excessively. If there was some dissatisfaction at home with Walter, it never got out of hand. Maier was away too often, and mother was averse to creating crisis situations.

Perhaps the most significant event in Munio's study with Walter came in late 1912 or 1913. It coincided with, and was precipitated by, the coming to Vienna of Pablo Casals, who was to play with the Philharmonic in the Grosse Musikvereinsaal. Maier was again away with Sigmund, so friends purchased tickets for Gusta, Munio, and Rachel. The boy had naturally heard much about the great Catalonian and was tremendously excited about seeing him for the first time.

Casals in the flesh more than lived up to his advance notices. He was impressively serious and scholarly on stage and created a powerful aura of expectancy even before he played his first notes. His solo works were the Boccherini B$^\flat$ and the Haydn D Major concerti. The demeanor of complete involvement was more than matched, for Munio, by the musical results. It seemed impossible that anyone else could have such an impact, both musical and technical, as Casals. His tone was warm and full. The melodies flowed freely from his bow; they rose over and beyond the orchestral accompaniment. The technique was so unnoticeable as to be rooted inextricably in the master's musicality.

Although Munio had heard much about great cellists such as David Popper, Charles Davidoff, and Julius Klengel, the truth, as all great musicians now recognized, was that Casals was truly recreating the instrument. Munio saw in Casals a benign uncle, only five years younger than his father, a symbol both to idolize and to emulate.

When he returned home, he demanded that his mother purchase the music for him that Casals had played. He had heard the Boccherini before, but the Haydn was new to him. It fascinated him, as it would for the rest of his life. He spent literally weeks figuring it out between periods of practice for his regular cello lessons. Finally, he surprised Walter one day by pulling the music out of his case and playing it. Walter was speechless. It was not a subtle or sophisticated performance, but it was there in the raw, with even a bit of the Casals grace. This kind of initiative Walter had not expected. It was a different order of bravado than the typical Munio "noodling." Perhaps there was even greater talent here than he had suspected.

When Maier arrived home he was overjoyed at the news of this accomplishment, especially when it was emphatically confirmed by Walter.

It was a rare person in Viennese musical circles who did not hear about Maier Feuermann's latest prodigy from Maier himself. Yet when the first flush of self-congratulation waned, Maier did little to follow it up. He did not envision in Munio the same kind of possibilities as in Sigmund, perhaps because of his current preoccupation with the career of the young violinist. Or perhaps it stemmed from his awareness of his own meager instrumental opportunities.

It is likely that the shadow of Casals also loomed large here. Casals was of Maier's generation. His overwhelming impact hardly made it likely that there were additional possibilities in what had never been a very large concert domain. There were increasing numbers of violin, voice, and piano performers of comparable caliber. Yet each was a unique artist able to carve out a successful and lucrative career. As for the cello, there were numerous competent players who ventured from their ensemble or teaching positions for some solo work. But with the exception of the unique Spaniard, no cellist could command a following that enabled him solely to concertize.

Maier's views reflected the musical consensus as to the possibilities of this avowedly important instrument. On the other hand, there were some who had not set limits to the possibilities in this dynamic musical environment. Such a person was the Viennese cellist Paul Grümmer, who had recently returned from England to resume his career. Grümmer had studied with Klengel and thus brought with him respectable teaching credentials, enough to have attracted a sizable class of students. In addition he was a fine cellist and obtained sufficient engagements, ensemble and solo, to spread report of his name around the traditionally close-knit Viennese musical fraternity. Later he would play with the Busch Quartet.

Being an ambitious cellist, Grümmer explored every possibility for advancing his career. He knew about the Feuermanns before he arrived back in Vienna, but he did not know at first about the youngest boy. Finding out as many details as he could, and appraising the situation carefully as to relative strengths and weaknesses, he saw quickly that the boy's talent was probably being underexploited. Being a few years older than Walter, cosmopolitan, and more committed to teaching, he concluded that a new arrangement was not foreclosed. He visited the Feuermann apartment with a clear and concrete proposition. If they would consent to switch Munio from Walter to himself, he would not only grant Munio the traditional scholarship, but would personally pay for a private tutor in Munio's academic subjects. But that was not all. As a bonus, he would grant an impressive cash stipend each month to the family for expenses.

To Rachel, who listened quietly to the mellifluous phrases of Grümmer, it was a dazzling as well as a perplexing offer. She did not like making a decision on such an important matter. Why did Grümmer propose it?

Was it to take advantage of their name? Maier was not at home to help, which was fortunate as well as unfortunate. For if he were, could he have resisted the temptation?

At any rate, there seemed no intrinsic need to shift Munio. There were enough aid and income coming into the house without more charity. Munio seemed to like Walter. They had already had their share of manipulation with Sigmund. If Kux heard about the offer, not to speak of their serious consideration of it, he would be troubled. Kux was too gentlemanly to say anything, but it would not be good. He had given them so much. And why Munio?

When she went to Dr. Harry Herschel, their friend, counselor, and doctor, to ask for his typically straightforward advice, he hesitated not a moment. His unequivocating advice was to reject Grümmer's offer, and keep Munio with Walter. He gave her no explanation as to how he reached this decision. Rachel sought none, for it confirmed her opinion. She forthwith informed Grümmer of their rejection of his proposal, with effusive thanks for his kindness.

What we have been relating reflects only the surface of a process that took place quietly, practically unnoticed in a way, and, fortunately, untouched. For a long while it was passed over as irrelevant to the main concerns of the Feuermanns' lives. It was a cumulative process that would have to be accounted for eventually, for they did not live in a vacuum. The incident with the Haydn Concerto and even the Grümmer episode did much to jolt them into some recognition. In the end it was the quiet inevitability of what had happened that stole over the Feuermanns and forced them to accept and understand the fact that Munio, too, was extraordinary.

He had started playing at a later age than Sigmund and for quite a while his playfulness seemed to indicate that he regarded the cello as a toy rather than as a serious commitment. Only at age nine had he been assigned to an outside teacher for a sustained period of instruction. In the beginning progress was good. But as time went on a cumulative series of surprising spurts had taken place, unheralded and almost without explanation, given the supposedly careful and didactic program Walter had planned for him. When the Feuermanns were finally convinced that all the incidents did not constitute a series of unconnected accidents, they naturally were delighted. Here in their own yard their uncultivated, scraggly weed had blossomed into a rose.

Maier now busily took advantage of Munio's competency. The brothers increasingly played in various informal ensembles at the homes of wealthy, influential, and cultured people. And it is understandable that Maier did not see beyond the possibility of a joint appearance of the brothers in the Brahms Double Concerto, sometime in the future. By the fall of 1913, at a time when Sigmund was enjoying unprecedented success, both Walter and Kux began to exert a certain amount of pressure to induce Maier to prepare a debut recital for Munio.

It was decided that the inaugural would be only a modest affair in a small hall in the Leopoldstaadt. This would be followed by an appearance with the Tonkünstler under the redoubtable Nedbal in Munio's favorite, the Haydn D Major. The announcements were given some publicity because of the Feuermann name. Indeed, yet another prodigy. But since young cellists were not the public rage, there was too small a market to draw any quick conclusions. And Munio's impact was somewhat muted, even for a child not quite eleven.

In the debut recital, the family recalled, Munio had a complete lapse of memory at one point. When this occurred, he stopped playing and just sat quietly on the stage, seeming calm, but puzzled by it all as he gazed out over the small hall. The pianist had as little presence of mind as Munio; he sat equally still. Maier, stationed in the rear of the auditorium had come prepared for any exigency. In an instant, he came running down the aisle, music in hand. He leaped up the steps onto the stage, grabbed a music stand which had been placed unobtrusively at its rear, opened the music to the appropriate passage, and placed it before Munio. He frantically pointed to a place where they could both begin, then backing off in front of them like a conductor, started them off together. Munio continued with complete unconcern. It was as if nothing untoward had occurred at all.

It had taken a bit of pushing to get Maier to break his pattern and arrange for Munio's debut, but now that the idea of a second prodigy had been planted firmly in his mind, he spared no time or trouble in exploiting what he fully expected would be another successful beginning. Sigmund had several weeks free in his concert itinerary and Maier found several concert openings into which the boys could be fitted. Concerts at Quedlinburg, Halberstadt, Tavia, and Abazzio (where Munio is reported to have played the Tartini Cello Concerto), and several others in Poland and Bohemia, would culminate in a concert at Bucharest.

The trip lasted just over a month, but it was memorable in that all three Feuermann males were now together, pursuing their mutual vocation. The concerts were unexceptional, a few short solos by Sigmund, a movement, usually the first, from the Brahms "Double," in which Maier had coached both boys, and usually a concerto played by Sigmund.

There were to be many such trips in the years 1914–1917, and they would not vary substantially in their character. In subsequent years the balance would be improved to the point that Munio would regularly play a few solos in addition to the Brahms. When Munio came to Klengel in Leipzig in 1917, the latter would reiterate constantly that the only piece the young cellist had in his repertoire was the cello part of the Brahms "Double." And while this was not quite accurate—the boy did have a few

Sigmund and "Munio," 1915.

solo opportunities in addition to the tours—Klengel was not far wrong.

The success of the concerts could not be disputed. Munio was especially ecstatic to be part of the musical establishment. Maier had obtained a beautiful yellow-orange French cello of 7/8 size, which the boy treasured. It was a hardship sale, and Maier, who had always reserved some cash for such an opportunity, was able to strike a good bargain for the instrument.

An instrument is often crucial to a performer's success, because it has a personality of its own. And if it fits the personality of the player, it becomes, in turn, an integral part of the player's body. Munio held onto this instrument until he left home, when he was already a good-sized adolescent. The cello was easy to play, bright in sound, and beautiful to look at. He grew into it in those years with remarkable ease.

Sigmund also treasured the Andrea Guarneri lent to him by Kux. Bucharest would later be a place of disaster for this particular instrument. After the war, Sigmund gave a recital in that city. When he was leaving to catch a train, he took a short cut across the tracks. He had grown heavy and was somewhat slow of foot, and as he hurried to avoid any moving trains, he tripped. Unfortunately his instrument case was decrepit and he fell with full weight on top of the violin. The case gave way and the violin was smashed. Sigmund always tried to avoid Bucharest after that incident.

Munio also had his troubles with Kux's instruments. His first full-sized cello was a dark red Nicolo Amati, which the family always claimed was the best instrument he ever had. It is possible that it was symbolic of Kux's great admiration for the boy, since he had acquired the instrument especially to lend to Munio. The particular disaster it encountered occurred in Köln, where Munio was also in transit, on a bus. As he climbed onto the slowly moving vehicle with his cello held behind him, an anxious rider with a metal-tipped suitcase got up beside him on the bus steps and cracked his suitcase through the cloth case into the belly of the cello.

The crack was so bad that major reconstruction was necessitated, and the forebearing Kux exchanged the instrument for a lovely Petrus Guarneri. Munio enjoyed playing on this instrument for a number of years, but disaster almost overtook him here, too. This occurred in the midtwenties when he was traveling by train. He had placed the cello, again in a cloth bag, on the rack above his seat. As he dozed, a passenger came in at one of the stops and chose the seat next to Munio. He proceeded to fling his suitcase onto the rack. At the first sound of contact between that object and his instrument, Munio was awake; and if he was not able to prevent the contact, he did save the cello from toppling down to the floor.

The Guarneri sustained only minor rib damage, but since it was a small model, and Munio felt the need for a bigger and more powerful instrument, he gave it back to Kux with great apologies and purchased for himself the fine, very large David Tecchler with which he began his recording career. The history of cello disasters was not yet over, but more of that later.

Kux's collection was legendary. Altogether there were sixteen of the very finest instruments obtainable including a rare sixteenth-century Gaspar da Salo. And he lent them freely to his young prodigies. In 1938, when the Nazis came to Vienna, there was an attempt to find the collection but it had disappeared. Ultimately, it was saved.

The years 1914–1917—in spite of the war, an extremely delimited concert career, and much material hardship—provided the Feuermann triumvirate with their high point as a family. Never again would they be together as they were at this time. To be sure, they were exploiting their careers in a serious enough manner. But the two ebullient boys were now almost a match for their ingenious father, and they found much that was adventurous or hilarious in every experience. The stories they brought home with them provided many entertaining evenings.

One of the favorite stories which they told on their father, and which in later years they related to characterize him to relatives and friends (and which Maier enjoyed as well), concerned one of their tours. They were traveling east from Vienna. The railway conductor came by to collect their tickets. As usual, Maier had purchased half-fare tickets for the boys. But there was a difficulty. Half-fare applied to those under twelve. And while Munio was perhaps six months over-age—and a good-sized child at that—Sigmund was already a sturdy adolescent.

The conductor gazed with some amazement at the tickets as he took them from the father. "Sir," he exclaimed with some anger. "These gentlemen are not under twelve! It is hardly possible." Maier met the challenge. He straightened himself, his sense of dignity outraged. His voice boomed out in rebuttal: "Don't you think I know what their ages are? This one," he pointed to Munio, "is only eleven, and this one," pointing to Sigmund, "is only eleven and one-half." The conductor glared silently for a moment and then collected their tickets, to the muffled but delighted giggles of the youngsters.

Munio's official debut was in February of 1914, with the Vienna Philharmonic under Weingartner. The boy's previous appearance had elicited enough interest and approval to warrant the sponsorship of the great conductor, who was assured that the younger Feuermann was a talent in his own right, not merely a pale reflection of Sigmund. There was even a hint that were the concert to be a great success with the public as well as critics, Munio could be included in the American itinerary.

As it turned out, the Haydn concerto went extremely well. Both Korngold and Kalbeck, the well-known Viennese critics who reviewed the concert, pronounced Munio to be an unusual cello talent, and a worthy addition to the family's musical reputation. The audience was especially taken with the image of the small boy, his beaming childish face, seated behind the awesome cello, managing with such aplomb.

While members of the family were well pleased with the results, no special note was taken of the occasion. In their own minds, they had already arrived, and they were now somewhat indifferent to the tangible as well as intangible excitements growing out of their position in the musical world. Just weeks earlier, Sigmund had precipitated a scene at the recital of the Viennese soprano, Selma Kurz. He had been engaged to play several short, light numbers between groups of songs the soprano was to sing. He would thus provide a few moments of rest for her, without distracting the audience from the major focus of the program—the voice. Sigmund's extremely fluent handling of the few technicalities, his luscious sound, as well as his complete composure onstage brought on a thunderous ovation. There were insistent demands for encores from this thirteen-year-old. These of course he had been forbidden to deliver, so the applause reflected a redoubled insistence. Backstage, the soprano was flushed with fury. She had not counted on such a distraction for her audience, and she vowed to her manager that never again would she tolerate a Feuermann on her program.

Thus they were surprised the morning after Munio's appearance with the Philharmonic when a delegation arrived at the apartment, led by one of their recently acquired friends and part-time manager, a Mr. Kolum, to see the new genius. A hurried family inspection revealed that Munio was nowhere in sight, so eldest sister Gusta was sent to look for him while the visitors were served coffee. Ten minutes later, Gusta burst through the door shouting that Munio would not come. "He doesn't care who's here to see him," she reported excitedly, "he's right in the middle of a whip-the-top game and doesn't want to come." The mother whispered angrily to her and Gusta ran out of the apartment once again. A few minutes later a thoroughly repentant and sheepish-looking boy made his appearance; the guests smiled benignly and nodded, "there now, a great prodigy, yet a regular little street urchin."

Before the end of the summer of 1914, most of the plans that had been made as a result of the debut had to be abandoned. The war had finally come. For a time there was an attempt to continue as before. France and England were of course removed from the concert itinerary, but Austria and Germany still held a large slice of Europe and much opportunity for the Feuermann "act." Through 1916, the boys gave many concerts to uniformly appreciative audiences and good critical notices.

Whenever they returned, with startling and almost mechanical simultaneity, the redoubtable Professor Knepfelmacher would appear to give them their academic lessons, usually to a resounding chorus of dismay from the brothers. Inevitably the departure of tutor Knepfelmacher brought forth father to lecture them for their lassitude and to reiterate

The Feuermann children: left to right, Rosa, Gusta, Munio, Sigmund, Sophie, 1915.

that the Feuermann household was a place of learning, not a playground. The impact of these lectures was less than decisive.

Increasingly there were concerts for war relief, and the Feuermanns, as good Austrians, participated whenever asked, usually repeating programs that they had given on tour. In the next year or two, the military situation worsened and serious shortages of food developed. It was not a time favorable to musical life. Yet in Vienna, it seemed necessary to continue the pattern, at least to pretend normality in one's private as well as public life. Music ran too deep to be abandoned easily.

In the second year of the war the undulating front line, pulsating back and forth with each new offensive and counteroffensive, dredged up increasing waves of refugees. The influx of refugees from the east, especially Poland, became extremely serious. In one of the first waves, partly goaded by Maier's insistent warnings, were the Hoenigsbergs, including Rachel's mother, Feige. They were of course given refuge in the Feuermann home. When Vienna was finally closed to all refugees, Maier made a point of keeping in touch with friends in Prague so the displaced who had made it to that city as a final haven might be looked after.

The elder Feuermann was now the patriarch of a large clan, and he reveled in the opportunity to make everyone's business his own. His commitment and enthusiasm were complete. Several of Shmuel Hoenigsberg's sons (there were six, all musicians) were threatened with the military draft. As in all wars, this was a possibility to be avoided at all costs. Maier launched a one-man campaign at the musicians' union to try to prevent this by getting the boys into one of the municipal ensembles, the Orchestre Populaire, the Philharmonic, or the military band. He had good contacts in all of these.

Wilhelm Wacak, who at that time was head of the union, was sympathetic to Maier's urgent pleading. He was sensitive to the need for preserving the musical talent of the city and for preventing as many as possible from becoming cannon fodder. Adolph Hoenigsberg, an extremely gifted trumpeter, was absorbed into one of these ensembles. A brother, Philip, a mildly talented cellist, was drafted in Prague and sent to Italy, where he turned up playing the bass for dances. Brother Max was also drafted, but he managed to wend his way into officers' clubs by playing the piano well enough to escape the front lines. Another brother, Joseph, was taken on by the violinist Suchy, a famous disciple of Sevčik in Prague, and spent several years with this master before Suchy's untimely death. By this time Joseph was able to support himself by playing in the pit in Prague theatres. And so it went.

Maier was always busy. He spent an inordinate amount of time arranging concerts, getting tickets, appearing at all the important functions. If there were few tours for the boys he did at least keep busy. And he still found time to play the cello. One of the boys' favorite father stories from

The budding virtuoso in Sigmund's old *"Wunderkind"* outfit, 1916.

these uncertain days concerned Maier's campaign against Hugo Kneppler, who has been described as the Sol Hurok of that era in Vienna.
There was a concert especially important to Maier, in which the boys were
scheduled to appear. Maier wanted everyone in his entourage to attend
and was, as usual, trying to get more than the normally allotted number of
complimentary tickets. He had always been something of a thorn to
Kneppler. This time, on his third appearance in one week at Kneppler's
office to lighten the impresario of a few additional tickets, and in the midst
of a tight financial squeeze, Kneppler finally threw him out of the office
with an exasperated cry of *"O, dieser Väter!"*

In November of 1916, Munio turned fourteen. Gradually, but perceptibly, he was turning into a man. The Feuermanns' friends now often
asked about their plans for Munio. The press of events, the war, the
hardships, had diverted them from this subject. However, both parents
began to realize that with Munio there might be alternative options.
Increasingly their thoughts turned to education. Munio was at a crucial
point, since he was at the age when his basic education should have been
completed.

In retrospect it is hard to understand why there was any question as to
which way his future lay. But at that moment there was still doubt. With
Sigmund, there was surety. He was a born violinist and too far along the
road towards an important concert career to think of alternatives. Munio,
playing on the cello—which in itself raised questions about his ultimate
success—was, in addition, a different kind of child. He was interested in a
variety of things besides music. He read quite a bit and was able to handle
most of his academic work. Where Sigmund could practice six or seven
hours a day with phenomenal persistence and concentration, Munio
barely squeezed out his two or three hours. There were too many other
things in the world that interested him.

Sigmund seemed the more brilliant and specialized. His memory was
unusual. Once the initial excitement of touring had worn off, he took it in
a very relaxed way, talked little about his experiences or even the world.
He would pore over encyclopedias and memorize long passages from
articles about people or events that interested him. As the war dragged
on, he became fascinated by the personality and career of Napoleon. The
walls of his room were covered with pictures, drawings, and maps that
concerned the life of this hero. But these interests did not seem to be
intellectually integrated. In general, Sigmund's musical interests dominated all else. He was now arranging various pieces for violin. All were
amazed at his ability to reduce from memory an orchestral score that he
had studied earlier, to piano and violin.

The Feuermanns, as typical Viennese, were aware that music was not
the only key to success. It still carried the stigma of indebtedness and
servant's status. Higher education, a university degree, and the civil

Kritikauszüge
über den Violinvirtuosen Sigmund Feuermann, Wien.

Berlin.

„Berl. Tagbl.", 23. April 1923.

„Bei Sigmund Feuermann interessieren die artistischen Leistungen wegen ihrer geschmackvollen Ausgeglichenheit und temperamentvollen Gestaltung.

Zürich.

„Züricher Tagesanzeiger", 12. März 1923.

„Symphoniekonzert. Der Künstler trägt seinen Namen mit Recht; denn ein feuriges Temperament zeichnet vor allem seine exquisite musikalische Leistung aus. Er spielte das Violinkonzert von Beethoven mit prächtigem Ton, zuverlässigster reiner Technik und mit sympathischem individuellem Zug.

Winterthur (Schweiz).

„Schweizer Musikzeitung", 28. April 1923.

„... Das ganze überschäumende Temperament, doch gezügelt durch künstlerischen Geschmack, zeigte sich in der glänzenden Wiedergabe des D-Dur-Konzertes von Tschaikowsky ... eine oft stupende Virtuosität in einem E-Dur-Adagio von Mozart in den Variationen von Corelli und endlich in der feurigen mit allen möglichen Hexenkünsten ausgestatteten ,Carmen'-Fantasie von Sarasate ..."

München.

„Münchner Neueste Nachrichten", 3. März 1923.

„Sigmund Feuermann ist ein Geiger mit großer Technik und einer makellosen Schönheit und Reinheit des Tones ..."

„Münchner Neueste Nachrichten", 25. März 1923.

„Der Geiger Sigmund Feuermann hatte auch mit seinem zweiten Konzert starken Erfolg, den er den ausgezeichneten Qualitäten seiner Strich- und Tontechnik zu danken hat."

„Münchner Allgem. Zeitung," 24. März 1923.

„Sigmund Feuermann ist Violinvirtuose großer Klasse. Sein gesunder, mächtiger und außerordentlich differenzierter Ton bei bewundernswerter Technik ..."

Frankfurt.

„Frankf. Generalanzeiger", 11. März 1923.

„... Sein Ton ist ergiebig, klar und von schönem warmen Anklang ..."

„Frankf. Nachrichten", 20. April 1923.

„Er gab Lalo und dann Tschaikowsky, die Noblesse seiner Tongebung und eine abgeklärte Ruhe, die besonders der schwermütigen Serenade des großen Russen zustatten kam ..."

Düsseldorf.

„Düsseldorfer Generalanzeiger", 15. Februar 1923.

„ Philharmonisches Konzert. ... führte uns der Geiger Sigmund Feuermann mit Beethovens Violinkonzert in Gefilde, die selbst mit Fokker, Eindeckern und Hängegleitern nicht zu erreichen sind ... wenn wir vielleicht sogar manchmal das diesem bebenden und doch so kraftvollen Ton lauschen, dessen Stärke am deutlichsten im Piano wird, ja in der gerade in dem noch schattenhaftester Zartheit tragfähigen und klangvollen Piano seinesgleichen sucht, wenn wir uns dieser unfehlbaren Technik, dieser feinen Phrasierung, diesem scharf profilierten Aufbau und vor allem diesem rassigen Temperament gefangen sind ..."

Köln.

„Kölner Tagblatt", 7. Oktober 1923.

„Sigmund Feuermann gehört zu unseren bedeutendsten Geigern ..."

Cassel.

„Allgemeine Zeitung", 23. Oktober 1923.

„... Die Giaconna von Bach für die Solovioline war die Hauptnummer für die Leistungsfähigkeit des Geigers ... Kristallklar, überlegen, sicher und beherrscht, in plastischer Fülle und wundervoller Abstufung entstand sie zum Leben ..."

„Casseler Tagblatt", 23. Oktober 1923.

„Der Geiger Sigmund Feuermann befriedigt in gleichem Maße die höchsten Anforderungen. Sein Ton ist im Piano von einer süß-sinnlichen Weichheit, durchströmt von jener faszinierenden Art des modernen Geigers ..."

Engagementsanträge erbeten an die Konzertdirektion:

Publicity sheet for Sigmund, 1924, photograph taken about 1917.

service were far more prestigious socially; these accrued a good share of titles and perquisities. Professor Knepfelmacher, even if he had his doubts about Munio's preparation, agreed that perhaps the next step was to have Munio stand for the examination for Gymnasium. Anton Walter also concurred that a few weeks' hiatus would not hurt and Director Kux was moderately favorable. The latter was well aware that with the end of the war Munio might become a musical anachronism in the family and be forced into ensemble playing, while Sigmund and father embarked on Maier's long-dreamed-of world tours.

The long weeks of preparation were an unbearable chore for the young cellist. Knepfelmacher appeared almost daily. Munio even sneaked an hour or two on the cello between tedious sessions with his books. While he hated to do anything under compulsion, the academic regimen was particularly onerous, and he whined incessantly.

Thus the entire household was relieved when the examination came and went. There were a few days of hesitant anticipation and even foreboding. Finally, Knepfelmacher arrived and closeted himself with the father. He departed as suddenly as he had come. The results had been conclusive. The Latin examination was a disaster. The other parts, Maier was told, were little better. Obviously Munio had not cared. "Let him be a musician, a scholar he is certainly not destined to be," the pedagogue had concluded sadly.

3

THE EDUCATION OF A VIRTUOSO

In the spring of 1917 a rare event occurred in the Feuermann family. Maier vacillated. He could not decide what to do with Munio. Weeks went by and all plans stagnated. In truth, conditions in the outside world were not conducive to the making of any plans. The family's situation was not auspicious, the war was increasingly a factor in the daily lives of the Viennese. It was going badly; catastrophe lurked on the horizon.

Musical activity had dried up. The year before, appearances by the brothers had helped keep things going. But even in Germany, contracts had not been renewed or expanded. There were the usual benefit concerts, now attracting fewer people. Chamber music among family and friends provided bright spots much sought after by all musicians, clustered ever closer together. Personal striving and study at least for the moment seemed pointless. Yet Sigmund was as assiduous as ever in his practicing, urged on by Maier, and stimulated by an occasional visit to Sevčik.

Maier had pinned so much hope on an early cessation of the war. He had planned so many glorious tours in his imagination. The whole world would become the arena for his youthful duo. It was the stuff of dreams, for the war dragged on while before his eyes the boys were sprouting into men. What was becoming of his *Wunderkinder?* Vienna, because of their forced incarceration, had, ironically, become a kind of ghetto.

As the memory of Munio's academic examination faded into the background, Maier's temporary inertia was gradually overcome by pressures that could no longer be resisted. Not only Rachel, but Director Kux and Dr. Harry Herschel as well, began to urge that Munio be placed in musical hands outside Vienna. For the first time Kux became an active and insistent participant in these deliberations. He had only that winter lent Munio a full-sized Nicolo Amati cello to replace the beloved small French instrument the boy had been using. Kux had been the first to notice that the time had come to place a good-sized instrument in his hands. It became apparent that spring, merely listening to his playing, that the tide of adolescence was beginning to wash over his youthful frame. There was greater strength in his playing now, and in a matter of a few weeks the period of raspy transition on the new cello gave way to a warmth and expansiveness of sound that raised exciting expectations in all who heard him.

Maier at last consented. The circumstances had indeed tied his hands. He would have to permit Munio to leave Vienna and his own close supervision. There were two good possibilities for Munio—Leipzig and Berlin. Leipzig did not have the wealth, power, or prestige of Berlin; yet there was still in those early years of the century a status to the provincial centers of Germany that reflected the decentralized state of things of the eighteenth and nineteenth centuries. Had not Goethe called Leipzig "*kleines Paris?*" At its distinguished conservatory, Julius Klengel had been teaching cello since 1881, and turning out a large number of fine cellists. He was also the first cellist of the Gewandhaus Orchestra. The previous year, he had witnessed the Feuermann brothers perform the Brahms Double Concerto under Artur Nikisch.

The other possible choice was the Berlin Hochschule, which was rapidly becoming the premier music academy of Germany. Hugo Becker, a highly respected chamber musician and soloist, was the cello teacher (Flesch-Schnabel-Becker Trio). Becker represented a scholarly and academic approach to instrumental playing. He was a typical example of the Berlin tradition of the violinist Joseph Joachim, now deceased, whose influence in this institution was still pervasive.

In fairness it should be noted that Joachim himself had studied in Leipzig, under Ferdinand David. Joachim was at that time still a boy and the officials of the conservatory boarded him out to a local family by the name of Klengel. This was Julius' grandfather, at that time a violinist in the Gewandhaus orchestra. Who is to say what mutual influences occurred in that home? It was from Leipzig that Joachim ventured forth under the sponsorship of Mendelssohn, Schumann, and later Brahms to found, in 1869, the Berlin Hochschule in that as yet semiprovincial city.

Becker, a strong, domineering musical personality, exercised the influence expected from such an august chair and attracted a large and devoted group of students. These students, steeped in Becker's own distinctive methodological approach to cello technique and interpretation, constituted a powerful group of advocates for the Berlin tradition.

The decision was difficult. It was Kux, the astute amateur cellist, who added the weight of his opinion before Maier's vanity could cloud everyone's judgment. It was the prestige of Berlin versus the utilitarian advantages of Leipzig. Kux stated categorically that it should be Leipzig and Klengel. Perhaps to soften the impression that it was his will alone that forced the decision, Kux noted to the elder Feuermanns that Leipzig was closer to Vienna than Berlin. In times when war had disrupted communication and transportation, this was a persuasive factor.

It was never explicitly mentioned as being decisive in their deliberations, but there were rumors of which all were aware that raised their apprehensions. Perhaps Kux knew more than he had told them. Yet the subject was too widely disseminated to discount. It was said, although with great respect, that the great Herr Professor Becker was a typical German autocrat. Even if the story was only partially true, the family could not take a chance on a potential musical disaster. Their experiences with Buxbaum had taught them to be wary. Then too, Munio had not grown any less opinionated in the intervening years. Sharing the same studio, master and student could catalyze a fair-sized explosion.

Gregor Piatigorsky has given us an insight, possibly somewhat embellished, of how Becker impressed him when he was a young yet advanced and talented novice in Berlin. This occurred some five years after Munio considered studying with Becker. It tends to confirm what has become the traditional evaluation of Becker as a teacher—that he destroyed far more talents than he nurtured.

A servant led me to the study of the professor's luxurious home. Becker and Ochi Albi, the student who had previously translated for us, were waiting for me.

'The professor wants you to forget you ever played cello before.'

'Yes.'

'You must start from the very beginning.'

'Yes.'

'Your right arm is your tongue; your left, your thoughts.'

'Yes.'

'You have no thoughts whatsoever. Even if you have, you must learn to speak first.'

'Yes.'

Professor Becker showed me how to hold the bow. He seemed pleased. He let me strike an open string. 'Professor is encouraged,' said Ochi Albi. 'He thinks you are gifted.' Becker glanced at his watch. He stood up. The lesson was over.

Ochi Albi accompanied me home. He spoke with great admiration of his teacher. 'It took the professor more than twenty years to solve the problems of the right arm,' he said. 'His method is perfect. He is a great man—a scientist and a true artist. I have been with him only two years, but my right arm is improving already.'

My German progressed very slowly and my practicing of holding the bow was boring. My second, third, and fourth lessons were quite uneventful except at the end, when I would make a bow and say, 'Gott sei Dank.' Each time it seemed to throw him into a rage. What did I do wrong? I wondered, wishing that Ochi Albi had been present.

At the fifth lesson the professor was unusually friendly and I was glad to see Ochi Albi again. He told me how highly the professor thought of me and how rapid my progress was. 'You learned to hold the bow in four lessons. Some can't master it in years. Your bow arm is in almost perfect position on all four strings. The professor has decided to make a great exception and begin to work with you right now on the finest music for our instrument.'

Becker spoke again and Ochi Albi translated. 'The situation is now drastically changed. You are not a pupil any more. You are ready to work on great music and therefore you and I are equals.'

'We have to be frank, and I expect you to express your opinions freely.' He took his cello and said, 'I will play the beginning of the Dvorák Concerto—only the beginning. After I have played, you will do the same. Then we will discuss the merit of each performance.'

He began. I saw a gust of resin fly, rise and fall in all directions. Ripping off the hair, his bow knocked on the sides of his cello. The stick hit the strings. After some noisy thumping on the fingerboard with his left hand, he stopped. I did not dare look at him. He asked something. His voice sounded happy. I looked at his face and saw that he *was* happy.

'Herr Professor asked how you liked it.' said Ochi Albi.

'It was terrible,' I said. Ochi Albi was silent.

'What? What?' Becker asked.

Ochi Albi pleaded, 'The professor wants to know. What shall I tell him?'

I hesitated. 'Tell him it was just fine.' I don't know what Ochi Albi told him. Becker's face was red. He looked at his watch and said the lesson was over. I bowed and said, *'Gott sei Dank.'*

'Heraus!' Becker screamed. 'Out of here, you conceited, ignorant mujik!'

In July, it was off to Klengel in Leipzig. As their young virtuoso, not yet fifteen, gathered up his suitcase and his precious Amati to board the train in the station, the family gathered around him for the last emotional farewells. Munio climbed aboard and waved to them from the steps as the train began to move. They all moved with the train for their farewells. A final voice calling out, "Munio, come back a second Casals." His high-pitched voice called out in instantaneous response, "No, I'll come back a first Feuermann." There was more significance to this remark than anyone could have predicted at the time.

Leipzig in this era still presented the visitor with a rich historical panorama. The destruction of World War II was to be irreparable. But now, in 1917, one could still trace in its street patterns, architecture, and physical scale, the esthetic qualities of its medieval origins. Originally a Slavonic settlement, Leipzig had been gradually populated by German settlers and invaders from the west. By the date of its founding in 1174, it was under the exclusive hegemony of Teutonic culture. The university came to Leipzig, as to Cambridge, as a result of secession. In this case it was the German students from Prague who sparked its development, a classic example of Slavonic retribution. From this time on, Leipzig played an increasingly significant role in the intellectual and cultural history of central Europe.

Built at the confluence of three rivers—the Pleisse, Elster, and Parthe—the city, by 1917, had grown to almost half a million people. Berlin was a larger, more boisterous and lively city in every way, politically, economically, and by now even culturally. Nevertheless, Leipzig had tradition, what one today would call class. The achievements of the past announced themselves on every block, at every corner.

As the boy left his *pension* in those early weeks to enjoy the fruits of his adolescent liberation by exploring the ancient streets, the oppressive atmosphere of war and defeat touched him not at all. The excitement and wonder of great achievement in the past stirred his imagination and hopes and confirmed to him the wisdom of choosing Leipzig. In 1519, here in the Pleissenberg Citadel, Martin Luther engaged in one of his earliest disputations. Leibniz, Germany's first great philosopher, was born here; Richard Wagner, too. Goethe studied here and utilized his memories of Leipzig in the writing of Faust. Lessing produced his first play in Leipzig. The philosophers Schelling and Fichte studied here and from here went on to greatness.

Others came to Leipzig to contribute their fame to its glory. For twemty-seven years, Johann Sebastian Bach was cantor of St. Thomas Church. Here in the closing years of his life Bach brought German music to its first high peak. Robert Schumann came to Leipzig to work and here composed his *Andante and Variations,* op. 46, and *Paradise and Peri,* op. 50. Importantly, for Munio, Leipzig was where a fellow Jew (if an apostate), Felix Mendelssohn, came, not only to compose, but to revive the Gewandhaus concerts, which had been started in Bach's time (1743) in the old medieval cloth hall. Mendelssohn gave distinction to the musical season by improving the orchestra and its programs as well as by reintroducing Bach's music to audiences that had so soon forgotten it.

Munio recalled the year earlier, when he and Sigmund had walked through these streets with their father. Maier had been especially eager and proud for the boys to play at the Gewandhaus under Nikisch, and had been emphatic about the superiority of German music and culture as compared, for example, with Slavic or Latin. Implicit in this adulation was an element of self-intimidation over the fact that they were Jews from Galicia. Though Galician Jews were themselves considered to be the intellectual elite of eastern Jewry, to the Feuermanns it was a tradition that looked backwards only. In places like Leipzig or Berlin, past and present were wedded to a vigorous and dynamic social and cultural *Weltanschauung* that put even Vienna in the shade.

These views were confirmed in all Munio's experiences. At the conservatory, in the boarding house, wherever one encountered students or teachers, there was an atmosphere of seriousness and commitment he had never felt in Vienna. But then, the newness of this life, the excitement of a mysterious and foreign city, which, in Munio's adolescent state, stimulated his senses far beyond his physical limits, could not lend his impres-

Munio, extreme right, at Leipzig pension, to study with Klengel, July 1917.

sions objectivity. Whatever the truth of his still largely inchoate thoughts, his experience in Leipzig could not help but be powerful. But of all his experiences in Leipzig, his encounter with Klengel was the most important. For the first time, Munio ventured out on his own on the cello, consciously and self-critically, not almost sub rosa as he had before.

Julius Klengel was one of the great teachers and musicians of the late nineteenth and early twentieth centuries. His was the third generation of an established musical family. He was destined for the cello early in life and never hesitated or deviated from his goal, which was fulfilled entirely in this city of his birth. His grandfather had played violin with the Gewandhaus Orchestra in the days of Mendelssohn, and stayed on for fifty years without ever missing a concert. And though his father was a law professor at the university, he was constantly at the piano, so that to the young Julius it remained a mystery for years as to what his father's profession really was.

At an early age Julius was apprenticed to the cellist Ernst Hegar at the Conservatory. Later he studied composition with Jadassohn. He developed a passion for composing and eventually combined his talents to produce a vast literature for cello, not only *études,* but an enormous number of solo pieces for cello in every imaginable chamber or orchestral grouping. His heroic productivity in composition was matched by his stamina on the cello. He equaled his grandfather's mark at the Gewandhaus. Becoming a member of this orchestra at age fifteen, he stayed on until 1924, fifty years, without ever missing a concert.

This important event was marked in that year by a performance of the master's own Double Concerto for Violin and Cello conducted by Furtwängler, then the orchestra's regular conductor. If Klengel had any thoughts of improving on his grandfather's record, they were frustrated by Furtwängler's rapid replacement of the old man. Klengel died in 1933. Thus he did not have to witness the tragic destruction of German musical culture wrought on his nation by the Nazis. His life ended while the fruits of his own work could still be experienced in a Germany that was at the center of Western musical life.

It is doubtful that his music will attain immortality—although this has yet to be evaluated fully—because of its technical difficulties. He did produce a score of extremely fine cellists—including Guillermina Suggia, Alfred Wallenstein, Joseph Schuster, Jascha Bernstein, Mischa Schneider, Benar Heifetz, Henri Honneger, Stefan Auber, Paul Grümmer, Gregor Piatigorsky, and, of course, his greatest product, Emanuel Feuermann. No other teacher, including Hugo Becker, could equal this record. The story is told how in the early twenties Emanuel Feuermann came to Berlin to appear as a soloist with one of the local orchestras. After the concert, an acquaintance and perhaps secret antagonist spotted Hugo Becker as he walked down the stairs. The gentleman came up to the haughty old cellist and nudged him, "Well, Hugo, what do you think?" he asked with a twinkle, "a student of Klengel. . . ." Becker stiffened and gruffly uttered two words, *"Ein Göttertalent."*

The closest approximation to Klengel's style and charm as a teacher was manifested in Leopold Auer, who probably did not equal Klengel in versatility. Both men had that rare ability to bring out the best in the student without literally teaching him how to play. Perhaps it was their intuitive sense of when *not* to touch or to interfere, rather when and how to guide, coax, and stimulate. The natural evolution of the classical forms of music necessitated an expanding level of musical and technical competence. This demand was met by a band of young talents that gravitated into the musical centers from eastern Europe. Physically these young from the east were no more capable than their brethren in former or later eras. They were merely fulfilling a need, and the contemporary social and cultural stimulant of opportunity to an already music-hungry generation was decisive. Those teachers who eschewed a stifling and rigid methodology of playing were most likely to see their flocks flourish.

Klengel was a selfless and contented person, his ego secure in his work. Indeed, he probably did not have time to probe the inner psychic dispositions of his students in order to attempt to solve their technical problems as certain later teachers have found necessary. Besides his composing and orchestra obligations, there were chamber music concerts, and not a few solo engagements. Later, many of his students would reflect on their good fortune in coming to him. He never attempted to mold them to his way of playing. If they played naturally and easily, he let them alone.

Klengel knew that this extraordinarily raucous and ambitious group of boys would move mountains to best each other. He baited them by hinting that one or the other of them had an able trill, or a good vibrato, spiccato, etc., and sent them on their way usually to spy good-naturedly on each other. It was a competition without painful consequences. There were opportunities, yet the stakes were not extremely high. There were in those days few lucrative jobs or possibilities for a concert career.

Perhaps most important of all was Klengel's love of all his students. Never in their memory could any of them recall an unkind or destructive word from this teacher. The sarcasm, the sadism that accompanied so much musical instruction, in that as well as in our day, were completely lacking. They were lacking as well in the Auer style.

Klengel would always listen attentively and quietly to his students' playing, and help with phrasing, fingering, or bowing, occasionally demonstrating. More usually his major activity was to puff on his ever-present cigar. (Few would venture to guess the real color of his thoroughly stained beard.) He would tell the story of one of his visits to a doctor for treatment of his ulcer. The doctor, noting his level of cigar smoking, strongly advised him to give it up for the sake of his health. Klengel asked the doctor whether he had ever smoked. The reply was negative. The cellist shrugged his shoulders and continued his cigar smoking to his final days.

The atmosphere at the conservatory was one of complete immersion in music. No one had to be urged to practice. Practicing went on at all hours of the day and night, in practically every home, rooming house, and building in the neighborhood. It was a veritable cataclysm of sound unrelieved except for the occasional carousing, practical jokes, and typical carryings-on of music students. Klengel presided over his class as if it had been his own brood. He was able to involve himself in their lives and their welfare, yet rarely interfere except when his help was needed. A devoted husband and father, in his habits, attitude of mind, and preoccupation with his art, he was a true bohemian. There was little in the blandishments of higher society to attract him. In fact he rather enjoyed observing the antics of his boys, from afar. They probably reminded him of his own youth.

One of his later students, the cellist and conductor Albert Cattel, recalls how he became ill one winter while in Leipzig. He found he was unable to practice and could not appear for his lesson. Sending word to Professor Klengel, he gave the reason for the cancellation of the lesson and requested a later makeup. The following day at the time usually set for his lesson there was a knock on his door, and the tall, thin old man entered. After enquiring solicitously for Cattel's health, Klengel took a bottle of wine from his coat pocket and placed it on the dressing table, saying simply that he hoped the wine would put him on the road to recovery. After a few minutes of conversation Klengel took his leave, but not before assuring himself that the young man had enough money for his personal needs.

As a cellist, Klengel was formidable. Indeed, many musicians considered him the Paganini of his instrument. Together with David Popper and Carl Davidoff, who were somewhat older, Klengel is thought to have opened up a wholly new level of technical accomplishment for the instrument. The sonatas and concerti he wrote are extremely difficult. Many a Klengel student has had to assure younger cellists that indeed the old man was equal to the demands of his compositions and often played them in public.

At the same time, he was still considered by his students to be of an earlier era of instrumental accomplishment. Casals had already established canons of cello sound and technique that made Klengel's approach outdated. It was not that Klengel had a wiry and scratchy tone. Recordings made in the late twenties, late in his career, testify to his ample and pure sound. However, his changes of position and movement on the instrument make the modern listener cringe.

Klengel had matured during an era when the technical possibilities of the instrument were advancing at an extraordinary rate. Much more was expected of the cello in those latter decades of the nineteenth century. Every cellist strove to be equal to or in advance of contemporary demands. Always, the goal lay in the startling possibilities being revealed by the violin, even as played by lesser mortals than Paganini.

At the turn of the century, however, the methods of achieving such results were yet to be perfected. The cello presented enormous problems. The distances to be traversed on the instrument were prodigious. Its girth and slowness of response (thickness of strings) evoked on the part of instrumentalists such as Klengel only superhuman physical efforts. And to add to these difficulties, cellists attempted to solve the problems with the same approach that was used when the cello had no more demanding role than figured bass accompaniment or parlor entertainment.

In 1917 Klengel was a mature fifty-eight, hardly an age to pause, step back to evaluate and revamp his technical equipment, in the light of what Casals had created as a standard. Similarly it is hardly likely that cellists such as Servais, Franchomme, or Piatti of an even earlier generation could have performed compositions such as Klengel's.

Even the most naïve cello students from eastern Europe carried with them to Leipzig a set of technical expectations that they considered to be far in advance of what Klengel set as his norm. He was even then felt to be a lovable, albeit old-fashioned, cellist. What was already the ordinary expectation of achievement for violinists—what Casals had shown to be possible on the cello—had transformed their own sense of what was possible on the instrument. When we consider the kinds of music that were then being played and written, from Wagner and Strauss to Mahler and Schönberg, we must acknowledge the existence of a silent but irresistible process of internal growth that encompassed even the art of performance.

There is a story which illustrates in a personal way what became a real historical factor in the transformation of modern cello playing. Benar Heifetz arrived in Leipzig from Poland shortly after the first World War. At his audition with Klengel he did his best, exhibiting not only brilliant technique, but passion, beauty of phrasing and sound. In his own words, he played like a Cossack. Klengel listened politely and without interruption to the young applicant. When Heifetz concluded, Klengel nodded appreciatively and said in an encouraging manner that the piece was well done and that Heifetz was an extremely talented instrumentalist. "However," Klengel continued, "you played it a little dry." Taking his cello, the old master began to play the same piece.

Heifetz listened intently but was increasingly nonplused. With every slide that Klengel made, the power and the beauty of the composition dissolved. Rather than enhancing the piece, as Klengel thought, the slides weakened if not destroyed it. In this we see illustrated a conflict of two esthetics, which could be decided only by the passing of the old. To his credit, Klengel saw the difference in ways of playing in this light and never forced the issue.

This discrepancy did not affect his students at all, for they valued his musical guidance and knowledge and his intimate understanding of the technical problems of the instrument. No matter how assiduous and talented a pupil might be, a fine teacher can show him valuable shortcuts to his goal—the product of generations of accumulated intelligence. Interpretively, Klengel represented a Germanic orthodoxy with regard to the classical tradition that appealed far more to this rising group of virtuosi than did the freer French and Belgian schools. His approach was favored even above that of Casals, who represented a more romantic and individualistic esthetic.

Feuermann's immediate reaction to Klengel's quiet but stringent standard of musicality was a positive one, for these canons were close to his father's preachments, though far more articulate. It was unfortunate that Maier had had neither the musical background nor the physical capacity to perfect and carry out his ideas. To say that Klengel was orthodox and classic in his interpretive renderings is not to deny his technical and tonal shortcomings. One can slide, shift, and bow in a way that we feel detracts from the music and at the same time still give the composer his due. Perhaps the issue can be phrased thus: Klengel's technical equipment came to him at an early stage in his musical development. It was part of his physical rhythms and thus far more difficult to modify in later life, whereas his interpretive approach to music was a result of mature and considered study of the repertoire undertaken at the source of the musical tradition.

That he did not truly understand the significance of the advances that had been made in cello technique is suggested by a story Feuermann used to tell about the master, a story that he used in his classes to illustrate his own approach to the instrument. By the end of the second and last year of Munio's study with Klengel, it had become public knowledge that Klengel had a unique phenomenon in Feuermann. He would joke with students and teachers, saying, "Now, I go to take a lesson from Feuermann." When pressed by others to explain Feuermann's abilities, he would reply that the boy had huge hands.

Told of this, Feuermann, at that time, had no answer. In later years he would pull his 5′ 7″ frame together, thrust his hands in front of a student's face and say "Compare!" As often as not, Feuermann's hands were smaller. Klengel's explanation, like so many explanations that use a structural argument to explain a musical talent, merely avoided a question difficult to answer. If you cannot explain a mysterious process, it is always easiest to resolve it through a gross physical explanation (huge hands) or by postulating a new mystery (unique genes).

We have been discussing the environment into which Feuermann came because it was important in forming his later attitudes towards music. Also, Leipzig and Klengel reflect the cultural milieu out of which a new kind of musical heritage was being formed. But as important as the externals of environment and teaching are, they provide only a partial explanation for the development of genius. Genius is not completely explicable in terms of external molding, although there is clear evidence that the early years of life, the accidents as well as the weighty inevitabilities, are crucial for the later flowering.

But Feuermann's flowering, in those two important years in Leipzig, was for the most part an internal process, the development of which lies largely hidden from explanation in terms of external facts or events. Feuermann himself looked back to those years as his most fruitful time of study, the period when he came to know the cello.

It is difficult to hypothesize how he was influenced or affected by the strangeness of his new environment and the awe with which he held both place and people. He was not yet fifteen when he arrived. The cello was the oasis, the familiar symbol of his own competence in a world that seemed to question the validity of that ethnic heritage and background which constituted his self. His personal lacks, given sharper meaning in that hectic, chaotic, frenzied place he called home, could not be sloughed off merely because he was a talented cellist. In his own home, he had been an appendage, dragged hither and yon by his father. First, he was the supporting actor, the prelude to the feature—Sigmund. Second, what were they?—performers.

To Maier their career was a great achievement, a vehicle to catapult the family out of the ghetto of Kolomea, now to rub shoulders with the great in Vienna, Berlin, Budapest. But art and its artists were still largely housed in the servants' quarters of society. Maier's attitude, forcefully communicated to the children, was still that of a supplicant—a haughty supplicant perhaps—always in abject reverence of wealth, status, and power. Now, as Munio's mind and body grew and he began to make his own judgments, he could see that his father was right. He and his fellow music students stood very small in the world. Even the great Klengel—he and they were no more than *klesmers*.

If Munio still retained the brashness of his childhood, it was now only a shallow overlay on a very timid and self-conscious boy. His surface behavior in later years may have appeared to belie it, but Feuermann had a deep inferiority complex, which he could never completely overcome. After he had tired of boisterousness and shallow student pranks, his room at the *pension* became increasingly a precious haven for himself and his cello. His maturation had released vast energies and emotions; he became supersensitive to all experience. His awareness of his limitations was yet suffused with feelings of an infinity of powers. As he practiced his instrument under these new physical conditions, this sense of possibility was increasingly focused on the relationship between himself, his body, and his cello.

No more the few hours of careless, sometimes desultory practice that had been the case in Vienna. The alternation of casual noodling and serious preparation of lessons for Walter was now transformed into hours of intense, committed practicing. Now he averaged six to eight hours a day, in short, one-to-two-hour sessions. During his breaks he would study his theory, find a piano that was not in use, improvise a bit or sight-read any music that was handy. Merely from copying his sisters, Munio would eventually advance, on the piano, to the Mozart-sonata level of proficiency.

Feuermann's diligence in studying those parts of the cello repertoire that Klengel assigned may have led Klengel to misinterpret the cause for the frenzy of effort that the boy put in. As noted earlier, Klengel would tell musicians that Feuermann came to him with only one piece of music securely in his repertoire, the Brahms Double Concerto. This may have been a comment meant to note the boy's prior subjugation to the violin, but it was not entirely true. Munio had studied most of the repertoire; indeed, he had performed much of it.

His eagerness reflected partly the importance of restudying the repertoire with a man who knew the ins and outs of every composition as few cellists knew them in that day. But more likely it reflected the music's newness and his own maturing. As Feuermann worked through the various compositions, new feelings and emotions were evoked that did not fit in with how he remembered playing them just a few short years ago.

Previously he had been a well-trained child dutifully going through memorized routines. He was an instrument created of other personalities. Being mature physically, quick and adept at learning, he soon had a fluency, even a precocity. In short, he was a talent. But without his teachers or his parents he would have been nothing. Everyone is enthusiastic about such prodigies. Sometimes, as in the case of Sigmund, the musical instinct can be so well developed as to manifest preternatural maturity. But those skills, while being important for future development, in no way assure future fulfillment.

The pitfalls come with adolescence and are manifested soon afterward. The child's personality is now transformed. Instead of being supported by the parental alter-ego, the child must confront himself as a self-conscious, self-motivated, and aware being. New muscles, energy relationships, and mental powers appear.

Those who fail to make the transition from *Wunderkind* to mature artist miss in one of two ways. Either they become oversized playing machines, retaining their mechanical childhood efficiency without the requisite growth of mind or personality, or they suddenly become aware, self-conscious, reasoning beings, and their physical capabilities fall apart in the conflict between cerebral cortex and spinal cord. There are many examples of both, not a few of whom missed on both counts. They disappear like super-novas.

We are far from arguing that talent can survive without proper guidance and training. Talent demands good, economical teaching. It always displays itself in the context of an existing social skill that is held valuable, in the fact that someone who cares places a violin or cello in a child's hands. Because the student shows an adeptness to learn, to focus mind and body on the normal problems of the instrument does not mean that he can be freed from the guidance of those learned in this skill, even those whom he is destined to surpass. The teacher can show the student in a condensed manner a multitude of clues, shortcuts, and options without which an untrained talent, even of gigantic potential, might fritter away his energies. A fine teacher has a logical understanding of the solution to problems, which the novice only feels intuitively and cannot quickly be secure about. A great teacher probably understands the physical capacities and limitations of his student far more clearly than can the student, even in retrospect.

Klengel was excellent in this respect. But he was constantly surprised by the manner in which Munio literally transmuted his instructions. It was as if every item of coaching, whether fingering, bowing, or phrasing, set off a unique combination in Munio's mind, for he would come back for the next lesson, obviously having taken the master's suggestions seriously, but transforming them to meet his own purposes. The years of playful experimentation on the instrument, imitating Sigmund on his violin, were being turned to his special advantage on the cello. The natural facility he had previously built up as a part of an intuitive growing into the instrument now needed permanent fixing. Munio had to concentrate all his physical powers and energies in a way that satisfied his hearing of the music on the cello completely anew. The notes were old, and the fingerboard and bow were familiar. What was new were the powers of manhood and the desire to achieve.

Every instrumentalist remembers those adolescent years when playing an instrument brings one close to orgasmic release. The better one plays, the greater the impact on oneself. Perhaps it is like the conquest of an especially desirable woman. To play an interesting piece of music with pristine attacks, hammerlike clarity of runs and scales, poising, releasing, and landing with grace over broad distances, securing a steady rhythmic pulse and a rich, beautiful sound, add up to an esthetic achievement of terrifying exhilaration. There is nothing more deflating to an intelligent and sensitive musician than muddiness and flaccidity. Agreed, these qualities are relative in every era. But every period of musical history has had gradually shifting standards of performance that do go somewhere. Feuermann intuited the direction of the change in his era and guided himself with an irrevocable internal logic towards its achievement.

The process of study was thus not a task to be completed, but a private act of love, of complete, selfless abandonment of his bodily instincts to this almost living organic instrument. In achieving what he attempted, he was discovering himself. The cello was his own body; he knew it as he was knowing himself. Hence there was no restraint or inhibition to the complete private revelation of himself. In the process the cello, too, gave up its ultimate mysteries and resistance.

Fortunately Munio was free of the musical and technical problems that prevent so many players from exercising the initiative necessary to fly straight to their goal. While Sigmund was being impaled on Sevčik's system, Munio had remained unnoticed. Yet he was absorbing what was important and meaningful for him. Without being driven to a childhood peak of accomplishment as Sigmund had been, he could accept at a more leisurely pace what Anton Walter offered him.

In Munio's mind, if not in Maier's, there were no reasons a cellist could not perform with as much facility as a violinist. Munio had played both instruments. The memory of the violin still lingered. The cello was much larger. But the hand position on the latter is far more natural and less debilitating than on the violin, especially when one is free (on the cello) to search for a position that is natural in terms of the musical effect. Munio's assiduousness in working out a technique that would match on the cello what had been done on the violin, given his new personal independence, might even have been his own way of replying to the unspoken brotherly rivalry with Sigmund that Maier had precipitated.

The extent of Feuermann's talent became clear to Klengel within a few months. Feuermann, as do all artists, delighted in telling stories of his own precocity. One story reflects this growing realization on Klengel's part. Munio had arrived one day at his home on Kaiser Wilhelm Strasse. A maid who had not previously met Munio answered his knock and upon hearing of his appointment with Klengel called up, "Herr Professor, there is a little boy here to see you." Klengel came down the stairs, chuckling, "My dear, that little boy is going to be a great cellist."

The endless hours and days of "Feuermann" practice continued throughout that year. For, once the basic insights of Klengel were absorbed and added to Munio's store of instruction, it was practice that stretched his capabilities beyond those of the day before. He ranged freely and widely over every area of the string repertoire—études, quartets, trios, orchestral music—with an untiring voraciousness. Perhaps this was the Sevčik way, all over again, but now modified by the will of this strong-minded, if socially timid, young man. If it was difficult, make it more difficult. But never ease the same strict canons of technical and musical accuracy.

One of the earliest delights of Munio's personal studies on the cello was the challenge of sightreading. It is hard to reconstruct the method by which he gained his particular level of fluency. But considering his complete absorption in and knowledge of the instrument, it is quite possible that, as sensitive a musician as he was, he could almost intuitively read the intentions of composers. With enormous concentration and a lack of concern for technical limitation, he could scan, far in advance, the message being translated into an almost reflexive physical response. It was a different kind of ability from Sigmund's phenomenal capacity to transcribe from memory much of the violin literature with its piano and orchestral accompaniments. Emanuel Feuermann had a notoriously poor memory onstage and many a night faked his way through sections of his program. Perhaps this was extreme stagefright, which never completely leaves most concert artists.

Klengel would recall to students in later years how one day he set before Feuermann a group of his latest études. In these particular études, Klengel intended to bring the student of attained professional capacity to what he thought were the limits of technical achievement on the instrument. He viewed Feuermann as a tremendously endowed student, but still rather inexperienced and wanted to see how he would approach this new challenge. Klengel suggested that Munio look over the music, while he fetched himself a cigar. Barely had he left the room when Feuermann began to play the first étude at full tempo. Klengel returned hurriedly and sat down at the boy's side while Feuermann raced through the entire manuscript. When he had finished the series of exercises, Klengel picked up the sheets of music, put them on the piano, and without another word returned to the main concern of the lesson.

Years later one of Feuermann's most talented students, Mosa Havivi, came to his apartment in London to present to Feuermann his newly composed and dedicated *Capriccios* for unaccompanied cello. It was a set of studies of formidable complexity and difficulty. Feuermann took out his recently acquired Stradivarius, sat down, squinted at the first for a second and then proceeded to breeze through it and each of the others at enormous speed and with unerring accuracy. Closing the manuscript, he handed it back to Havivi and, in a somewhat sarcastic manner, commented offhandedly, "I used to write music like this."

This was not an expression of deprecation. If Feuermann was defensive about the achievements of others, it was because he was respectful of all abilities and wanted to understand what others could do as an aid to his own improvement. Like all musicians he was intensely competitive and jealous of his achievements. But he was ever alert to the achievements of others, and carefully noted them, so as not to be caught napping.

As he matured, however, this tremendous drive to improve himself, aiming for a goal that always eluded him, was focused only on his instrument. The cello was his only musical passion. He had no grandiose musical or creative ambitions à la Casals, who wanted to be, in addition to a romantic and "recreative" cellist and conductor, a composer of large-

scaled works. Because Feuermann limited his domain of musical endeavor, his efforts were far more intensively focused.

His was the third generation of a family of performing musicians.
Leipzig, to which he had been sent to sharpen his skills, was at the center
of musical activities in an era when musical specialization had reached its
apogee. The explosion of musical life in the earliest decades of the
century had in the years after World War I excited a much greater degree
of specialization than had ever before been attained. To survive the
immense competition in evidence in Klengel's class or elsewhere, in performing, composing, or conducting, it was necessary, though it had not
been a few decades earlier, to concentrate, not divide oneself. The many
instrumentalists who had descended upon the music centers of Europe
and America had effectively discovered the heretofore underdeveloped
possibilities of their instruments. They goaded each other, even as the
composers and conductors of that day were kept in a state of intense
competition. At the time, after three hundred years of its existence, the
secrets of the violin family were finally revealed, in a climax that has
occurred in few art forms. Indeed the possibilities of the symphony
orchestra (in the classical forms themselves) caused musical life to stir and
pulsate with a vigor that today we can appreciate only in retrospect.

It takes relatively little effort in our own day to acquire the wherewithal
for comfortable middle-class living. In central Europe before 1914, the
struggle necessary to maintain oneself at the fringes of bourgeois existence was formidable. True, society was opening up. But it was difficult to
know when one might lose everything again, to be relegated once more to
the *shtetl*. We can thus understand the tremendous striving of a Maier
Feuermann and of thousands of his contemporaries. This was passed on
to the third generation. But here it was transmuted, softened into the
drive to achieve status, to merit success and admiration, to conquer
formerly restricted institutions.

At the conservatory in Leipzig, they came in the dozens, chiefly Jews, all
hungry to be best, to squeeze into positions of even modest bourgeois
standing. With Munio, more was demanded. He had to be better than
Sigmund. Not only the walls must be breached but the citadel itself taken.
Fortunately for this happy young man, the efforts were a labor of love.
Music was both his appointed craft and his great emotive passion. He
wanted to achieve great things, but achieve them in the right way.

Even as saintly a man as Klengel was a symbolic object of this competition. The students, probably including Feuermann himself, took an inner
delight in being able to best this old establishment figure. No matter that
the Klengel family had climbed out of the misty anonymity of
eighteenth-century German peasantry to gain its foothold in society. To
these young Jews, only the given reality of a dualism between *they* who
were in power and *we* the disadvantaged and oppressed minority was

meaningful to them. It is interesting to note, though, that they accepted the rules of the game. Western musical culture became theirs also; and in thus accepting it, they would share the burden of carrying it into the future.

The intensity of competition among the students is illustrated by an event that took place in the Klengel home. The Sunday morning teas over which the master presided were an established musical tradition at the conservatory. Each week students would gather at the house and perform solo and chamber works with their professor. —n this particular instance Klengel had notified one of his students, Jascha Bernstein, that he wanted him to play that Sunday. Bernstein, one of Klengel's many prizes from east Europe, later would be first cellist under Toscanini in Palestine and assistant principal cellist with the NBC Symphony. Klengel had mentioned that he wanted to audition a work for three cellos that he had just written. After refreshments, Klengel brought out the stands and set them up, putting a sonata part on each.

Klengel looked towards Bernstein and directed him to an outside stand and then did the same to a boy Bernstein had barely noticed earlier and whom he did not know. Before Bernstein could glance up from the music to question his teacher, Klengel had gone to get his cello. Jascha was dismayed, the part said Cello III. Before he had arrived in Leipzig, Bernstein had already established himself as a noted prodigy and had toured all over eastern Europe. Here in Leipzig, now a mature student, he had received a reception that inclined him to consider himself one of the master's premier talents. Yet it was obvious that Klengel now intended this unfamiliar bespectacled young boy to play the second part. He was outraged and hurt, but did not say a word or look at Feuermann. The other students seated themselves around the room and waited. Klengel returned and sat down between them at the center stand. He opened his music. A quick glance proved to Bernstein that the situation was even worse. Klengel would be playing second cello and the boy first. This had never happened in any of the earlier musicales. Was it a joke? He gained control of himself and waited.

They began to play. It seemed to last forever. The music was not bad. Little different from most of Klengel's pieces—romantic and technical. From the perspective of many decades now past, those few minutes—that were like months to Bernstein—can be smiled at with philosophical acceptance. After all, the boy was Feuermann. Bernstein heard playing that morning that neither he nor any of the others thought possible. But that day, Bernstein's dismay was so complete that he could not touch the cello for many weeks.

By the beginning of his second year in Leipzig, Feuermann's name and reputation had begun to spread throughout the conservatory, and even to the musical environs beyond. What had been his own secret world of aspiration and achievement had to be shared with the outside. Now began the shaping of the public man, a process that turns into an affliction for many performing artists. Here in an environment of public as well as private self-awareness and testimony, the famous Feuermann personality took shape, a personality which for many was an irresistible endearment and for others a persistent outrage against good manners.

He was, to be sure, endowed with a quick and potent mouth. Munio was never at a loss for words. Yet all who knew him well testify to the fact that his tongue was a shield, the defense of an extremely sensitive and open person to the shallow impositions that a public figure must endure from acquaintance and stranger alike. To every action there is a reaction; and Feuermann's verbal darts were a way of displacing these impositions. His sarcasm, his wisecracks and clowning were his method for projecting his natural defensiveness into an aggressiveness that complemented rather than impeded his cello playing.

It is easy to commit all one's feelings to solitary practice or performance for one's close friends. But once it is necessary to appear before the general public, this display of one's innermost reactions and feelings becomes much more difficult. Under these conditions an open, naïve person may have additional difficulties in his interpersonal relations. He would hardly want to open himself up further. Thus appears the public mask; all too often it overflows life, into art.

It sometimes leads to careless playing. And if not to sloppy playing, the instrumentalist may hide behind performances of mechanical objectivity. The masks are varied. There are styles of personality that are culturally selected. They constitute a varied and utilitarian palette for those performers with thespian abilities and these performers tend to assume them as standard—the *grande dame,* the witty sophisticate, the reserved European intellectual. Feuermann's mask was at least his own. It reflected a dimension of his personality that was real and convenient, yet it effectively hid a sense of idealism and enormous striving, indeed a measure of personal arrogance and pride in his own achievements.

The story is told how towards the end of Feuermann's stay in Leipzig the students had arrived once more at the Klengel home on a Sunday morning only to be told by Frau Klengel that they would have to carry on without the master. He had not been able to return home in time following a concert engagement. The youngsters went about normally, gathering up their tea, coffee, and cake, always plentiful and delicious to these semi-starved students. They all knew when Munio had arrived. Hardly had the door been opened for him when his high-pitched voice piped out for all to hear, *"Frau Klengel, wo ist J-u-l-i-u-s?"*

Back in Vienna the news of Munio's successful study was received with gratitude. The boy wrote glowingly about his work with Klengel and the musical activities at the conservatory. In addition, the parents were hear-

Munio and father, Maier Feuermann, in Leipzig, 1918.

ing reports through the usual musical grapevine about their little "cello talent," and how he was making a name for himself in Leipzig.

The war was over now and Vienna was attempting a psychic renewal. Austria, bereft of its hinterlands, was a shell of its former power and wealth. Musical life had become sharply circumscribed, as support from neither government nor philanthropic resources had been reestablished. Yet peace had come, and with it the opportunity for normality. The family was keenly involved in rebuilding Sigmund's concert career, for in the last two years it had completely stagnated. Gusta, the oldest sister, was working and thus added to their income. Maier had not yet been able to bring their affairs back to what they had been in those few good years before the war. There was the usual glut of orchestral musicians and ordinarily competent teachers in Vienna. Too, he had lost many contacts by being away on tour with the boys. He could no longer turn to account his being the father of *Wunderkinder*.

In the summer of 1918, after Munio had completed his first year with him, Klengel wrote as follows to Director Kux in Vienna:

Dear Sir:

I have presumed to write to you in the interest of our dear Munio Feuermann. I want to request that you allow our young cellist to perform in public this fall, from October on. The boy wants to play in public and I agree that he ought not waste his art only on four walls. I am sincerely convinced that he is going to be very successful. It is possible that his first concerts will necessitate some financial sacrifice. It is my thought that he should give solo recitals in Leipzig, Dresden, Munich, and perhaps in other large cities. As soon as we shall have received your consent, we shall inform you about further details, such as programs etc. As for the Gewandhaus, it was an impossibility, too late. However, I have got the promise that he definitely will get an invitation in Winter 1919–1920.

It is necessary that I reiterate, in all sincerity, that of all those who have ever been entrusted to my guardianship, there has never been such a talent as this gifted one, Munio. Well, good luck for our divinely favored artist and lovable young man.

With greatest respect,

It is not remembered whether the faithful *mitzayin* Kux was able to raise the money for this venture. At any rate the second year was as rich a fulfillment of promises as the first and, at the very least, Klengel had the pleasure, as he held forth in the first cello chair, of looking forward to the appearance of his star pupil with the Gewandhaus Orchestra. It was the prophetic fulfillment of a youthful career that had begun similarly, only then with his father sitting in the rear of the cello section of the Tonkünstler Orchester in Vienna.

How can Feuermann's gift be explained? So many explanations of great talent fall back upon the mystery of genetic endowment—a divine gift. But this sidesteps the issue. It is difficult to believe in the case of instrumental talent involving such a complexity of factors—physical, mental, psychological, and social—that it is somehow an ineluctable, deterministic gift that *must* be expressed and that the Paganinis, Rachmaninoffs, and Heifetzes are merely the blind purveyors of genetic accidents.

A more likely explanation lies in good coordination and morphological equipment—good hands and fingers that are to be found in a good proportion of our youths. An examination of the modern symphony orchestra is testimony to what generally good teaching can do for the average level of string performance, and thus supports this contention. These symphony instrumentalists can usually whip through their own solo-concert repertoire with great facility. One might say then that the basic physiological equipment is a necessary condition for greatness, but never a sufficient condition.

What is not usually emphasized enough in the creation of an extraordinary artist such as Feuermann is intelligence—critical, perceptive, and aggressive intelligence—for if intelligence is not expressed verbally it often goes unnoticed. Finally, intelligence without strength of will, persistence, and ego will lead inevitably to an undeveloped performer.

These conditions still need a social and cultural environment for their nurturing. The remarkable Feuermann home was such an incubator. An important factor for Emanuel was that he was the second son of this musical family. It helps to explain his relatively quiescent early development, and then his later spurt. Again, Leipzig was a fortunate place to be during his adolescence. Thus, not only circumstance but his inner capacities freed him from the debilitating elements of that unusual home background.

An examination of the background and development of the truly great musical performers would probably demonstrate the importance of perceptive intelligence and strength of character. The recollections of Pablo Casals support this view. Taken by his mother to study in Barcelona at age eleven, Casals was almost immediately forced to fend for himself. With only eight or nine months of cello playing in his background, the young Casals found an opening for cello in a trio at the Café Tost. There at twelve, he acquired the on-the-job technical and musical wherewithal necessary to manage his job.

He had a musical background. His father was the church musician in his home village. Pablo had now seen the accomplishments of the local Barcelona cellists and thus he had a model of what could be done. The instrument had to be mastered and he had the heritage to do it. Fortunately there was no one to tell Pablo that progress on the cello could take place only at a predetermined rate. His teacher in Barcelona, weak as cellist and teacher, was humbly aware of this and allowed the child full scope.

In the Spain of 1888 there were few models from whom one could glean either ultimate limitations or current possibilities, merely rumors and dreams about events in the musical centers north of the Pyrenees. With an economy of effort, maximum concentration, and an inner serenity as to his place in the world, Pau (Pablo) Casals in a short year or two created for himself the technique and style that satisfied his own musical needs and standards and eventually established these ideals as the standard for cello playing throughout the western world.

A somewhat similar situation existed for Feuermann. Everything in his environment bespoke progress and advance. There was no heavy, inert tradition of established practice. His brother Sigmund was a living exemplification of what could be achieved with a stringed instrument. Casals was the distant idol that exemplified to him the worth and possibilities of the cello. Feuermann had to grasp these environmental clues and build them into his own personal vision of achievement. It was the Leipzig years that provided, at an opportune moment in his development, for those quiet hours when Feuermann flirted with the unknown and permanently revolutionized the playing of his instrument.

4

COLOGNE: JOURNEYMAN

The executive committee meeting of the faculty of the Gürzenich Conservatory broke up in an atmosphere of consternation. Professor Abendroth left the room muttering that he would write again to get some clarification. It was hard to understand why Klengel, ordinarily such a dependable person, would put forth such an outlandish proposal.

It was true that the death of Professor Grützmacher was sudden. But certainly in all of central Europe and among the innumerable students and acquaintances of Klengel, there was a more appropriate candidate for the Gürzenich position than a sixteen-year-old boy. After all, Cologne was not the end of the world. Indeed, the position of professor of cello at the Gürzenich Conservatory was one of the more important in all of Germany.

Friedrich Grützmacher, the younger, one of the most esteemed musicians of that era and the last of a line of distinguished string musicians going back to the beginnings of the nineteenth century, had died suddenly at age fifty-four, leaving an enormous gap in the Cologne institution. Not only had he been its cello teacher, but also the cellist in the Gürzenich Quartet (of which Bram Eldering was first violinist). Also he was the first cellist in the orchestra and a chamber-music coach. The executive committee was searching for a distinguished replacement.

The committee's great hope lay in Leipzig with Julius Klengel, who not only had the best students but, better than anyone else, understood what was meant by an excellent cellist. He could therefore be relied upon to make an appropriate suggestion, whether or not the person was his student. Klengel had recommended Emanuel Feuermann, a sixteen-year-old student of his from Vienna. A sixteen-year-old for a position that was advertised as carrying with it the rare appellation of full professor! A variety of sardonic remarks came from the sober and distinguished panel of musical scholars in Cologne. Eldering recalled the violinist Feuermann, who had been a fantastic prodigy before the war, but knew nothing of this child.

In due time a second letter from Klengel arrived and was read to the assembled group. In it Klengel, with great emphasis, reaffirmed his selection. He stated that never in his experience had he known such talent. The boy's abilities on the instrument, his natural musicality, his assiduousness and intelligence had forced him to conclude that Feuermann was the greatest cello talent of his day. It would be a grievous error to rule out his candidacy merely because of age. In closing Klengel noted that it would only mislead the distinguished committee of the Gürzenich were he to imply that there were second or third choices, even amongst contemporary and well-practiced mature cellists.

This document impressed, especially so since the candidates who had been interviewed or had been suggested by others—some of whom were quite well-known—were for the most part middling, if respectable, craftsmen. Abendroth and the others agreed to take a look at this phenomenon. Soon after, a letter was written and eventually relayed back to Vienna, where the boy had by now returned for his summer vacation.

The Feuermanns were delighted, especially Maier. What an opportunity, a professor no less! Things in every way seemed to be looking up. Maier had been reëngaged by the Tonkünstler and Sigmund was soon to embark on his first extended European tour since the war. There were thus great expectations and the family gave its blessings for the trip and held high hopes for its outcome.

The audition proved to be traumatic for everyone except Munio. His attitude was careless to say the least. At sixteen, what did he have to lose, an interesting trip, a new city? During his performance with the quartet, he giggled and exploded into laughter at some of the slides and missed notes of the various members. There were some ruffled feathers. After all, they were sightreading to audition *him*. But from the first there was never any doubt. He was all that Klengel had said he was. In fact their excitement was such that they hustled him back on the train rather quickly, saying they would write to him in Vienna very soon.

The entire faculty met the following morning. After several hours of lively discussions they decided. Abendroth ran to meet his advanced conducting class, which had been waiting patiently for him. "Gentlemen," he panted as he entered the classroom, "the faculty has had a unique experience. It has witnessed in the playing of the young cellist Emanuel Feuermann abilities of unimaginable scope. He is truly a talent of the utmost rarity. In spite of his age we have agreed to appoint him to the faculty. Feuermann will be a brilliant jewel in our crown."

Munio had hardly arrived back home when the letter came. But there was a disappointment. While the position still carried with it all the responsibilities that Grützmacher had held, and though the salary was excellent, the title of professor was to be withheld. No beardless sixteen-year-old professor for Cologne!

Now that the tension had broken and illusion and dream gave way to reality, the implications of this appointment had to be faced. Mother Feuermann was not happy at the prospect of letting her youngest son leave home at such a tender age. Who would take care of him, feed him, be sure he got to bed on time? What if he became ill? Why not study a few more years, perhaps in Vienna, where life was beginning to pick up now?

Maier, too, began to have reservations. The sequence of events had been wrong. Munio was the child, the playful, not the studious one. Sigmund was the serious, devoted student of the violin. It was Sigmund whose future had been planned out so carefully, nurtured and protected. The professorship, the academic environment seemed so right for the elder boy. And yet it was the careless, carefree one, for whom everything seemed to come so easily and accidentally.

No matter, it had to be accepted. Rachel insisted, however, that Munio not go off by himself. Germany was in revolution and no one knew what the outcome would be. Gusta, their steady, loving "proxy mother" would accompany him, set up an apartment, feed and care for him, and stay in almost daily communication with the family.

On their arrival in Cologne in September of 1919, Gusta and Munio were met at the train depot by an older student at the conservatory, Michael Taube, who had written the family during the summer and had arranged to rent a small apartment for the pair, within walking distance of the conservatory. Taube, a jovial young cellist, originally from Lodz in Poland, explained to the Feuermanns that Eldering had buttonholed him in June after the appointment and emphatically told him to stick to Feuermann, to take care of him while he was in Cologne. Taube commented as they taxied to the apartment that he was not much of a cellist and that his interests were more and more being concentrated on piano, accompanying, and conducting. But he would avail himself of the privilege of taking cello lessons from the young master.

Gusta may have had a natural competency in the home, where she had had to substitute for the mother so often. But barely twenty-one, she was yet a waif in a foreign land. It was Munio who took the initiative in suggesting new sights to see. Since the school year had not as yet started, they spent the first few days, with Taube as their guide, wandering through the shrines and narrow alleys of the old city. Despite the recent conclusion of the war, Cologne was already experiencing an enormous economic expansion. There were building and bustle everywhere. Cologne seemed different from Leipzig—so much newer and more hectic, in spite of its ancient central areas.

The Emperor Claudius founded Cologne in A.D. 50 at the insistence of his wife Agrippina, who had been born on a rural estate in that area. It had served first as a military encampment. From the eighth through the thirteenth centuries it gradually grew, when trade on the Rhine River, along whose banks the lovely village was nestled, enhanced its fortunes. Not only herring, wine, and weaving, but religion helped it grow. Its Gothic cathedral, begun in 1248, represents this era. A university, sponsored by the citizens of Cologne, in imitation of more venerable institutions elsewhere, was founded in 1389, and by the following century had a student body of over a thousand. This was an international era for the Kölner, symbolized by their Hanseatic allegiances. They had communities in London, and several in Scandinavian cities. The university student body also reflected a Lower Rhine cosmopolitanism fostered by the river. So prosperous was the town that in 1414 it could afford to expel the Jews. The Catholics were now capable of handling the monetary tasks usually assigned to this opprobrious people.

The sixteenth century brought religious controversies. The gradual ossification of the guild system slowed the expansion of the city just as it had begun to approach a peak of prosperity and power. Reaction further set in with the ostracizing of the Protestant minority. Its effect was to denature the university of any intellectual ferment.

When Napoleon entered this city in 1794, Cologne had 40,000 people, of whom only 6,000 had civil rights, and a university that had collapsed and was about to dissolve (to be supplanted by the University of Bonn, thirty miles to the south).

The steamboat trade and the railroad in turn in the midnineteenth century quickly changed Cologne's fortunes. By 1870 the population had multiplied five times to about 200,000 and the growth would soon necessitate the elimination of the old Hanseatic walls. By the beginning of World War I, there were between 475,000 and 500,000 crowded into a sprawling, grimy, industrial Cologne.

The Gürzenich, which was built between 1441 and 1447 as a combination dance and festival hall, meeting house (for the Diets of the Holy Roman Empire), and first-floor market place, had in this same year (1919) seen the efflorescence of a new, democratic university, which had joined in the musical events given in the building. The stock exchange, which had used the Gürzenich since 1875, had been recently moved to more modern and appropriate quarters.

Not too far away the conservatory had prospered with increasing vigor since its founding in the early part of the nineteenth century. In its search for teachers it represented a wealthy and expanding municipality ready to compete with better institutions in central Europe. It now welcomed musicians of all racial, religious, and ethnic backgrounds. On one of the youngsters' early excursions, Taube had nodded towards the Gürzenich Hall as they passed across Hay Market Square and commented ironically that the Jews had indeed returned to Cologne.

Youth has its problems, for its possessor as well as for those amongst whom it resides. Indeed the period was one of democratization and enlightenment. But for those faculty members and administrators of the Gürzenich who had been nurtured in the well-ordered paternalism of imperial Germany, this new faculty addition would necessitate a formidable adjustment. And after the first excitement of the appointment had worn off, how many second thoughts there must have been. Perhaps some recalled the words Aristophanes put in Aeschylus' mouth about an earlier youthful hero: "No lion's whelp within thy precincts raise; but, if it be there, bend thee to its ways!"

Fortunately, at this point in his professional development, Emanuel Feuermann was certainly no lion. There were many moments of trepidation as he approached the day of his appearance at the conservatory to begin the year. The actuality was not to assuage his fears. He arrived promptly at Dr. Abendroth's office in the small brownstone conservatory building on Dagobert Strasse to introduce himself and be taken on the scheduled inaugural tour of the building and to meet the faculty. Unfortunately the secretary had stepped out for a moment and the waiting room was empty. On her return, seeing Munio standing there with his cello, she peremptorily ordered him out of the office, stating in an officious tone that no students were allowed in the chamber. When Munio explained who he was, she gasped in humiliation and hurried out to fetch Abendroth.

The jarring newness of things was soon normalized through that neutral enemy of idiosyncrasy—routine. The cello students, the quartet, his role as first cellist of the orchestra, together with the need to prepare for his recitals—all this made a heavy burden for a young man. But it was in the workaday musical chores that one could forget one's age and immaturity and aggressively, even retributively, flaunt them at strangers. In the cello lessons Munio did little more than demonstrate. His students, usually much older than he, literally shrank into the walls as they watched and heard him tear easily and devastatingly into music with which they had to struggle so mightily. Later, having relaxed a bit in his newfound assertiveness, he would lecture them on their smoking habits, not yet having fallen prey to the habit himself. If the weather allowed, he would adjourn the class to the tennis courts, where he was in process of picking up some bourgeois refinements.

The heavy schedule and the changed hours he had to keep caused one near-disaster. In Leipzig, Munio had gone to bed as a rule about eight o'clock. Now he had to adjust to a musical life where concerts normally began at that hour. The first quartet recital was a long one. And what with a full day of teaching and rehearsing, Munio began to feel the hour as they launched into the final work of the program. The quartet had an unusually long and dull (for cello) slow movement—an unending sequence of open strings. Eldering noted that though a *piano* was called for from the cello, Feuermann was producing an ultra *pianissimo*. A puzzled glance revealed that the boy was about to doze off in his seat. A nod to the second violinist in the direction of Munio immediately produced a sharp, but discreet kick on Munio's right shin that elicited a momentary *szforzando* from the boy and a rejuvenated alertness for the remainder of the composition.

Eldering was of enormous importance for Feuermann during these years. It was his firm support that decided the faculty and Abendroth to hire Munio. After all, as head of the string department and the quartet, he would have to live with this whelp. He was another Klengel, having a mature understanding both of the needs of genius and of its youthful excesses. Eldering was in his middle fifties, at the peak of his career and fame. He had come to Cologne in 1903 after the departure of Willy Hess, who had left to go to Berlin as concertmaster, ultimately to the Berlin Hochschule. His apprenticeship, first under Hubay and then under Joachim, gave him impeccable credentials. In his playing and teaching he was a marvelous amalgam of the great schools. Hubay had studied with Vieuxtemps and thus Eldering, a Hollander, had absorbed the stylistic subtleties of the Belgian school along with the serious and almost literalistic Berlin tradition represented by Joachim. And, to be sure, he suffered somewhat from Joachim's technical rigidities.

A story is told about Eldering's most famous student, Adolph Busch. Busch, like so many other German violinists of that day, was half pedant, half instrumentalist. He had committed himself to promoting the quartets of Max Reger and was attempting in his quartet to do what the Juilliard Quartet would achieve later with Bartok's quartets—make them an accepted part of the repertoire. At one concert the cellist, who happened to be Paul Grümmer, blundered momentarily in the third movement of a long Reger quartet. Not content with picking up the pieces where they were, Busch solemnly announced to the consternated, but intimidated, audience that the quartet would start over from the very beginning.

It was this kind of complete commitment to a new dimension of the string repertoire that was so good for Feuermann. Heretofore his chamber-music experience had been for fun and entertainment in the homes of well-placed amateurs or among family and friends. Eldering himself bore up rather well under the grimaces and giggles of the boy, whenever someone slipped. Feuermann treated himself with equal harshness onstage. A year later, at a concert with the Gürzenich Orchestra in Cologne for which his entire family had come from Vienna, he smirked and broke into a broad smile after he had missed the first octave jump to a high "A" in the last movement of the Schumann Cello Concerto. The parents glanced knowingly at each other. "Our Munio!"

The decisive moment in the introductory phase of Feuermann's career came on an October evening in 1919 in the ornately wooden-pillared and -buttressed great hall of the Gürzenich, replete with murals of an ages-long tradition, and looked down upon from captain's-walklike balconies, their several rows filled to capacity. Even below, the thousand or so in the audience—front, side, and rear on their high-backed wooden chairs—completely surrounded the young cellist as he struck the vigorous opening B minor phrase of the Dvořák Cello Concerto. Much curiosity had been aroused by the news of the new "professor" acquired by the conservatory. This was the moment; would the reality come up to the publicity? The result was a sensation. No one had ever expected such sounds to issue from a cello. The lovely Kux Amati had responded with unbelievable clarity and brilliance, considering the small, thin, childlike figure that played upon it.

It was obvious backstage as the well-wishers lined up that a new dimension had been added to the cultural scene of the Kölners. One of those who offered congratulations and added significantly "will communicate with you soon" were Paul and Emma (Oma) Reifenberg. Reifenberg was one of the city's leading businessmen. He owned a large factory that manufactured trimmings for women's clothing and did business throughout Europe. Educated in Westphalia, he had come into the family business, prospered, and subsequently abandoned his Judaic heritage, much to the scandal and scorn of the city's Jewish community.

With prosperity came the devout and typically German earnestness in cultivating a proprietorship over musical and artistic affairs. And with businessmanlike acuity, Paul realized that in Feuermann there existed not merely a local curiosity but a find of potentially international stature. Whereas the great peripatetic artists of that period had been marching through his living room and guest book with monotonous regularity, it was his intention to ensconce this young man within the Reifenberg compound as a permanent cultural enterprise.

Barely two days had passed when a chauffeured limousine appeared before the tiny apartment of Munio and Gusta to spirit the young man away for lunch in the Reifenberg mansion. It was a monstrous gray stone building of forty-two rooms located in the southern suburb of Bayenthal, in a breathtaking setting overlooking the Rhine.

Paul Reifenberg was a person of enormous energies, Prussian efficiency and toughness. He ruled his fiefdom of five children, wife, and assorted other relations—who arrived and departed at regular intervals—with an iron hand. Everything that was done in his life had to

Munio with W. Kux's Amati, in Cologne, 1920.

be done at peak determination, and was usually attended by success. In spite of his background, everything about Reifenberg exuded a kind of Calvinistic moralism in his striving for salvation through work and commitment. Being two generations out of the ghetto stood him well in his own self-transformation and he now determined that in these twilight decades of his life he would effect a similar transformation for this child of the Galician ghetto. Now in his sixties, with a family ranging from adolescent boys of Munio's age to little five-year-old Eva, Reifenberg realized that none of his three sons had either the capacity or the will to achieve anything near what Munio gave evidence of. He was indifferent to the fact that this commitment was in the arts. Music and culture were as much a part of the general moral and intellectual challenge as was *geschäft* (business). The problem was to do something well, to be intolerant of any other goal than to reach the pinnacle of one's field of endeavor.

It took no time at all for the Reifenbergs to inquire fully into Munio's affairs, both locally and in Vienna and Poland. A cursory visit to the apartment, to meet Gusta, convinced them of the need to take immediate steps to change Munio's lifestyle. The suggestion was soon made to Munio, and communicated by letter to the family in Vienna, that the boy's mode of life was wanting in the extreme. The little apartment was dingy and primitive. The boy could not be cared for adequately and could gain no experience in the amenities in such an environment. The implications were clear. Munio's way of living was too reminiscent of Galicia to satisfy the Reifenbergs. Their solution was to establish Munio in a large two-room apartment in the home of one of the managers of the Reifenberg factory, one Joseph Steinberg, an uncle of the conductor William Steinberg. This apartment had been used by the Steinberg son, now away at the university. Here Munio could be cared for, cooked for, and taken care of by the household maid, and thus concentrate on his career in a modicum of comfort.

Gusta, greatly relieved, shortly returned home to Vienna. She had hardly ventured out of the apartment, was shy and lonely, and felt completely ill at ease away from her beloved Vienna and her irascible family. Later this situation would generate a certain amount of hard feeling on the part of the Feuermanns. At the moment however, they were impressed and overwhelmed by this strong-willed show of philanthropy. Then, as the full dimensions of the Reifenberg "takeover" of the destiny of their Munio became manifest, they grew embittered and characterized the event as the "casting out" of Gusta from Cologne, rather than as a beneficial sponsorship by the Reifenbergs.

The academic year 1919–1920 was a transitional one. There were only a few concert opportunities. The engagements came in for the following year and in goodly numbers, too. Munio had an enormous number of adjustments to make—musically, to a new and demanding regime; socially, to act the young music teacher and performer amongst his older peers both at the conservatory and in the Reifenberg home, where the greats of musical Europe appeared—Casals, Fritz Kreisler, Hoffman, Walter Gieseking, Andres Segovia, Fritz Busch, *etc.* He could now laugh at his age and appearance, as when he gleefully wrote home reporting a lecture he had received on the bus from a passenger, who, noting his cello, told him that if he worked very hard, he might one day approach the great young cello professor at the conservatory.

The following year, 1920–1921, Emanuel gave several solo recitals in addition to his regular duties. These took him to Berlin, Munich, and Vienna, among other towns. His family felt less anxious now about his safety, since he had returned for the summer apparently as sound as ever and showing healthy signs of manhood and maturity.

The impact of the Reifenbergs was now seen in his meticulous diary of the concerts and places that he visited. At about this time we also see Munio beginning to catalog a growing repertoire of solo works, adding them to the store acquired under Walter and Klengel. As he lists the towns and studiously copies out the salient sections of his reviews, the number of times he visits the towns, the number of concerts in the year, the total over the years and his available repertoire—both concerto and recital pieces—one can almost visualize a young chef perusing the qualitative possibilities available to him in satisfying an ever-hungrier clientele. It constituted an objectification of a role in life of which he was becoming increasingly conscious. He was learning to add a measure of Germanic system and discipline to the drives necessary for survival he had absorbed at home and carried with him to Leipzig. The Reifenberg environment was beginning to teach him the value and necessity of sustained efforts which, grafted onto his independently won technique and personal identity, were to be an invaluable addition for the long, competitive siege.

The year 1921–1922 was better yet, especially as his tours were now under the sponsorship of the distinguished Berlin management of Wolf and Sachs, the same management under which the brothers had appeared in the Brahms Double Concerto with the Berlin Philharmonic in 1914. The redoubtable Louise Wolf had apparently decided that the eighteen-year-old cellist could now be considered more than a flash-in-the-pan child prodigy. So well had his fortunes fared that he appeared triumphantly at his parents' silver wedding anniversary party with a mink stole for Rachel. This visit coincided with the decision of the entire family to maintain their Austrian citizenship rather than becoming Polish citizens, as was now their option, since Kolomea was again part of the Polish Republic.

Munio was carving out a small niche for himself in the concert world. He made regular solo appearances in Riga, Warsaw, and Prague. In Prague, both he and Sigmund appeared, a week apart, with George Szell as accompanist. As the engagements came in at a rate of twenty, thirty, and then forty appearances per season, the conflict with his Cologne duties became apparent. Inevitably one or the other would suffer. Several events decided the question.

On October 16, 1922, Munio performed in a recital of the Cologne Trio with Eldering and Uzielli, a pianist on the faculty, in Trier. The review in the *Rheinische Zeitung* was highly favorable and noted approvingly that Feuermann was the replacement for Friedrich Grützmacher and that it was good to see the young (Feuermann) learn from the old (Eldering). Feuermann had been on the staff for three full years, time enough, it seemed to him, for a local critic to register the changes in the Gürzenich. After all, this was not new information.

In mid-November Feuermann had been engaged to fill in on a program of the local men's glee club in Magdeburg, a concert that took place in a large ballroom there. The reviewer's comments about the soloist were:

> Good violinists are rather rare nowadays, but good cellists are even rarer. In our prosaic times one ought yet to frame them in gold. It is striking that the people of Magdeburg knew nothing of an artist as phenomenal as Feuermann. Are we living on an island of exiles? This young cellist has long been recognized in southern and western Germany as the best cellist we have in Germany at the moment. People here do not even know anything about *the* cellist, the Spaniard Pablo Casals. True, we cannot afford to pay him any more. But he was celebrated in the rest of our fatherland as early as 1910. Why didn't our townspeople invite him then? And why does Feuermann, the only one in Germany that we can at least secretly compare with Casals, have to present his lovely art accompanied by a piano that was played wretchedly, unmusically, and unappreciatively in a dreary restaurant in the midst of the roaring basses of the teachers.
>
> The D Major Concerto by Haydn which he executed in superb style ought to have been accompanied by Volkmann and the municipal orchestra. It is an inexcusable imposition to allow him to play this masterpiece to the jingling accompaniment of a piano. Those who heard his rendition of the Chopin Nocturne or the Sarasate Gypsy Airs are aware of his unlimited technique. . . . the intensity of his timbre. . . . in turn warmly dreaming and then ecstatically temperamental.
>
> Why don't we find his name in concert programs? Wouldn't it be great if the Rebling Glee-Club could interest him in taking part in a symphony concert?

In Enzbote late in January, quite a different reception was evidenced. The critic noted that the music society had purchased a new Bechstein, which had arrived in time for the Feuermann recital. Too bad, the critic added, that it had not arrived a week earlier in time for the Walter Gieseking concert. In February, 1923, Feuermann played the Brahms

Double Concerto with the Berlin Philharmonic and Gustav Havemann, the successor of Adolf Busch as professor of violin in the Berlin Hochschule (Busch had by now organized his quartet). The performance won Feuermann rave reviews.

He had now been at the Cologne Gürzenich for four years. The advice that came at him from all sides, seconded by the Reifenbergs, was that Cologne now held him back. Kux in Vienna also felt that Feuermann was too young to continue such an apprenticeship indefinitely, as well-founded as it had been. Only his parents had doubts. And these were predictably economic. To Maier the position at the Gürzenich was a sinecure, to which would ultimately be added the official title of professor. Why give it up for the peripatetic life of a concert artist? Sigmund himself, although he had innumerable engagements, found it difficult to secure really lucrative contracts, given the enormous competition of this era.

Munio's own feelings were reinforced more by the persuasive voices of the strangers than by his family's strong objections. There were so many places he could go if he were free, and he was only twenty. There were things to learn on the cello that he felt he could do now only if he were away from the scholastic environment.

Every free moment he had had for his own study during these years had been devoted to expanding his repertoire—new concerti and solo pieces by Toch, D'Albert, Strauss, Reger, arrangements of violin pieces he had only half-heartedly developed before. The classical sonata repertoire had to be fixed, and a broader selection of Baroque music mastered. Before he had become aware of the significance of it, he had accumulated a library of music that would rival that of many violinists. It was a veritable passion that he continued throughout his career, to place before the public a cello literature that would represent the enormous expressive potential of the instrument.

In accumulating and studying the music, he had had scant time to involve himself in it. In essence his playing, though brilliant and musically correct from a Hochschule standpoint, was still essentially that of an extraordinarily talented student. He was aware that only through constant reiteration on the concert platform, under a diverse set of performing exigencies, would he learn about his own needs and potentialities on the instrument as well as begin to explore the inner nuances of the music. He had to learn to relax and find his own particular voice in performance itself.

Symbolic of his growing emancipation was his first venture across the Channel to London's Aeolian Hall in June of 1923, only a modestly successful venture. The following fall, Wolf and Sachs had proposed Italy and Poland for Munio as part of a European tour. He would have to resign.

This was not a propitious time to break loose from the security of Cologne. Germany was going through a period of economic chaos; and Austria was nearly as badly off, the situation compounded by serious political crises. Yet the fact that he was twenty years of age and was able to do so many things that he had previously had barely time to dream of compensated for his inevitable pangs of insecurity.

Bruno Walter had returned to live in Vienna that summer of 1923. He had had to resign in November of the previous year from the conductorship of the Munich Opera. And though he had a number of conductorial engagements while he was, so to speak, between jobs, he was receptive to young Munio's suggestion of teaming up with Sigmund to form a trio. The family Feuermann was overjoyed at the thought that this might herald a return of their son to Vienna, since he had by no means broken with his Cologne sponsors and cohorts, in spite of giving up the teaching job. The brothers also decided to offer themselves as a tandem for the Brahms Double Concerto, something they had not done for a number of years.

The debut of the trio was in Düsseldorf, in the Dumont-Lindemann Theatre, and the reception a fine one. It served as a model for the trios that Feuermann would periodically bring together in Berlin, New York, and California. They played a number of recitals that fall. But an engagement in New York that winter and in the spring of 1924 forced Walter to withdraw. It was a mutually satisfactory solution to a situation that had no future. Walter's style of playing was not compatible with that which the brothers, particularly Munio, had developed. Walter represented the older Viennese romantic esthetic as regards tempi, rhythm, and interpretation, in almost direct opposition to the more rigorous and literal training that was the fruit of the newer, or perhaps German, school. The parting was amicable and the boys filled their remaining commitments with the pianist Hans Hoppe, accentuating their varied solo abilities more so than they had with Walter. A sample program:

Beethoven: Trio, op. 70 no. 1
Bach: Chaconne (violin)
Handel: Passacaglia for violin and cello
Bach: Air for cello and klavier
Tschaikovski: Rococo Variations
Glazounov: Violin Concerto

Walter bore no ill will toward his obstreperous young colleague and remained a close friend to the end. There was something about Munio which, in spite of all the arguments, bickering, and sarcasm he might inflict, no one could take seriously or literally. While he was a devoted *Musikant,* he was always just a grown-up child. Munio's unique solution to the internal-external relationship that all musicians must come to terms with, was to remain a perpetual fifteen-year-old.

Those musicians who understood the nature of the problem in terms of their own accommodations took him in their stride. In the four years at Cologne, Eldering was continually excusing Feuermann's gauche public behavior. He knew what was behind it. Munio was able in this way to balance his utter seriousness and lack of affectation on the stage with his desire for privacy off the stage. His pranks constituted his armor, though after a while he was hardly aware of it.

Several years after he left the conservatory, he returned to Cologne to play. As he was about to begin the Schubert *Arpeggione,* he spotted his old friend Michael Taube with the pianist Emil Hauser in the audience. Hauser had played the Schumann A Minor the night before in a concert Feuermann had attended. With a grin in the direction of his two friends, Feuermann began his recital with the first *expressivo* piano phrase of the Schumann, C B A, which fitted the A minor opening of the *Arpeggione,* and then continued right on with the Schubert and the rest of the program as if his friends did not exist.

In 1925, in Winterthur, Feuermann performed the Haydn D Major Concerto under Herman Scherchen. Scherchen was a profuse perspirer. As the concerto proceeded and Scherchen's conducting became more animated, the sprinkling of moisture became a shower, an inundation, much to the discomfiture of Feuermann, playing downwind. He showed no annoyance during the performance. The moment it was over, however, he took out his handkerchief and unfurled it amidst the applause and bowing, and proceeded to dry his face, head, and neck in a conspicuous manner. As Scherchen followed him into the artists' room, Feuermann called out, in full hearing of all, "Ich bin getauft worden" (I was just baptized).

Anyone around Feuermann for very long would get some kind of "treatment." Only a very few—those of whom he was in awe—remained immune. George Szell was not among the latter. Szell, a near-contemporary, had accompanied Feuermann when the latter performed in Prague early in their careers. In fact Feuermann during the twenties probably performed with every professional accompanist then working. The tradition was to utilize any talented local pianist, of whom there were many.

Feuermann had come to Düsseldorf to give several recitals, perhaps as part of his trio work. It was home ground; he knew everyone in town. Thus he was aware of the impending arrival of Szell to begin his conducting career as head of the municipal opera. Knowing of Szell's excellence as a pianist, he suggested to the local concert society that several additional chamber music events could be added, with Szell as the participating pianist. Arrangements were made and announcements and posters

Emanuel Feuermann, about 1925.

printed. When Szell stepped off the train a week later he was greeted by these posters announcing his recitals. Feuermann had conveniently forgotten to approach or communicate with Szell about the matter. Szell, a serious person (perhaps that is why Feuermann did it), was furious; yet he played the concerts.

For six years Feuermann was truly a journeyman in music. Every year between 1923 and 1929 he set forth diligently on his assigned tour, which added up to a total of fifty to seventy solo appearances a year, so that by the end of the period he had appeared in almost three hundred different communities in all of Europe, the majority, of course, being in Germany. In spite of the difficulties of travel and the physical abuse involved in this heavy schedule of concertizing, he did not quail at the burden. He was of course very young. And he also realized that as good as he thought himself, there was purpose here.

His task was clear. He had to ground his technique, to purify it, to bend it, subject it to his own will, to the subtlest beckoning of his mind whenever and wherever desired. To explore the inner nuances of the music, he had to learn to relax and find his own particular voice in performance itself. Munio perceived that this could only be done through constant reiteration on the concert platform. The mental control achieved in his own study had to be made total in concert. He must make his body obey his mind.

Most modern soloists start out with roughly this same vision of concert performance. But the difference between intent and achievement is a variable dependent on the ability to master a technique cognitively and that intangible called natural physical talent. When the gap between intent and achievement is not bridged, eventually the artist must rationalize his failures and make do with what comes easiest. Feuermann would later put this minimum necessary difference at 5 percent. But for him it was the 5 percent at the very peak of what could be thought possible on the cello. Never solo, he would tell his students, if you will lose over 5 percent of your technique and interpretive control. The two elements—technique and interpretive control—grew to be synonymous as he matured.

As these years rolled by, Munio began to approach at least the technical side of this vision. There are more frequent stories of his growing lassitude when it came to practicing. His playing now reproduced his intent onstage, his body responding to his commands. His intense concentration would be seen in his sucked-in cheeks and puckered lips. Klemperer, observing this at a concert in Berlin, would whisper puckishly to a companion, "Look, he is blowing the cello away."

Joseph Schuster, solo cellist of the Berlin Philharmonic following Piatigorsky (1929) and later first cellist of the New York Philharmonic (1936), and indeed one of the finer cellists of this era, first heard Feuermann perform in the Brahms Double Concerto with Sigmund early in the twenties. Some years later they spent several weeks together at the Semmering resort outside Vienna. They chummed around, played tennis, and swam. Schuster was positive that Feuermann did not touch his cello that summer. He cheerfully allowed his nails to grow at will. One morning a call came through asking Feuermann to substitute the next day for the indisposed Arnold Foldeszy. It was for the Dvořák Concerto, accompanied by a Spa Orchestra. Schuster went along and witnessed an extraordinary performance. Certainly the cellist's flabby muscles gave evidence of fatigue after the performance. Nevertheless, Feuermann's proverbial ability to call forth his technique even after a layoff of a number of weeks testifies to the enormous cerebral control he had over his body. He knew himself as few instrumentalists do. It can be speculated that the cause lay in the hours of completely critical and self-scrutinizing practice in those two crucial years of maturation in Leipzig.

The Feuermann family would recall the summer of 1929, when he posted his greatest triumph—the purchase of his first car. He had wanted to buy a car several years earlier, but Paul Reifenberg insisted that instead he ought to return the small Petrus Guarneri cello to Kux and purchase a cello more suitable for concert work. Feuermann agreed and came up with his Tecchler. The summer of the automobile he returned home to Vienna, religiously lowered the strings of his cello, packed the instrument away in his room, and "took off for Europe." He did not return to play on it until September, a few days before his first concert of the season.

After six years, anyone would tire. If there was a goal that drove him on, it was the vision of a new and exciting resting place—Berlin. Berlin was not only the cultural center, where all his friends were gravitating, but it was a city within which he might once again establish his independence. He could not go back to Vienna. Sigmund had departed three years earlier, first for a concert tour of the United States—aided somewhat by one of Munio's new-found friends, the wealthy cellist, Gerald Warburg—and then to teach in New York as well as to play. Thus Munio was the only son the family could turn to. Gusta was now married; Rosa was engaged to Adolph Hoenigsberg, her first cousin and a trumpet virtuoso; Maier had "retired" from the Tonkünstler, complained regularly about his intestinal troubles, and took to the spas for the waters.

The person who drew him home was Sophie, the youngest. She was now a pianist of great talent. By 1927 they had begun to appear together. Munio was eager to do what he could for her, but what with two brothers ahead of her, he feared she would have an uphill battle asserting her personality. Otherwise, Vienna was not attractive any more, it was stagnant and replete with sad, tense memories. Munio was twenty-six, but the family still remembered him as an obstreperous child.

On the other hand, his other home, Cologne, was great fun. The

Reifenberg mansion was his own. As Paul grew older and weaker, Oma had begun to depend upon Munio and absorb more of his energies. The sons were almost outsiders—enigmas. Both daughters, the older, plump Lili, and Eva, now a delightful teen-ager, looked upon him as a knight bringing excitement and energy into their prosaic existences. There was a built-in dilemma in such a situation. To what extent could his career be absorbed into the cares and woes of those around him without compromising his inner creativity?

The 1927–1928 season had been a great one. Artur Schnabel and he had been engaged for ten days in the Soviet Union. Feuermann was impressed with the people, the conductorless orchestra in Moscow, the Leningrad Philharmonic under Nicolai Malko, the young Raya Garbousova and her mother, a very talented duo, and so much else in this experimental society. He wanted to return, even if the monetary rewards were thin. In a later tour, 1932, his fee was paid with a supposed early J. B. Guadagnini violin.

In July of 1928 he received a contract from the publisher Benjamin to revise the Lee Cello Schule, recognition Feuermann coveted. He.had even cut a few discs for Parlophone—salon pieces . . . but . . . there were so many competing now—Foldeszy, Schuster, Mainardi, Kindler, Salmond, Cassado, Suggia, and the very talented Russian Piatigorsky, who was a meteor in the musical world. Just three years earlier Feuermann had soloed in Vienna with the Berlin Philharmonic. Before he came onstage, the huge Piatigorsky entered and stood at his first-desk position. When Feuermann came out, there was a murmur of amusement. Those in the audience recalled the unique contrast of the two great cellists, something like Mutt and Jeff. Though Piatigorsky was now the rage of the German concert public, he was too "charming" a musician, Feuermann felt, to stand in the way of what must now be his ultimate destiny, the Berlin Hochschule.

An opportune moment was near. Hugo Becker, close to retirement age, was anxiously awaiting the opportunity to return to his two estates in the Tyrol and northern Italy. Becker, a man upon whom great wealth had been bestowed by the banker Edgar Speyer, had grown into an increasingly weary and anachronistic figure in the rapidly overheating musical environment in Berlin. An ultra-Prussian nationalist, Becker was now a citizen of hated France, a turn necessitated by the freezing after World War I by the Allies of his hoard of gold deposited in foreign banks. Since he had been born in French Strasbourg before 1871, he renounced his German citizenship and thereby made himself eligible for the recovery of these accounts. He could now anticipate a leisurely retirement in resplendent circumstances.

In early September, 1929, this post was only an anticipatory fragment. However, by mid-September, Piatigorsky had resigned from his trio with

Sigmund and cousin Abraham Hoenigsberg in Vienna, before the start
of Sigmund's American tour, 1925.

Sophie Feuermann at the beginning of concert career and partnership
with Emanuel, 1927.

Joseph Wolfsthal and Leonid Kreutzer. The United States was beckoning, and Wolfsthal immediately approached his friend Feuermann. Both were "Galizianer" and they had formed a close friendship in the last several years. Wolfsthal was the youngest son of the Professor Wolfsthal of Lemberg to whom Maier had brought Sigmund in 1907, and who had been touted by his father as almost in the class of Sigmund. His older brother Max, also very talented, was now having difficulties maintaining the impetus of his concert career, the competition had become so fierce. But the younger Wolfsthal, at twenty-nine, was flourishing. Not only did he have a successful trio, but he was solo violinist of the State Opera Orchestra under special contract. He was a favorite of Richard Strauss, who often requested him to do the solos in his various operatic and symphonic works. And now he was a popular professor at the Hochschule.

Feuermann accepted Wolfsthal's proposal with alacrity. No sooner had he done this than the trio almost dissolved. Piatigorsky showed up one evening with his new manager, Merrowitz, and pianist Vladimir Horowitz. They needed a fiddler for their American tour. Wolfsthal was Piatigorsky's choice. Feuermann, Kreutzer, and several others were present at the audition, which featured a very complex modernistic piece by Carl Schnitika, a personal favorite of Merrowitz. The performance was a mess. Wolfsthal was a guileless gypsy. What he felt, he did. He thought the work was awful and halfway through it he started to improvise. Feuermann, sitting behind him and reading the music, was the only one to notice it, so absolute was the cacophony. He roared. Finally Wolfsthal could contain himself no longer and burst into uncontrollable laughter that brought the performance to a halt. Merrowitz was incensed. Ultimately, the young Russian violinist Nathan Milstein accompanied the others on their trip to the New World.

The first week in October Feuermann gave his inaugural trio recital. The reviews were warm and the Berlin musicians noted with satisfaction that a dependable cello part contributed mightily to its success. There were earlier complaints that Grisha (Piatigorsky) could never be relied upon to play the same notes in any piece twice. He was ever a capricious Russian "muzhik" onstage. Later that same week Feuermann played a solo recital, again in Berlin. The reviewer commented:

> The young cellist Emanuel Feuermann is a great and fine musician in addition to being a master of the technical dimension. I heard him play a solo sonata by Hindemith, vigorous in its emotional side, vivid in the finale. It is almost a dramatic work, suffused with technical finesse that could be solved only by a first rate talent like Feuermann. He executed it eminently in every respect, as he did likewise with other, smaller pieces. They were excellently accompanied on the piano by Hermann Hoppe. One should try

to interest Feuermann in Berlin. As far as I know a professorial chair for the violoncello will shortly be vacant.

Not much persuading would be necessary.

Four days later, on October 9, Feuermann played again, this time away, with the Hamburg Symphony in the Brahms Double Concerto, with Carl Flesch. It was a crucial appearance, since Flesch, Wolfsthal's teacher, was head of the violin department at the Hochschule, a great scholar and pedagogue of the violin and, most recently, personally antipathetic to Wolfsthal. Flesch felt that Wolfsthal had certain character defects not appropriate in a teacher at the Hochschule. Wolfsthal was an impetuous bohemian and unfortunately Feuermann was somehow implicated both by friendship and by his own reputation as a prankster.

Munio, however, was ultra-careful. Flesch, having limited facility, needed all kinds of performing concessions from his partner. Feuermann obliged so unobtrusively as to make it seem natural; thus the ensemble was flawless. There was mutual satisfaction and much congratulating.

Two weeks later Feuermann was notified of his appointment as professor of violoncello at the Berlin Hochschule für Musik.

Tecchler Cello

5

BERLIN: PROFESSOR

It was Easter, 1930. The Rhine flowed placidly through its green banks, passing Bayenthal Gärtel on its way toward the towers of Cologne, and then on to the sea itself. There was no visible indication of the turbulence now overtaking Germany at the very beginning of this new decade. In the Reifenberg mansion on Oberländer Ufa, all was pleasant and congenial, at least on the surface. There was even happy excitement. Munio had come for the holidays. He would stay until the sixteenth of April, when he would again play with his old colleagues of the Gürzenich under Abendroth.

It was important both to him and the family that he spend a week or two with them. Since Paul Reifenberg's death, they all seemed to depend upon him, Oma especially so. Superficially, this new dependency of the well-born Reifenberg clan on its erstwhile protégé seemed eminently understandable. Was not Munio a professor at the Hochschule and in the words of a number of critics the "premier" cellist of Germany? Yet at twenty-seven, Feuermann, especially when he came to Cologne, had to remind himself he was no longer the Galician kid from the streets of Leopoldstadt.

Munio had arisen fairly late this particular day. Nothing was scheduled except a visit from Oma's young cousin Gerhardt Hertz. The young man was about to graduate from Gymnasium and was trying to settle upon a career or profession. He loved music dearly and was entranced with the violin, upon which he practiced with great assiduity, helped not a little by a J.B. Vuillaume violin his parents had bestowed on him as a token of their approval of his endeavors. But now they were troubled, for he had decided to embark on a musical career. In their opinion it was not the appropriate choice for a young man of his background and education. Gerhardt disagreed, and at the suggestion of his Tante Yetta, who was staying at the Reifenbergs', decided to ask Munio's advice.

Upon arriving, Gerhardt was ushered into the music room where, Vuillaume in hand, he greeted Munio, who entered in a bright silk dressing gown. It was a warm greeting. They had not seen each other in several years. Munio, of course, commented on Gerhardt's maturation and growth, which, it should be noted, was in the latter instance modest. "Well, what did you bring with you?" Munio asked, peering into the folio óf music Gerhardt held. Gerhardt pulled out the Handel Sonata no. 5 in D Major. Munio took the piano part and sat down at the Bechstein to look it over while Gerhardt tuned his instrument. They played through the slow opening movement and into the second movement. Munio suddenly stopped and asked, "What else do you have?" The Mozart D Major Concerto was set upon the stand and they both began, Munio carefully following him with a piano version of the orchestral accompaniment. After a page or two, Feuermann again stopped. "Can you play the cadenza?" Hertz nodded and dove in.

When Gerhardt had finished, Feuermann motioned him to stay put, rose, and went over to the other side of the room to a massive mahogany-paneled cabinet. From one of the drawers within which was housed the extensive Reifenberg music collection, Munio brought back with him the Beethoven Opus 18 String Quartets. He took out the second violin part, handed it to Hertz, and told him to look over Number 6, the Scherzo movement, while he got his cello. Placing the first violin part on a stand, Feuermann tuned his Tecchler and announced, "I will give you three bars for nothing. This is the rhythm." He proceeded to count off, first in three and then in one, at, to Hertz, an appallingly rapid sixty-three to the bar.

They began, Feuermann playing the first violin part, which is in thirds with the second violin, on the cello, in the violin register. It was too much for Gerhardt. Both the syncopated rhythms and the tempo caused him to break down three or four times until, mercifully, Feuermann stopped. He muttered, "Not so good," and asked the violinist for some scales with varied bowings. That shortly concluded, he waved Gerhardt's violin into its case and stood quietly for a moment, chin in hand. Gerhardt, still trembling with embarrassment and exhaustion, straightened himself up for the inevitable judgment. "Look, Gerhardt, why do you want to try to make a living on the violin? There are so many terrific violinists who can barely eat today. You play well . . . but. . . . Look at us. We came from Poland. We never knew anything else but the instrument since we were tiny children."

Feuermann picked up his cello, sat down and started to demonstrate by playing octaves at terrific speed—legato, staccato, jumps, separated and connected bowing—over the fingerboard—and in rhythm. "You see, this comes naturally. We don't have to—and we can't afford to—struggle on the instrument. Gerhardt, you are a bright fellow. Why don't you go to Professor Golad in Freiburg and become a music critic and make lots of

money criticizing us?" Hertz, obviously disconsolate, politely thanked
Munio and left. The future had been decided for him. In September of
that year he would be in Vienna at the Academy studying theory, in
addition to the piano, with a brilliant young teacher named Sophie
Feuermann. Later, in the United States, he would make his mark as a
distinguished Bach scholar at the University of Louisville.

Feuermann was flourishing. He was barely in young manhood, yet his
career now seemed to be touching a new peak of achievement. His salary
at the Hochschule was excellent; students were coming to him from as far
away as Roumania, Palestine, and Japan. He had more than he could
handle in the way of concert bookings; and, in spite of the depression, the
fees were good, the reviews ever better. The piano trio with the dour
Kreützer and the aggressive Wolfsthal had been replaced by a new,
exciting, and challenging combination with Wolfsthal and the phleg-
matic, yet energetic, genius Paul Hindemith on viola. They had embarked
on a series of recitals featuring the literature of the string trio, which
would yet display their individual solo abilities. The combination had
caught on and they were now committed to numerous recitals. There
were few similar combinations of the kind that could put together such
talents. The string trio does not necessitate the ensemble blending of the

The string trio: Feuermann, Hindemith, Wolfsthal, 1930.

string quartet, but it requires the full technical and solo capacities of concert artists as the other form does not. The three performers here probably represented the greatest talents on their instrument in Germany at the time. And this fact was quickly evident to a large audience of music lovers.

Feuermann's enthusiasm and success in this new milieu were not merely a product of his newly-attained musical achievements. The environment of Berlin contributed much. Before the war, all the talent and genius seemed to be concentrated in Vienna. But it had a hierarchical culture in which the great creators in every field were intimidated and inhibited by their own deprivation and a class society that placed upon musicians the stigma of second-class citizen. Now in Berlin, even in a world rapidly coming apart, the democratic environment, as it had long before in Athens in the last days before the Spartan debacle, produced a brilliance of intellectual and artistic achievement that in its intensity momentarily obscured the gathering storm. One cannot here mention all those names in literature, architecture, drama, art, science, philosophy, and music that gave to Germany and the Berlin bohemianism a deep creative thrust. Its position at the zenith of European cultural achievement, and its fragility in the face of the forces that would soon disperse it, reflect the paradox that underlies all great eras of cultural attainment.

Feuermann was one of the heroes of this generation. He was deeply serious about his art; yet he was important enough not to be serious all the time. In his classes at the Hochschule he would hardly need to open his mouth. Just to play, he catapulted over a hundred years of accumulated technical and interpretive tradition in performance on his instrument. His entire generation was laying down standards of performance that might well rest as the final synthesis of the musical possibilities inherent in this instrumental medium.

Merely to communicate to the students how clean technical articulation might give rise to a whole chain of new relationships in interpretation was in itself revolutionary. Feuermann taught his students to separate the composer's intentions from the accumulated concessions to technical incapacities of prior cellists; only in this way could they establish entirely new canons of what constitutes musicality.

Feuermann would not at this stage in his career, if indeed he ever could, teach his advanced students how to rebuild their techniques. However, he could now perceive, as he probably could not have in Cologne, what they were doing wrong, in concrete physical as well as aural terms. He could advise them about their posture at the cello, the shape of their left and right hands, and how to move cleanly and musically about the instrument. For the rest, they would have to transfer their external physical attributes to an internal organic synthesis. Again, he probably was not at the stage of intuiting the unique differences in bodily structure and personality that

give rise to different approaches in playing so as to be able to correct
subtle, inherent aberrations. Only a rare teacher has this ability. Feuermann's prime capability, especially since he did not as yet push his students as systematically as he would in later years, was to exemplify a new
standard of playing and free his students to their own devices of emulation. Finally, as a teacher he was fun to be with, and this was possibly one of
his strongest pedagogical qualities.

His fellow musicians found his enthusiasm and energy exhilarating and
exhausting. The fourth-floor apartment he had rented on Franken-Allee
was always crowded with musicians and suffused with music. His
Fascino-Osetto was forever roaming Berlin and its environs, as he visited
and concertized. As a driver, he was notorious for his innumerable near
and minor scrapes. Friends recall his intoxication with speed, the races
and pranks with his car and those of his friends. One entire morning was
spent in an apparently senseless, except to those involved, game—to block
the garage and parking space between himself, Hindemith, and another
musician.

Another recollection is of a trip to Munich to join the trio for a concert
there. Feuermann started two days early so that he could make a leisurely
drive, since it was a lovely spring. As usual he loaded the trunk with
several extra spares. Tires being what they were in those days and Feuermann's driving being what it was, he was forever getting flat tires. He
finally arrived in Munich an hour before the concert, nonplused and with
none of his spares usable any more.

One evening, on returning from a concert, he invited several friends to
his apartment. Others kept showing up until there were enough musicians for a chamber orchestra. Music naturally ensued. Someone finally
suggested a rather obscure sextet that Feuermann did not have. The only
music available was on the other side of town. Feuermann volunteered to
drive the owner of the music to his apartment to fetch the parts. And so
they set forth onto the streets of Berlin at 2 A.M. They literally whizzed
through the half-deserted avenues. The breakneck speed began to make
Feuermann's passenger somewhat uneasy. He soon became visibly frightened and called out, "Munio, you are passing through the red traffic
lights." Feuermann casually yelled back to him, "Don't worry, I'm color-
blind."* It is not recorded whether or not the passenger was comforted by
this information.

His color blindness got him into all kinds of traffic scrapes, including an
almost-serious collision with a trolley car. Usually the confrontations
consisted of the typical driver-driver or pedestrian-driver disputes as to
who had the right of way. Feuermann was never loth to exchange insult
for insult with his momentary antagonist.

---

*So, too, was Sigmund.

The seemingly casual attitude taken in Germany in regard to vehicles and their drivers was in sharp contrast to the necessarily highly regulated American traffic system. In fact Feuermann was ever in fear in America of revocation of his driving permit because of his congenital defect. Franz Rupp recalls an auto trip with Feuermann in the latter's old Hudson about 1940. They were on concert tour and traveling between Washington and Philadelphia. As usual Feuermann was driving over the speed limit, and talking just about as fast, when a motorcycle police officer overtook and berated him soundly while checking his registration and license. When the policeman had departed, Feuermann silently placed the ticket in his inside jacket pocket and drove on, but at greatly reduced speed. He said not a word until they reached Philadelphia.

To his close friends Feuermann always remained the same—a simple, intuitive, almost childlike person, yet with a sharp, instantaneously perceptive mind. From knowing him as a person, one could never guess his station in life. In the context of the outside world, to society, he was egotistical and brash. On occasion he would even act the role of accomplished virtuoso to the neophytes in a group. At a gathering in his apartment sometime in 1932, someone suggested that all hands were available for Schubert's Trout Quintet except the bass. On tap for the performance were Bruno Walter, piano, Szymon Goldberg, violin, Michael Taube, viola, and Hindemith, who had volunteered to play the bass if one could be found at 11 P.M. Feuermann turned to Goldberg, who—in spite of his new membership in the string trio as well as his job as concertmaster of the Philharmonic—was still a youngster, and peremptorily asked him to take Gerhardt Hertz, who was also present, and borrow a bass from a Philharmonic musician who lived nearby. Both Goldberg and Hertz obediently agreed to go and transport the monster the several blocks, that music might be served.

There is more to this occurrence than the simple pulling of rank. Feuermann, as probably did many other musicians, made many demands upon his colleagues, as to job opportunities for himself as well as for friends. There existed a tradition of self-help amongst these musicians, which at least in Feuermann's case went back to his own father's example. You never demand for yourself alone, but for the progress of the art. The Feuermanns, in demanding help and opportunity for their children, served the same cultural interests as did their wealthy patrons. Talent served all of society as well as the individual in question. In turn those who succeed are obliged to help the young, talented, and as yet unrewarded ones.

As jealous of his own abilities as Feuermann was, he was always vitally interested in any new skill that might be developed by other instrumentalists. It was as if a new capacity had been uncovered in nature and, personal pride notwithstanding, his obligation as an artist was to note and examine it. In sum, the line of responsibility to the art connecting him with the past had not yet been broken. The demands to receive and give help within the context of the law of the artist-musician could not be dissolved. This was a fundamental restriction on personal advancement that every member of the craft was expected to observe.

If any consistent picture of Feuermann can be drawn, it is that from his earliest years his potential for a sharp, terrorizing tongue existed, a potential fulfilled with the coming of success, as fears of retribution for his personal style diminished. Friends would often caution him after his frequent verbal skirmishes with themselves or others, "Munio, don't be a *shegitz*" (a common gentile). Else, as described by others, he was the perennial *lausbub* (a little rogue).

The Israeli violinist Wolfgang Schocken, then a neophyte professional in Berlin, recalled a party given by Mrs. Hans Von Bülow for Aloys Haba, the quarter-tone composer, and one of a galaxy of composers in that city in those years. The cream of Berlin musical society was in attendance. In addition there were a number of amateurs and philanthropists, the latter always necessary at these affairs. One of these, a noted sponsor of musical events and an amateur musician himself, was a somewhat pompous German of the old Prussian school. Feuermann, spotting him standing close by and disregarding the possible consequences, stepped momentarily away from his own group to bring him over, ostensibly to be introduced to the "famous." The gentleman was grateful for the opportunity and beamed with magisterial anticipation, until he heard Feuermann's unctuous enunciation, "Hier ist die grösste Schüttle in Deutschland." The burst of laughter from the assemblage reddened the poor man's face, and he shrank away silently, humiliated.

The first recordings made by Feuermann date from about 1925 or 1926, but were released later. They are short salon pieces, such as *Träumerei* and the *Abendlied* (with harmonium accompaniment). They are, admittedly, timid performances. The playing is correct, the sound full. Only slight inflection in the interpretation can be noted, not much personality but, on the other hand, no yielding to the salon nature of the music. Feuermann seems unsure as to the correct role to play on these discs. There is a slight regression in style in that there are far more slides than are reported of his public performances during this period. One feels that the cellist was making an effort to sound like other cellists then recording, without becoming sentimental or careless.

From the period just before 1929 and onward, Feuermann assumes a more assertive style, and makes a continually restrained and disciplined attempt to reproduce the composer's intentions musically. With each succeeding recording of the *Swan, Träumerei,* or Chopin's $E^\flat$ *Nocturne,* one hears the gradual emancipation from the influences of the styles of

other cellists and from the internal restraint, built out of an almost literal
respect for the written music. The playing is always straightforward, with
none of the idiosyncratic shaping that most romantic instrumentalists
would give it. Yet the phrasing is there, giving the listener just enough to
make the piece interesting, tantalizing him to go back and listen once
more to the impeccable technique and the understated nuance.

One of the first recordings he made in Berlin was Saint-Säens' *Allegro
Appassionata,* an ordinary romantic potboiler. Feuermann plays it straight,
at great speed, yet with elegant phrasing in the *cantilena* sections. One gets
the feeling that through his playing he is enunciating a simple rhetorical
question. Have you ever heard this piece played so cleanly, so that its
technique reveals rather than obscures the lines of the music? It is completely understandable that at twenty-six or twenty-seven years of age, he
is not reshaping the music "subtly" and "profoundly." His technique is so
remarkably new that it stands by itself as a musical contribution of fundamental importance.

If one turns to one of the last pieces recorded in Berlin (1932–33),
probably on his new Montagnana cello, Popper's *Hungarian Rhapsody* with
Paul Kletzki and the Berlin Philharmonic, one hears another simple
romantic piece played with extraordinary subtlety and restraint. The
music represents a classical rendering of the gypsy tradition, a common-
place among late nineteenth-century composers. It alternates slow
melismatic passages with fast *czardas* sections. Feuermann's interpretive
freedom shows evident advance in the three years that probably separate
these recordings. The slow passages flow easily within the rhythmic
framework and the fast sections have enough rhythmic hesitation to the
forward momentum to make the entire production a truly tantalizing
achievement. The *Rhapsody* recording is a musical gem and shows off the
throaty Venetian cello to its best advantage. Feuermann's control in every
transitional phrase gives the listener a real sense of the growing realization of mind over matter that the cellist was aiming for in his concert work.

The most famous recording of this period, and the first to open up an
audience for Feuermann in England and the United States, was the
recording of Dvořák's B Minor Concerto with the Berlin State Opera
Orchestra. This performance was conducted by his old friend, and now
perennial recording accompanist, Michael Taube. By modern standards
this 1930 set of discs has a primitive sound. In addition, as in many
recordings of this era, the orchestra's playing leaves much to be desired.
Yet the overall impact of the performance as well as the clarion assertiveness of Feuermann's Tecchler come through decisively. It is mid-Berlin-
period Feuermann at his most typical. In spite of the two takes and the
omission on the rejects of a few ragged spots, it is still not a flawless
performance. Feuermann played too freely ever to play spotlessly. Typically, it is not a highly inflected interpretation, yet withal, a completely

integrated one. Some will argue that it is too straightforward and that Feuermann's literalness detracts from the flow of the various themes and moods one into the other. And it is true that here and there the changes are somewhat abrupt, though still within rhythmic and textual authenticity.

The cause of this lack is more a technical one rather than one of musical insensitivity. Feuermann's first commitment at this point in his career was to his vision of technical precision and clarity. He had attained freedom of movement on the cello by abandoning the reaching, pawing, and hesitating that characterize the accommodations of cellists who must perform with less than his physical mastery. Although immaturity is a good explanation for Feuermann's inability to weave the varying stylistic and technical moods into a seamless interpretive whole through the use of slides, portamento bowing, greater nuances in his right- or left-hand attacks instead of his typically assertive and concrete delineations, it is not the only explanation. It is Feuermann alone who was first able to probe the technical problems of this piece of music with such complete results. The mushy romanticism of others was in reality a capitulation to lack of capacity.

Thus Feuermann was in a sense exulting at his achievement, which, while technically unique, is still completely musical and typical Dvořák. Also, he was still relatively inexperienced with the recording medium. And since the Dvořák represented his first recording collaboration with orchestra, he probably played a bit more tightly than in public performance. Every new medium demands experience before one can utilize it to its utmost. Only so much can be immediately transferred from the concert hall with an audience to the concert hall with a microphone. Finally Feuermann had no models of the Dvořák interpreted by cellists he truly admired. His was a ground-breaking performance, which indeed probably became a model or a challenge upon which Pablo Casals built six years later when he recorded the concerto with George Szell and the Czech Philharmonic.

In fact, a comparison between the recording made in 1936 by the fifty-nine year old Catalonian and the twenty-seven year old Feuermann of 1930 yields some interesting contrasts in the evolving cello traditions. There is no doubt, when one hears the old master's Dvořák, that one is listening to a powerful musical personality. Casals as interpreter stands definitely to the fore. Perhaps, as many have commented, Casals would have been a masterful musician no matter what musical medium he had chosen. On the other hand, even in 1936, one notes that, especially in contrast with Feuermann, the revolution begun by Casals on the cello was an uncompleted one.

Throughout the recording, and especially in the course of the demanding first movement, it is evident that part of the interpretive shaping engaged in by Casals is a shaping to avoid the technical demands of the piece. There are numerous concessions. There are tempo changes in rhythmic transitions to allow for repositioning. There is often the raspy sound of effort, there are notes cut short, and passages are swallowed, yet all done in terms of a musical design that one almost accepts as representative of orthodox playing.

Shortly into the first movement there is a passage, repeated later in the movement, that calls for a flying-spiccato arpeggio passage. Feuermann had played this passage with breathtaking literalness, his bow propelling the notes with pearl-like clarity. Casals plays the passage legato; it is almost obscured by the orchestral accompaniment. Yet the effect of the Casals passage is quite musical. It all points to the fact that the old master had by this time come to terms with his capabilities. Even toward the conclusion of the first movement, in which he shows palpable signs of running out of steam—can a cellist be still as capable at fifty-nine as at twenty-seven?—his playing, though fuzzy, is still under musical control.

Casals' entire performance reflects the great difference between the eras he and Feuermann represented, which through the quirk of fate were reversed as far as longevity and musical influence are concerned. Casals made it possible to be musical on the cello. He made a giant step forward in technical and musical emancipation. But once he achieved his musical goal, to bring the cello to an interpretive par with his contemporaries on the violin—Sarasate, Ysaÿe, and Thibaud—he halted. All that he achieved musically was done in spite of his available technique rather than because of it, as was the case with Feuermann. The final climb to the pinnacle of instrumental mastery he left to his younger colleague.

It is certainly true that without drive and self-centeredness there can be no achievement. And when he later examined his life amongst all the stars in Berlin, Feuermann would have to admit that, for all the camaraderie and close musical associations, his relationships were not warmly human and intimate. Each of his colleagues carried along with him the burden of effort out of which his achievement had been built. And essentially it was a closed document, to be read only by its owner. Feuermann was the same. Only one friend could be really called an intimate. That was the pianist Franz Osborne, whom he first met in Cologne. Osborne was a talented young man, a fine pianist in an era of great pianists. His father, Max Osborne, was a well-known writer and critic, associate of many of the great dramatists and art historians of that era, a man into whose home the elite of the Weimar Republic was welcomed.

Unlike the Reifenberg mansion, the Osborne home was not a place where the patron asked the greats to sign a guest book. Franz had a distinguished father to compete with in an intellectually allied field. The thrust, the drive to achieve concourse with the great, was not there, as with

Feuermann. Franz had associated with the great all his life. And thus, he fell in easily as an associate and confidant of Feuermann. They fitted each other's needs perfectly. Franz was from an "establishment" Jewish home, and Munio was to be one of the greats.

Munio of course fulfilled his musical destiny even after the world of Weimar fell apart. Later it was obscurity for the Osbornes—father, now an old and forgotten intellectual, and son, one of a horde of refugee pianists. Feuermann did everything he could to aid the Osbornes in eventually settling in the United States and obtaining citizenship papers. With regard to Franz, he used his tours, to the annoyance of some, to attempt to scour up a teaching position for him in one or another of the colleges at which Feuermann often played.

Another important and pregnant association was tragically short-lived. This was Feuermann's musical relationship with Joseph Wolfsthal. In the short two years of their close association it is probable that Feuermann was moved to see new possibilities in his own playing that heretofore he had not been ready to consider. There is no doubt that the power and impetuosity of the young violinist played a role in evolving Feuermann's attitude and approach both to people and to music. Essentially, Feuermann had been, and was after, a timid person. The recordings of 1930 show a wholly new definition in his playing.

The general experience of playing in the trio with Wolfsthal and Hindemith was crucial. It was an association of artists with a common esthetic. More, they discovered and shaped each other's playing through the fact that each was in a class by himself on his instrument. Hindemith was the oldest, and moving irrevocably towards a full-time preoccupation with composing. Yet in his quiet manner he brought his musicianship fully to bear on the literature that was their joint enterprise. For, not only was he the greatest of the young German composers of the day and its best violist, he was probably the greatest purely German string player around.

As far as string instrumentalists were concerned, Feuermann thought Wolfsthal to be in a class by himself, along with Heifetz and Milstein, the most talented of the young violinists of that era. Wolfsthal was an extremely confident person with an ego that perfectly projected his musical capabilities. His sound was open and pellucid. It had less of a worked-over quality than Kreisler's or Heifetz's. Between 1928 and 1930 he made a number of recordings, short encore pieces as well as recordings of the Mozart A Major with Frieder Weiszmann for Parlophone and the Beethoven Violin Concerto with Manfred Gurlit and the Berlin Philharmonic for Gramophone. In addition there is an earlier, privately recorded performance of the Mendelssohn concerto that exemplifies his immense talent, yet still shows a musician in need of schooling and discipline. No doubt, in spite of their later and mutual hatred, Carl Flesch did give the impetus to the flourishing of Wolfsthal's talent.

Of the commercial recordings, the encore pieces and the Mozart concerto are uncommonly brilliant and beautiful performances. But it is the Beethoven that constitutes one of the unique achievements in the recorded history of violin performance. It is as spontaneous and natural a playing as could be imagined. One's immediate impression is that of a musically and technically supremely educated gypsy. The attacks and releases of a magnificent right arm, the articulation of the left hand, the presence in the sound of the Joseph (filius Andreus) Guarnerius violin all add up to a wondrous experience.

Like Feuermann, Wolfsthal is not impeccable technically, in his spontaneity. He occasionally lands slightly flat. But Wolfsthal will not paw, he takes chances, even if there is no second chance. Wolfsthal refused to make second takes. He would play a piece through only once. It was now or never. Even Feuermann allowed himself the extra luxury of a second chance. Wolfsthal threw himself into performance with such ferocity of concentration that he felt another performance would inevitably lose too much to be worth the additional physical and mental effort.

However, the lack of technical perfection does not in any way detract from the impact of mastery. The playing, technically, compares with Heifetz's. It is less intense and it is light in sound, being cleaner, his impetus clearly enunciated; yet overall not quite so impeccable. As compared with Milstein's playing, it is certainly not so sweet nor so highly polished. Yet it is far more vigorous and impressive. Stylistically Wolfsthal shows a real sense of difference between Mozart and Beethoven. The scales in the Beethoven come through with an unbelievable momentum and inevitability that reveal the architectonic power of this concerto as few violinists have been able to do.

Had Wolfsthal not had that moment of bravado at the audition, had he not upset the applecart for the American tour, we might have heard much more of this musician. But the audition of 1929 was not atypical for Wolfsthal. He had been hired to play in one of the great homes of Berlin early in the fall of 1930; it was a private concert before an invited group of notables. The fee agreed upon was one thousand marks. Several days after the recital, a check for five hundred arrived. The host, a wealthy businessman with the traditional disdain for musicians, had felt he could hedge on the stipulated fee. Wolfsthal impetuously ordered five hundred marks' worth of flowers to be sent to the lady of the house, whom he felt was somewhat sympathetic to his art. Prominently displayed in the huge basket of flowers was a bill for five hundred marks, clearly marked "paid." A week later a check arrived for the full fee.

Wolfsthal was a true friend in need during the only bit of personal unpleasantness, even scandal, that marred Feuermann's career at the Hochschule. As is inevitable with a vigorous, young bachelor musician, many young ladies were attracted to Feuermann. Among his many stu-

dents, there were several women, one of whom became extremely suscep-
tible to his charisma. The young professor was at first flattered and
possibly even reciprocated the young lady's infatuation. However there
was no possiblity of a serious alliance and Feuermann soon withdrew any
thoughts or actions that might have given rise to hope on her part. The
young woman did not abandon her quest and in fact began to shadow him
when he was away from the Hochschule. She would often be seen waiting
outside his apartment building. Often Feuermann would find her lurking
in the oddest places, having had no premonition that anyone else knew his
patterns of life. He was worried; he cancelled several of her lessons and in
general took evasive actions so as not to run into her. The greater the
lengths he took to avoid her, the more determined she became to impress
her presence on his mind. Finally she made an inept and futile attempt at
suicide.

The imbroglio now came to a head. Her brother, a violin student at the
Hochschule, directed a number of allegations against Feuermann to the
administration. Feuermann was asked to shift his students temporarily to
Enrico Mainardi, the second cello teacher at the Hochschule. Feuermann
was now at loose ends. How does one handle such matters? He was
haunted by the terrible fate that overtook Fritz Steinbach at the Cologne
Conservatory several years before he had arrived there, which students
and faculty used to recount with considerable dread—"there but for the
grace of God go I." Steinbach was the predecessor of Herman Abendroth
as conductor and director of the conservatory. He was at that time the
greatest conductor of German origin then active. This all came to a
sudden end when in 1914 a girl student leveled a series of personal
accusations against him. The board of overseers, very serious and
punctilious Germans, viewed even the slightest lack of correctness as a
fatal lapse. Steinbach was dismissed. He died in obscurity three years later
(1916), ignored and abandoned by everyone.

To add to Feuermann's personal distress, tragedy had recently over-
taken his family. His beloved older sister and protector Gusta had died
after a horrible, prolonged illness. Several futile operations on her brain
had only made her plight more pitiful and had shredded the Feuermanns
emotionally. This young "mother" had been crucial in providing a measure of stability for the younger children in days past; and now, when a life
of her own had been newly embarked upon with so much hope and
expectation, she had been snatched away.

It was at this point that Feuermann's friends intervened to extricate him
from a situation that appeared to be getting beyond his control. Mrs.
Osborne personally drove him to a rural retreat outside Berlin where he
would stay for several weeks, while Franz and Joseph Wolfsthal, among
others, took up the battle in Berlin. This was after all 1930 Berlin, not
1914 Cologne.

Wolfsthal himself had caused a minor stir with his whirlwind courtship and marriage of Olga Szell. The latter's marriage with the conductor had disintegrated and was in process of dissolution when the ardent violinist appeared on the scene. Wolfsthal thus threw himself into this *cause célèbre* of Feuermann's with a will. He refused the brother of the girl entrance into his chamber-music classes and threatened to quit the Hochschule and take his students with him if the rights of the accused were not protected. And though Flesch was the master teacher in the violin department, the thought of losing Wolfsthal, a magnet for the younger, more talented violin students, in addition to Feuermann and possibly others, did not appeal to the administration.

The tack worked; the matter was dropped quietly. Feuermann resumed his teaching. Mainardi, seeing that he would be second cello teacher indefinitely, decided to leave, much to Feuermann's satisfaction. To the questions about Mainardi at the Hochschule, Feuermann would reply with relief, "*Er ist aweck.*" Even with no real competition, it was better to have none at all.

Joseph Wolfsthal died on February 3, 1931. He was thirty-one years old. On the prior November 19, he had attended the funeral of a mutual friend of Olga's and himself. Olga would have gone, but their baby was not well, so Wolfsthal went by himself. The hillside was blustery and cold that afternoon and Wolfsthal came home thoroughly chilled. He had a rehearsal that night at the State Opera, and a performance that included several solos the following night. There was, in addition, a full regimen of teaching so that, without the needed rest, he developed a severe cold. By the middle of December he was in bed with influenza and a high fever. Home medical treatment did not help, what with his casual attitude towards his illness and his constant restlessness. However by Christmas, he had to admit that he was very ill. His fever mounted and the doctor announced that he had pneumonia. Even when removed to the hospital and given the best medical treatment possible, he showed no improvement. He lingered on throughout January, sapped of his vigor and slowly slipping into unconsciousness.

Musical Berlin was stunned. How could one explain the loss of a man so suffused with vigor and life? Of all the departures of musicians at the Hochschule, Wolfsthal's seemed to be the most incredible. The attempt to understand the event, to come to terms with it and accept it, became increasingly difficult, especially after the funeral. Friends and family alike focused their frustration, their sense of unaccountable loss on Carl Flesch. How could he, the teacher of this man, his own protégé, have acted as he had in January, when he well knew that Joseph's life was ebbing away? Flesch had arranged to have Wolfsthal's students transferred to his new favorite, Max Rostal. How could one explain such indecently insensitive actions?

Old memories were dredged up. A year earlier in a quartet recital, Flesch, acting as first violinist, had stumbled over an up-bow staccato passage. Wolfsthal, having to repeat it a moment later, played the same passage in one down bow, a much more difficult feat, especially as so perfectly accomplished. Backstage, Flesch would later mutter to Wolfsthal in obvious pique, "You had a better teacher than I."

It was in this context, added to his bohemianism as well as his increasing popularity with students, that the famous telephone call from Harriet Kreisler was made to Olga Wolfsthal, not long before Joseph's death. Joseph had borrowed a Guarneri from Kreisler, who had a great collection of instruments, for use in certain recordings. Joseph had continued to play on it even after the recordings. While it was never clearly proven, apparently Mrs. Flesch had put through a call to Harriet Kreisler to persuade her to have the violin returned. Flesch probably did not want his student to get too big for his britches.

Years after Joseph's death the mutual hostility of the two was still to be reflected in Flesch's memoirs. Flesch notes Wolfsthal's accomplishments as a violinist—what a remarkable bow arm!—but sadly reflects on the probable ultimate lack of success of the young violinist, had he lived, because his defects as a person would have limited his potential as an artist.

It is, to be sure, pure argumentation to contest Flesch's statement, written some eight years after Wolfsthal's death. No one can predict the eventual outcome of the maturation process, even for an artist as accomplished as Wolfsthal was at his death. But from Flesch's own statements about Kreisler's Viennese period of stagnation, when the latter could not even obtain a desk position in the Court Opera, due in no small part to his bohemian behavior as well as his truly unique style of playing, it is dangerous to extrapolate personality and lifestyle into a prediction of what will ultimately emanate from an individual's character.

In one other respect Flesch's evaluation of musicians, especially violinists, is suspect. There is evidence that Bronislaw Huberman was a far meatier instrumentalist and interpreter than Flesch was willing to grant him. Keller, the translator of Flesch's memoirs, was himself forced to comment on the vendetta the pedagogue carried on against Huberman.

Feuermann's attitude towards Flesch was ambivalent. He would be the first to admit that this cool-hearted teacher was a better scholar than player. There were many things Feuermann had learned from him, since he himself had yet to verbalize many of his own intuitive approaches. And since he would have to continue to work with Flesch at the Hochschule, with the latter a far more powerful influence than himself, he tended to ignore the entire affair. His own world had been rocked from so many sides recently that he avoided pointless confrontations.

On the other hand, when he saw Rostal filling in for Joseph, he expressed a special, if quiet, disdain for this musician. For Rostal was a shadow as violinist, musician, and teacher, next to his late friend. And yet Rostal as Flesch's heir-apparent was prospering on what Joseph had created.

Several years later in London, at a private concert and reunion of a number of the Berlin group, Feuermann had occasion to play trios with Rostal and his own friend Osborne. In the very first Beethoven trio, Rostal had difficulties in managing a fairly difficult passage. Feuermann immediately mocked him in imitation in the same range on the cello "A" string. This error occurred again when the passage was repeated a few moments later. This time Feuermann chose the upper reaches of his "G" string to imitate Rostal, who was already fire-red in embarrassment. The violinist, a moment after the last incident, stopped playing, picked himself up and growled, "I will not tolerate such nonsense," and walked away towards his violin case. Several guests rushed forward and attempted to soothe his feelings, meanwhile casting furtive glances in Feuermann's direction. Feuermann fired back, waving his bow mockingly in Rostal's direction, "Let him go, let him go, we'll play cello sonatas."

As in all things, time is the great healer. These were troublesome days in Germany—political fragmentation, riots, a depression. Even the death of a dear friend could pass into the background. And even Wolfsthal would have to be replaced. The engagements for the trio, not only for the present season (1930–31), but especially for the following year, kept coming in. Feuermann and Hindemith were formidable names. They decided to try out their young colleague Szymon Goldberg, currently concertmaster of the Philharmonic, who they felt, even at a youthful twenty-one, was the best violinist in Berlin at that time, after Joseph.

The new union was quite successful, as the violinist was completely amenable to their own canons of musicality as well as technical accomplishment. Goldberg had been concertmaster of the Philharmonic for over a year and had appeared in a number of recitals over the years, so he was fairly seasoned. In his natural deference to his elders, Goldberg provided a new equilibrium amongst the three, one which they had to admit might even be a healthier blend, since Joseph's had been a very dominating personality. Goldberg, while marvelously fluent, was also well schooled musically in the Flesch tradition, and indeed had a touch of incipient intellectualism. His scholarly approach, taken in balance with a shy temperament, was a charming contrast to their earlier pattern. And since Szymon's playing was open and pure as well as technically clean, it completely held its own in the trio. This can best be seen in the trio's later recording of Beethoven's Serenade, op. 8, and the Hindemith Trio recorded in London in January, 1934.

Their mutual attitude towards the trio was one of musical dedication but professional avocation. It was a second or third preoccupation for each. In the case of Feuermann it was a new medium in which to test his competence. For Hindemith it was an opportunity to play the viola again professionally without being immersed in the routine of orchestral work as he had been in years before. Goldberg of course saw this as an opportunity to advance his burgeoning career as a solo violinist.

They had engaged a part-time secretary, a daughter of the conductor Schenfluke, and she proved most efficient at making contact with various concert societies. The engagements came in at a gratifying pace. Even so, the trio only rehearsed when about to embark on a concert tour. The agreed-upon pattern was to play through the particular work three times without interruption or comment. This would allow each to reacquaint himself with the music, to listen and adjust for blend and also to allow Hindemith a warm-up period to get back into the swing of playing the viola. He rarely played otherwise. Yet his amazing recuperative power, symptomatic of his immense versatility as a musician, was such that he was always ready for the hard sessions. His was playing of enormous technical facility, perhaps broader and less pristine than the others'; but it was fluent and blended extremely well with the outside voices.

Even after their warm-up rounds, the trio never engaged in much debate, as is supposed to occur in other ensembles of this sort in which strong musical personalities coexist. In fact there was little conversation. They would demonstrate to each other what they thought should be done. There existed a sympathetic musical bond of respect, and all discussions were to the point and avoided personalities. They wanted to get on with their work and had little time to luxuriate in musical quibbling. Feuermann, increasingly showing confidence in his musical taste, would do a great deal of demonstrating as compared with the others—he could reproduce their parts on the cello as fluently as they could play them. There was usually little to fault his point of view and the interpretations invariably bore his strong shaping influence.

The programs included—in addition to string trios of Beethoven, Reger, and Dohnanyi—a solo Bach Suite or Hindemith Sonata by Feuermann, or else a Bach violin partita played by Goldberg, Mozart violin and viola duos, and the Ravel violin and cello duo. The Hindemith Second String Trio was composed for the group and both Goldberg and Hindemith were wont to recall jokingly the day they sightread it, Feuermann blitzing through his part, cigarette hanging from his mouth, smoke curling up into his eyes. It was, as usual, deadly accurate. Hindemith invariably had difficulty with several passages and the others needled him regularly about the necessity for composers' writing music that performers could play.

In general, life was good during these brief years in Berlin. Feuermann's classes were full; students from all over the world sought him out. Things had never been this way in the days of Hugo Becker. The

Hochschule was now a truly international music school, perhaps the greatest on the Continent. Feuermann had no competition anywhere in Germany in his position as professor. Old Julius Klengel was long gone from the Leipzig Conservatory, enjoying a fruitful retirement in his beloved home city.

Added to the teaching at the Hochschule were the many solo concerts he was getting (at good fees in spite of the depression), the trio concerts, and small but helpful supplements from his recordings. There was even a hint of an offer for a tour of the United States. The actual offer came for 1933–1934. And while it proposed five hundred dollars per concert it did not provide for orchestral appearances, nor did it allow enough rest periods between concerts nor enough repeats of programs. He would have to carry with him a large repertoire. He finally wired the NBC Concert Bureau that he would wait until the following year.

A number of factors, besides the economic disadvantages of sacrificing his European career, caused him to postpone the venture. In Cologne had blossomed a lovely damsel, Eva Reifenberg, the youngest of the five children of Oma and Paul and the one for whom he had been a playful older companion when he arrived in Cologne in 1919. She was then a very young child and he was her "Uncle Munio." Her maturity had come about so recently and his feelings evolved so suddenly that he had yet to come to terms with them. He was in the first place the male psychological support to that household. In addition he had certain class trepidations about the appropriateness of a serious relationship, given the fact of his origins.

There was also a cloud in Vienna. All was not well with the Feuermanns. The problems were now in the main unrelated to Gusta's death, but they were exacerbated by her absence. Munio did not often go back, and, when he did, it was only because of the necessities of his career. It was not a matter of negligence or abandonment, for his ties with the family were stronger now in one important respect. Sophie and he were playing together more and more often. She was an extremely intense and serious pianist, with none of her brother's outward *joie de vivre*. There were the inevitable big brother-little sister tiffs, especially when Sophie felt that Munio was not acting in public or towards his students as the great, all-knowing musician he was supposed to be. In fact this complacency about his professional image often confused outsiders and perhaps lowered their estimation of him.

He was serious when it came to the big things. One of the most important responsibilities he had was to bring Sophie before a larger public. She would always play a number of solo pieces on their programs, somewhat in the character of a joint recital. Musically it was good experience for both of them. For Munio, Sophie was much better than practically all of his accompanists. And when the reviews were especially warm to her efforts, he glowed in her success. Yet in an era of great pianists and numerous Feuermanns, he realized that she faced insuperable difficulties in making headway in a concert career.

To an extent Sophie's criticisms of his lack of seriousness echoed the feelings of a number, of Munio's friends. They were buttressed by a modest slap on the wrist from critics who had heard him in the past and now noted a certain casualness in his playing. Turning thirty, he was probably trying to make too much of his unprecedented ascendancy. He had too many irons in the fire and did not have the stability in his life that would allow him to tend equally his various professional responsibilities.

He had recently bought a new American Buick, big and powerful. He roared all over Germany, attempting to mix his social life with his musical career. Often he would arrive at a concert hall completely exhausted. If this happened two or three times in a row his recuperative powers would inevitably fail him and he would play casually and carelessly, as he would never have dared just a few short years earlier.

Feuermann played this way one evening in Zurich. In the audience was Toscanini, a former cellist himself, who had followed Feuermann's career with great interest. After the program one of Feuermann's acquaintances came backstage to inform him laughingly that Toscanini had muttered a number of times from his seat, "*il porco, il porco!*" Usually Feuermann's sense of humor would have allowed him to overlook such an adverse comment. But coming from the Maestro and for such real cause, it was hardly funny that night. Later it would be one of the good Feuermann stories Munio told about himself to the press. But this was only after he had redeemed himself with the great conductor.

Even such minor setbacks did not diminish the pace he was setting for himself. The Buick was in virtual perpetual motion between a triangle made up of Berlin, Cologne, and Vienna, the last the least inviting destination, but a necessary one because of his sense of obligation to family and the musical importance of this still-great cultural center. He was in London with the trio in the spring of 1932 when he visited Hill Brothers, the important violin dealers, to have his cello adjusted. While he was there, Alfred Hill showed him a cello of the Venetian master Domenico Montagnana, which he had just acquired. It had not been used in generations and was in perfect condition. Feuermann seized on this glossy red-brown instrument as a panacea, a new turn in his playing.

Admittedly the Tecchler had begun to affect him adversely. It was very large and though it had a clarion quality, which penetrated and soared over orchestras, it did not blend as he would have liked it to in the trio. It was aggressive. And then, in recital especially, when his energy ebbed, it was a struggle to play because of the long reaches its size demanded. Were it possible, he would have liked to reclaim the Petrus Guarneri of old Kux and use the instruments depending on need.

But the mysterious Montagnana fascinated him. It was about thirty inches, a moderate length, but quite wide in ribs and breadth and thus had an intriguingly rich sound, even if it was stiff and unresponsive. Hill assured Feuermann that the cello needed a great deal of playing. But when it was worked in, he would have a unique solo instrument. He reminded Feuermann that after Stradivari it was not the Amatis or Guarneris or even the Guadagnini and Bergonzi families who made the best cellos. Rather it was Montagnana, Tecchler, and Gofriller, first-class makers of lovely violins, but supreme carvers of cellos. Certainly Casals had not been handicapped by his beloved Gofriller.

Feuermann was persuaded. He needed the experience of the new physical and aural relationship that the Montagnana promised. And its beauty overwhelmed him. He arranged to sell his Tecchler for a relatively modest price, he was so eager to get his new instrument. He agreed to the price of thirty-five hundred pounds for the Montagnana—a munificent amount for those depression days—which cleaned him out. He soon was able to carry forth the Montagnana, ensconced in Hill's magnificent oak case, and set himself a regimen of practice to break in the instrument. It surprised him how slowly it went. And when he telegraphed Hill to register his concern, Hill wired him back that two or three weeks of playing were hardly enough, that it would need at least two or three months.

The instrument led to several minor imbroglios during the rest of the trio's tour. In two cases complaints were served by the local managers because, while Goldberg and Hindemith would be onstage playing, Feuermann would use the time backstage in the artists' room to practice on his cello. Since these rooms were rarely soundproofed, the cello sound penetrated to the audience, giving the duo a weird counterpoint. It mattered not a bit to the other two, as their own foibles were many.

A concert manager in Holland wrote to their secretary, thinking that she represented a larger agency, denouncing Hindemith in no uncertain terms. Towards the end of their tours and invariably at the end of a long program Hindemith's viola would seem to gain in weight and Hindemith would let it drop from his collarbone so that he would not have to support so much weight with his left arm or bow at such an extreme angle. The violist, who even then was quite corpulent, had a large Tecchler viola. The complainant noted that most of the women in attendance felt that it was obscene that Hindemith should rest his instrument on his very protuberant abdomen, and that his behavior detracted significantly from the seriousness of the music. However, he did add that despite Hindemith's nefarious habit the three men played so divinely that he was impelled to reengage them for the following year.

It should have been a foregone conclusion from the earliest days of

1929. The social and economic instability, the accumulated unavenged military grievances, the extreme polarization of the body politic, all pointed to an inevitable disintegration of German society. The intellectual and cultural ferment that had been given increasing impetus in the decade since World War I was spurred even as the abyss widened. Rarely in European history, as the historian Peter Gay has noted, had the artistic and intellectual achievement of a cultural elite so engaged the attention of a nation.* And yet, as with a super nova, the brightness was prologue to its imminent extinction.

Bruno Walter reported that, as early as September of 1930, Feuermann and he had spent an evening together listening to the elections for the Reichstag in which Hitler's party polled well over six million votes and overnight became one of the largest in the nation. Feuermann, always excitable about political affairs, left the apartment visibly disturbed, calling out to Walter as he departed, "It's all over with Germany, all over with Europe."

By January of 1933 the prophecy was near to realization. With dramatic inevitability the facade of the Weimar democracy crumbled and with it, its culture. First the elections of January put Hitler into power as chancellor. On February 27, the Reichstag was burned. Anarchy and chaos followed. New elections, quickly set through pressure by the Nazis on Hindenburg, still did not yield them an absolute majority. Nevertheless, enabling legislation, purportedly to bring stability to Germany, gave Hitler virtually dictatorial powers for four years.

Almost immediately the crunch of the boot on Jewish musicians began. The Nazis made innumerable efforts, at first tentative, but ultimately inexorable, to purge Germany of its "undesirable alien elements."

Bruno Walter, arriving back in Germany in late March, 1933, to conduct in Leipzig and Berlin, was forcibly barred from both concerts, receiving in Leipzig under the Gewandhaus statue of Mendelssohn several farewell bouquets of flowers tearfully offered up by intimidated but devoted citizens. In Berlin, strings were pulled by the liberals, to no avail. Goebbels and Goering were unmoved, and at any rate a good Aryan, Richard Strauss, had volunteered to substitute for Walter. There were other German musicians who thought they could coexist with the new order, to work from within to humanize it and perhaps to protect those who would stay. Furtwängler, Walter's Berlin competitor, was one such. For years he would appeal to musicians to come back and play in Germany, not to mix politics and art. Few heeded him and finally events forced even Furtwängler to an accommodation.

Artur Schnabel was giving a series of concerts featuring all the Beethoven sonatas during this same season in Berlin (1932–33). He had already

*Weimar Culture, New York, 1969.

signed contracts for the important Brahms Centenary Festival to be held the following year. The last three recitals, all to be broadcast over the state radio, were to be given in February, March, and April. These three concerts did take place but were not broadcast over the radio; the Nazis had forbidden it.

The day after the final concert on April 28, a call was received from the manager of the Brahms festival informing Schnabel that plans were now indefinite for the following year and that Schnabel would have to re-negotiate with the new director. Schnabel cut him short with the now famous, "Though I may not be pure-blooded, I am fortunately cold-blooded. Good luck to you," and left Germany forever.

Throughout this winter Feuermann had been carrying both his teaching at the Hochschule and a heavy concert schedule. He was in Copenhagen in March when things were going badly in Berlin. A reporter from a Copenhagen newspaper, the *Berlingske Tedinde*, a German-language publication, requested an interview. Feuermann was hesitant, yet could not refuse. The interview took place on Thursday, March 9, 1933, and was prominently headlined:

A DIALOGUE CONCERNING HITLER AND GERMAN MUSIC
The State-Radio-Symphony's great Prof. E. Feuermann is an artist and not a politician

Tonight's concert of the radio symphony orchestra was conducted by Prof. Nicolai Malko, Leningrad, with the famous Austrian cellist Prof. Emanuel Feuermann, from the Berlin Academy of Music, as soloist. Professor Emanuel Feuermann, who is visiting Denmark for the first time, is staying here at the Hotel d'Angleterre. Yesterday afternoon we interviewed the youthful 30-year-old celebrity. "I have toured throughout Europe and I have played all over since my early youth," said Professor Feuermann. "I have been a Professor at Staatlicher Music Hochschule in Berlin for the last four years. My entire family is involved in and earn their livelihood through music." "Is German music growing at present?" "Yes, it is, I am convinced that Germany will keep her leading position in regards to music." "What is the relationship of modern music to classical music in Germany." "There might exist some tensions, but modern music will never be able to supersede classical music. People like Wagner, Bach, Brahms, and Beethoven cannot be put aside by new kinds of musical forms. The works of those great masters originated in the soul of the German people and they will be supreme elements in the musical life of our country for ever and ever."

Germany Lives to See a Great Epoch

"By the way, what do you think about the events of the past few days in Germany?" "This nation is going through a great epoch. But I am a musician and not a politician. I am not able to express myself about political problems, which by the way are so enormous and serious that even those

who deal with them daily, are not able to understand the actual events."
"What are your opinions of Hitler?" "The President has chosen Hitler to be
Chancellor and the elections last Sunday showed that the majority of the
German people stand behind him." "Why has he obtained a majority?"
"Well, you see, sir. I am an artist and not a politician, but it is beyond all
doubt that Hitler is a great personality. By the way, since I am a publicly
appointed Professor, I cannot make a judgment about the Chancellor while
I am a guest abroad." "How does one understand the upheaval after the
election?" "One sees fundamentally very little change in spite of the upheaval's drastic nature. It came about legally and without bloodshed. The
German officials behaved in one way during the upheaval, the way of duty.
They are still following it." "Do you think Hitler's reign will endure?" "Yes, I
think that Hitler will be in power for a very *long* time."

With the concert in Cophenhagen over, Feuermann left Denmark for
Vienna. He had a series of engagements in Austria and Switzerland with
Sophie that would prevent his return to Berlin before mid-April. On
March 27 a letter was sent by the director Schünemann to Feuermann
notifying him of the intention of the State Music Academy not to renew
his contract beyond its expiration date in July, and that further communication would be sent to him if necessary. There was a great tumult in
Berlin at the Hochschule and even Schünemann is purported to have
attempted intercession with Gustave Haveman, a former violin partner of
Feuermann, now minister of cultural affairs for music. Feuermann's
students, both Jew and Gentile, unanimously announced that they would
resign from the Hochschule were his contract allowed to lapse. To no
avail. On April 8, Schünemann was forced to send a letter informing
Feuermann that he was being given a "leave of absence" from the
Hochschule, pending the expiration of his contract, a typically German
bit of official punctiliousness.

Feuermann immediately returned to Berlin. It was there that he felt the
full impact of recent events. Many others were in similar positions. At the
same time the pressure on the Jews was just beginning. For a while the Jew
could exist if he could find means to do so. It would take time to transform
the old bureaucratic governmental system. In spite of his purported
prophecy of Hitler's long tenure at the helm of Germany, Feuermann
could not help believing or hoping that reason would eventually prevail
and that Germany would right itself. He had committed himself, not only
his present ambitions, but his future dreams, to the presumption of a
career here in wonderful Berlin.

Feuermann, in those early weeks of 1933, when the outcome was still in
doubt, had firmly rejected an offer from the Vienna Academy. He could
not even consider returning to Vienna. He drove to Cologne to pick up
Oma and Eva for a trip. Perhaps he could clear his mind while doing
something for fun. They headed south. In Perugia he wrote to his friend

Bronislaw Huberman, whom he felt was one of the most politically astute of all of his musical friends. A great and worldly violinist, Huberman would give him some solid practical advice, and maybe even a helping hand.

Brufani and Palace Hotel
Perugia

April 17th, 1933

Dear Mr. Huberman,

In accordance with your kind invitation, may I remind you that you agreed to try to achieve something for me in London. You would thereby open a new country to me which I more than need. For myself it would be best if I could still play in May/June, even more perfect if once with you and once alone.

I have actually been fired by the Hochschule. Nevertheless one assumes that there is still hope. What is your opinion of Furtwängler's letter? Of course it is easy for him because he did not act on his own behalf, but he is *the first one* who dares to speak up.

We—Mrs. Reifenberg and her daughter Eva, myself as the driver—are engaged in a magnificent trip. Just as one thinks that the climax has been reached, another surprise occurs which throws the preceding into the shade. (Lago Maggiore — Bergamo — Verona — Vicenza — Venice — Padua — Bologna — Ravenna — Urbino—now Perugia and Assisi—Rome in the end. Wonderful!) I hope that you, too, will find peace soon. Take a beautiful trip yourself!

With fond greetings and in reverence
I am yours

Munio Feuermann

Greetings to Miss Ibekken.

Bronislaw Huberman   Brussels, April 25th, 1933
SPECIAL DELIVERY

Dear Feuermann:

I just received a letter from Warsaw, in which I was told that they have turned to you—namely because of my manifold interventions—in regard to the performance of the Brahms Double Concerto on May 7th.

I can tell you a secret, someone else had been considered (although not yet engaged permanently) but I claimed that you as one of the victims of the German anti-semitic actions, apart from the artistic point of view, deserved preference. Now it is up to you to come quickly to terms with the people. I would advise you to send a cable to the Warsaw Philharmonic.

I talked to Holt about you and of course bragged very much. I believe that

you could write a letter to him and mention me. In May I shall be back in
London and then in addition I will talk to Mr. Tillett from the B.B.C.
Enclosed are my addresses,
With fond greetings to you and Mrs. Reifenberg
I am yours,

Berlin-Westend
Franken-Allee

June 11th, 1933

Dear Mr. Huberman:

I still deplore the fact that we could not play together in Warsaw and
Prague. What I was offered in Warsaw was only expenses and I believe that
especially there I may claim a little more. By the way I never told you how
delighted I was that you apparently enjoyed playing together with me. I
showed it, though, didn't I?

Now follows a long story because I want to ask for your advice. Perhaps
you will spend some minutes on it, maybe even on an answer. I believe that
you are the only one to give me appropriate advice in this matter.

For a long time, I have resisted the idea of going away from here. Now I
have almost decided to do so. . . . And my choice would be London. I will try
to create a substitute there for what I have lost here. Do you think that I shall
be successful there? I was almost convinced, but now Dr. Schiff wrote to me
that the BBC has refused me a contract. But a great introduction is absolutely necessary, isn't it? Did you abandon the idea of playing together with
me in London? I believe that this would be the right kind of introduction. As
far as I know there are no real cellists in London. How could I be presented
in the most savoury way? How could one make them notice the wealth of
vitamins and calories which apparently exists in my performance? I have
great confidence in you, but I do not want to bore you of course! Unfortunately I am convinced that England can jolly well continue to exist without
me, but I hardly believe that one can conquer a country with such a feeling.

I intend to go to Cornwall or Scotland in the summer and then remain in
London.

Will I receive an answer in the near future?
Affectionate greetings, to Miss Ibekken as well,
I am yours, with reverence,

Munio Feuermann

P.S. Hindemith showed me charming pictures of Vienna and told me about
big successes.

Bronislaw Huberman   Montecatini, June 20th, 1933
Professor Emanuel Feuermann
Berlin

Dear Feuermann,
If you promise me that for the entire future you will discharge me of any

responsibility as far as my advice is concerned, I do believe that the choice of London as centre would prove promising for you. During the last years music there has experienced a great upswing as far as institutions and performances are concerned as well as interest, quality and quantity of the audience. And you will not encounter much competition from the local celebrities. It is only a question as to whether you will get permission for permanent residence without any trouble. Are you still Austrian? If not I would advise you to become one again. But perhaps your status as banished German Jew might facilitate your task all the more? If you were Austrian I could recommend you in any case to the Austrian ambassador, Baron Franckenstein, a music-loving, amiable and helpful man who would perhaps even arrange a special reception night for you on my suggestion.

As to the prospect of playing together in London before long, I do not want to express myself today yet, but you can be sure that I will take advantage of an opportunity if I see one. I have even something special in mind, but I do not want to express myself today in order not to disappoint you, which might happen, after all. In any case, this idea, if at all, could not be carried out before spring, but, in the meantime, as I said, please, do not count on anything yet. This idea, in particular, depends only to a small degree on myself, but in larger part on factors over which I have no influence.

By the way, I think it is quite appropriate as a matter of principle that you do not impose yourself on Germany; just move away. After all, there are two sides to every medal and in the case of the German artists and scholars, from my point of view it will eventually be more a question of the Germans losing a good measure of those cultural agents which made them appear great in the eyes of the world rather than a matter of the affected Jews who will lose their positions. And if the Jews are to be expelled from their positions anyway, then the German nation should not be spared the cultural loss by the Jews' sentimental lingering-on in Germany, a loss which will certainly be revenged in the future. Considering that, I would like to combine the saying of a German king with an alliteration in Wagnerian style:
Macht eiern Dreck alleene, ihr Brider,
Geiget die Geige, ihr geifernden Gois,
Schabet das Cello, ihr schäbigen Schufte.

A final letter from his friend Bruno Walter, himself a Berliner, added support for Feuermann's London aspirations and generally confirmed all that Huberman had advised. There were no cellists in London to compete with Feuermann. Walter recommended the conductor Adrian Boult of the B.B.C., a non-Jew sympathetic to the plight of the now-exiled musicians and again, Holt, the influential Jewish manager. He would write both on Feuermann's behalf. If Feuermann needed him he would be in Salzburg until August.

There were many who did not heed the warnings. Perhaps they were the perennial optimists. Or perhaps they had too much to lose by picking up and leaving Germany. To their everlasting misfortune they stayed on.

Early in July Feuermann closed up his Franken-Allee apartment, packed his most precious personal belongings and drove to Vienna, where he briefly deposited a number of articles at his parents' apartment and drove to Paris. Wolf and Sachs had suggested Paris, where they were now situated, over Vienna, as a way station until more permanent headquarters could be established. Vienna was far too unstable and was already undergoing a gradual fascist strangulation.

The added advantage of Paris was that it was closer to Cologne than was Berlin. The Reifenbergs were still there. They hoped they might survive, since the prescient Paul Reifenberg had had all his children baptized in the Lutheran Church, an avowedly formalistic act, which in the end did not erase the taint of non-Aryan blood.

There were dozens of émigré Jewish intellectuals in Paris at this time, each having to confront his personal crises in his own way. Arnold Schönberg was there, reconverting to his original Jewish faith. Feuermann had known about his work on a cello concerto, based on themes from an eighteenth-century composer by the name of Monn. Feuermann had talked to Schönberg briefly about it in Berlin, and had wanted to premier it. The prospect appeared even better now. It might be the perfect vehicle to introduce himself to the London musical public. He had been warned that the English, always somewhat uninterested in Germanic instrumentalists, were now flooded with refugee musicians and in spite of their sympathies would be won only by unusual musical means.

Schönberg was hesitant to commit himself. He was trying desperately, and so far to no avail, to obtain a position in the United States (eventually he would obtain a teaching job at the small Malkin Conservatory in Boston). Secondly, he too was looking for the proper vehicle to introduce his concerto and give him the greatest professional mileage from it. He was honest enough to tell Feuermann that he had already sent a manuscript copy to Casals and was hoping that the master cellist would introduce it. Feuermann renewed his claim on Schönberg but did not press it.

Earlier nibbles from Columbia (English) for a recording contract with the trio now bore fruit. The recording would take place in London during the group's fall-winter tour of the British Isles, Belgium, and Holland. Goldberg had been dismissed from the Philharmonic and was already out of Germany. Hindemith, a non-Jewish German, was still in Berlin fighting a rearguard action for his friends, but was still interested, and able to carry through his commitments with his colleagues outside Germany.

In September, Feuermann received several communications from the Jewish Kulturfarband of Rhein-Ruhr asking if he could, despite the short notice, give a series of recitals in the various synagogues of that area in October. It was dangerous now to return to Germany. Although it was not illegal to play there, the Nazis would resort to the most brutal tactics to disrupt and abuse any who might try. However, the committee pledged its discretion and secrecy, promising that only "our circle will know about your coming."

It was more than a visit to support his intimidated and frightened constituency in those familiar towns. It was a small act of affirmation on his own part to realize who he was and whence he had come. He crossed the German frontier and appeared in the synagogues of Cologne, Krefeld, Aachen, Essen, and Bochäm between October 14 and 19, 1933.

He was soon off to London to establish himself there preparatory to his recording and concert debut. There was in addition the possibility of a separate recording contract for himself if his London appearance warranted it. The recording of the Dvořák Concerto with Taube and the Berlin State Opera had been widely heard and praised. Thus there was an anticipation of great success.

While in London he pursued the Schönberg matter. The latter's letters from the United States were short and cryptic. The composer was hesitant. He had now "accidentally bumped into Piatigorsky," who was also interested in the concerto. The Russian, like the Austrian, would have to await the negotiations with the Catalonian. Schönberg did tentatively propose an arrangement whereby all would get a chance to perform it, at a fee. But this possiblity apparently did not jell. Casals eventually abjured the opportunity. He had tried it out in private. In all likelihood it proved too difficult technically for the master to perform in public, even were he more sympathetic to its neo-classical veneer. Eventually, Feuermann would premier it, first in London with the London Philharmonic Orchestra under Beecham in the fall of 1935, then in Los Angeles, where Schönberg would ultimately reside and teach, with Otto Klemperer and the Los Angeles Philharmonic, in 1936.

The last weeks of 1933 were a turning point for Feuermann. The freshness of the London environment made him conscious of how jaded he had felt with the Continent. His new buoyancy made him realize that to make London only a springboard for renewing his European ties might not be the best move to further his career. He was over-exposed, somewhat dulled, even inconsistent, in his playing. It is possible that with his always-heavy concert schedule his audiences began to look upon him as a comfortable, not too special visitor. It was evident that he had needed this change.

Friends recall seeing him at a reception held on December 1, 1933, by the Austrian Ambassador Franckenstein, at which Henri Temianka is said to have appeared. Feuermann was everywhere, approaching a variety of dignitaries, busily making notes concerning people to talk to for whatever opportunities were available. His mundane enterprise here, too, was a deceptive cloak. Feuermann's outward lack of aloofness and grandeur was an almost consciously applied mask, if paradoxically still the real man.

The rest of the trio arrived shortly, and since the recordings were now scheduled for mid-January, they interspersed their several concerts with a number of furiously serious rehearsal sessions. The recordings were to consist of the Hindemith Trio No. 2, the Beethoven Serenade, op. 8, and the Hindemith Sonata for solo cello. The Columbia people had a natural anxiety to put the trio on discs now, because it might be dissolved any day, what with Hindemith's continued residence in Nazi Germany.

They were in fine fettle, comparatively rested and well-practiced. Hindemith, particularly, displayed his enormous gifts on the viola. The ensemble was impeccable, even classical in approach, the Beethoven being markedly restrained and idiomatic. Even today, that recording (Beethoven) has yet to be surpassed in pure beauty and clarity of sound. It must be recalled that Goldberg was still in his mid-twenties, Hindemith the oldest, not yet forty.

The Hindemith Trio comes through with enormous impact mainly because of the trio's technical freedom and precise, yet fluid, ensemble playing. Of the three major pieces, this one has the greatest immediacy. The solo sonata played by Feuermann presents an interesting problem. Its technical difficulties are immense and complicate the problem of making music out of it. Of necessity it requires subtlety. And Feuermann achieves this musical end to an amazing degree, assisted in no small way by the ease with which he handles the technical problems. Yet the impact of this relatively short piece is probably not what it should be. There is a strained quality to the recording, which on close examination is not due to anything inherent in the music or the performer. Rather, it seems that after more than one year of being "played in," the Montagnana cello had not as yet been subdued.

The choice of a proper instrument is crucial for a concert artist. Too often he stumbles into a decision and has to live with it for better or worse. How many have the wherewithal of a Kreisler, to luxuriate in a half dozen 'Strads' or Guarneris amongst sundry Gaglianos, Guadagninis, etc.? If a player is not strong, an instrument will bend him to its own way. Given even a strong-minded player, without the requisite experience to recognize the problem, player and instrument can battle to a deadlock for years, without the cause being known. Some instruments serve one purpose—orchestral, chamber music, various kinds of solo playing—better than other, equally fine instruments. It is all a great mystery, dominated to a large extent by chance, and fraught with the possibility of endless experimentation.

In the case of a solo artist such as Feuermann, two basic demands must be served: (a) the character of sound transmitted to audience or microphone, and (b) its responsiveness under the fingers and to the ear of the performer. The Montagnana, for all of its entrancing physical beauty and superb condition, and even granting a quality of sound which for certain pieces (such as the Popper *Hungarian Rhapsody*) could be ravishing, was basically wanting.

It was deep, rich, and bassy, intriguing on the lower strings, but in general it had an over-extended response. The upper registers had character, a typically throaty quality that one often encounters in cellos. Still, this detracted from its capacity to project with brilliance and clarity, as had Feuermann's large Tecchler. The sound on all strings seemed to remain in and around the instrument. It was intense, sometimes husky, even nasal. The player could easily sense these characteristics, especially in crucial interpretive situations. He could never be completely free in rapid passages.

There are those instruments upon which one's slightest touch evokes an immediate, open response. The sound is out and away. Some instruments even give all that they have in terms of reserves immediately and completely. In such cases, flexibility as well as character is greatly limited. The Montagnana, on the other hand, needed constant pulling, its sound was never truly freed. This could impede the player, in delicate and plastic passages where spontaneity and lightness were needed, or in molding and shaping a phrase. It was as if, wanting to create a clay pot, one could never get the clay off the hands and onto the form.

The recordings were finally cut and in process of being auditioned by the trio to decide which of the various takes would be synthesized into their final versions. Considering this was their first experience as a group with this medium, it had gone rather easily. Szymon Goldberg recalled that the whole process varied little from their typical rehearsal sessions. After about forty-five minutes of playing Feuermann usually called for a break. They would then pause for a few minutes and continue again for the same length of time until another recess would be necessary. Part of Feuermann's fatigue was certainly mental. He expended enormous energies in concentration, always having some new task that he had set for himself to master. But the strain was physical as well, and he would often complain that his bow arm had tired.

Feuermann, especially relieved that the whole procedure had been completed, was dismayed when the production manager presented them with a new problem. When the playing time had been totaled they found that enough remained for one whole side. Could they play something to fill up one side? Goldberg immediately reminded them that he had to leave in the morning for Brussels to fulfill a solo engagement. The trio was not to play in Brussels until several days later, thus both Hindemith and Feuermann were free. Otherwise they could all return in ten days. Columbia could not wait.

However, with a twinkle and a smile, Hindemith volunteered that perhaps he could resolve the dilemma. He would compose that evening, a three-to-four-minute duo for viola and cello. Tomorrow Feuermann and he would record it. Agreed.

That night Hindemith was up till all hours writing and playing. Goldberg rose early the next morning. When he checked Feuermann's room he was informed that the cellist had already left for the studio. Since the violinist had an extra hour before departing, he detoured to the studio to bid his colleagues au revoir. They were already cutting the first take. Since Feuermann had only arrived thirty-five to forty minutes before Goldberg, there could have been but little time to practice and rehearse the piece. It seemed awfully technical.

Hindemith informed him that the piece was entitled *Scherzo*. The éclat and professional sobriety with which both men handled the challenge of this extraordinary composition impressed itself indelibly on Goldberg's mind. It was one of those moments that in recollection illuminates the meaning of greatness. This little duo, recorded in January, 1934, can still be heard.

Montagnana Cello

6

THE TRAGEDY OF SIGMUND

In every area of importance to a culture, and in which there are great rewards for unique ability and achievement, those who "arrive" are naturally subject to scrutiny. The mysteries of greatness, its genesis and development, even the criteria by which society assesses it, provide a fascinating problem for enquiry. But along with the genius, the virtuoso, the artist, there are those who, while also vastly endowed, fail. Some are stunted early and thus are lost to sight. Others show vast potential on their way, then flag and slip gradually into obscurity. The mystery is still there.

By early 1934 Emanuel Feuermann had attained a worldwide reputation. Even if of modest dimension, his mark had been made. And while there still remained a Casals, in a class by himself, Feuermann was one of two or three cellists strongly contending for second place and ultimately the mantle of the then fifty-seven-year-old Spaniard. With Feuermann's impending May debut in Wigmore Hall, London, and the July recordings of the Brahms. E Minor and the Beethoven Variations for Columbia, his reputation in the English-speaking world would be further enhanced. In August he would be off on a world tour. His managers felt this would complete the triumph that was his due and establish him as the crown prince of violoncellists. By the time of his expected return in late winter 1935, New York and the United States would have been made cognizant of his abilities and his shift away from the central European cradle would have been complete.

As in all things, this necessitated a campaign, a plan. The world was in turmoil. New relationships had to be established; the old patterns of German musical life had to be abandoned, forgotten. This was good, Feuermann had become convinced. As he now looked forward, some of his earlier patterns of diffidence in concertizing made him shudder. He had been too comfortable, too successful for his ambitions to have been realized. But it was still an enormously successful and self-confident young artist of thirty-one who here looked back, a man with a definite future.

There were those—acquaintances and critics—who felt that things had gone too easily and naturally for one so young, and predicted for him only a modest future. But these for the most part were unaware of the conditions of his youth, the enormous effort and self-discipline that had catapulted him out of his familial environment and into his present role. It was this persistent drive that still carried Munio forward and undergirded his great ambitions, occasional bouts of smugness and self-satisfaction notwithstanding.

The same environmental, familial, and genetic conditions that bring greatness also exhibit a regrettable penchant for inducing tragedy. The Feuermann family had already lost Gusta in 1929. It was but the first of a series of blows, just when their life's dreams seemed about to be fulfilled. Perhaps the most searing and ultimately the most corrupting to the inner integrity of this family was the tragedy of Sigmund.

What made it so difficult for the parents was the suddenness with which they had to adjust to this new reality. They were even then trying to forget about Gusta's horrible ordeal. Simultaneously they were being bombarded by an avalanche of reports about Munio's unbelievable triumphs in Berlin.

Sigmund had left for the United States in 1925. And while both before and during his absence there were hints of problems, in general they felt that Sigmund's career would eventually fulfill the promise of the earlier years. They knew that his career had not flourished since the war. But then, it was a time when a horde of Russian violinists had swept into western Europe and America.

And though the invitation to America was helped along by Munio's wealthy and generous American friend Gerald Warburg, it did involve a debut, a tour, and an invitation to teach violin at the New York College of Music. They had heard via the grapevine that Sigmund was not concertizing extensively in the United States. But being so far removed they had no reason for concern since "extensively" meant different things to different people. His letters were neutral and typical of Sigmund, which meant uninformative.

Finally the letter came that he was returning. He had been gone for five years. Naturally the parents were elated. The blow came at the railway station. Sigmund had changed. He seemed old and tired. He had gained weight, lost much of his curly hair. But most of all, and it shocked them in a grotesque way—for it was when he smiled wanly that it somehow thrust itself at them, his head seemed to have become disproportionately large. Above the deepset eyes his forehead bulged and towered over the rest of his face. Sigmund was then thirty-one.

The visual shock was only the first of many. It was a different Sigmund.

To be sure he had always been diffident and aloof. But now he seemed almost to demand withdrawal for himself. Few words or memories could be elicited from him. His room took on the quality of a refuge or fortress. And into it he retired, partially, from life.

It was true that, with hardly an hour or so for some rest and a good Viennese meal conjured up by Rachel, he brought forth his beloved Guadagnini from its case and played. Maier had not wasted a moment to nag it out of its secure hibernation. It had been so long since he had heard Sigmund play. It satisfied a thirst long unquenched.

As the weeks went by a pattern appeared. It was evident that Sigmund had returned to the family hearth in order to go into semiretirement. He made no move to renew his concert career. Because of the enormous impact of the Feuermann name (Sophie, too, had a large class of students, stimulated by her appearances with Munio), and his own earlier reputation, he attracted a number of students. But he did not encourage this side of his musical career either.

Sigmund's earlier peculiarities, his phobias (insects, spiders), his consuming passions for Napoleon and encyclopedias, were undiminished. His practicing knew no consummation. Hour after hour within his private redoubt he would fiddle away, occasionally halting to correct a fingering or to clear up a technical passage. The playing was even more remarkable than in the past. It was fluent and brilliant, and precise to the point of being automatic. Perhaps that was it.

Through constant nagging by parents, family, and innumerable friends, he finally was persuaded to give several recitals. It was then that some of the more objective-minded friends—but never the Feuermann parents—began to see a pattern and cause for his malaise. Sigmund's body played the recital, but not his heart or his mind. For those who were hearing him for the first time or indeed were not well-acquainted with his playing, the impact was startling. But for the more sophisticated, the realization came through clearly. His development had come to a halt.

There was a great debate amongst both family and friends as to what might be done. Even professional advice was called in. But the solution lay in the diagnosis of the problem, about which there was at first no sense of agreement. Sigmund seemed neither interested in nor aware of the problem. In fact he seemed not even to suspect that the audiences were, by and large, unaffected by his playing. Both Rachel and Maier remained adamant: the audiences of this era were vastly inferior to the prewar musical public. The end result was that Sigmund, inevitably, stopped playing in public.

As we have noted, there had been hints as to what was gradually occurring, even before Sigmund had left for the United States in 1925. But they were so gradual during those eventful years following World War I, that they were not noticed. Sigmund had resumed his career after the war at about the same time that Munio had gone off to Cologne. It had been a successful start, too, in spite of the fact that he had been so much more encapsulated in the defeat-ridden Austrian capital than Munio had been in Leipzig. Szymon Goldberg recalls that in 1920 in his Polish home town of Pyatkov, the impending recital of Sigmund Feuermann caused a stir in the community. Goldberg's father took the young violinist to hear Feuermann. It was his recollection that the recital was a rousing success, and a memorable event in the eleven-year-old's life.

Other friends recall a 1922 recital in Czernowitz (then in Rumania), which was a neighboring city to Kolomea, and almost home ground. An overflow crowd in the auditorium had to be seated onstage. In this familiar and comfortable setting, Sigmund gave a ravishing performance of an old specialty of his, Tartini's Devil's Trill Sonata. Of particular note were his fluency, the sweet sound and the bravado of the playing. In 1923 and 1924 the reviews were in the main glowing throughout Germany and the east.

Zuricher Tagesanzeiger

March 12, 1923

The artist bears his name with justice; a fiery temperament displayed his exquisitely capable musicality. He played the Beethoven Violin Concerto with a splendid tone, a pure and reliable technique and with a quality of sympathy and individuality.

Dusseldorfer Generalanzeiger

February 15, 1923

Philharmonic Concert

The violinist Sigmund Feuermann brought the Beethoven Violin Concerto to a realm that could not be attained were one to have a scaling ladder, monoplane, or Fokker biplane. Let us for the moment omit reference to the work, to consider the violinist. One first becomes aware of a tremulous yet penetrating tone, which is strong and clear in lyric passages. He is equally capable of the appropriate sonority in passages of the most shadowy delicacy. There is an unerring technique, fine phrasing, sharply profiled architectonics and above all, encompassed in a passionate temperament.

If Wolf and Sachs did not summon him to Berlin it was probably because he had made his intentions clear to remain in Vienna with the family. Indeed perhaps one Feuermann on their list was enough.

Munio had by then left Cologne and the brothers began to renew their old collaboration with a trio (Bruno Walter pianist for a time) and in the Brahms Double Concerto. Munio still deferred to Sigmund, taking second place on the programs, although George Szell testified that even then Munio was far superior to Sigmund. He accompanied them both. But this may be hindsight.

There can be no doubt that Sigmund's hold on his audience was less dominating than Munio's. The competition amongst violinists was fierce and Sigmund did not seem able to loose himself from his home ties. The old saying perhaps holds true that "nothing can come of a Viennese until he has left Vienna."

The review in the *New York Times* for Sigmund's American debut on December 21, 1925, in Aeolian Hall had been favorable:

> Sigmund Feuermann, a violin prodigy of fifteen years ago in Vienna and London, introduced himself to a musical audience at Aeolian Hall last evening playing with Emil Friedberger the B minor Sonata of Respighi, who also will be heard as a guest here. Mr. Feuermann gave to the Italian composer's restless harmony a wealth of honeyed tone and plastic phrase, with naturally less of a rugged contrast than appeared in the ensuing Bach *Chaconne for Violin Alone.* The player's own arrangement of Mozart's *Turkish March* was among his later pieces, others being of Tchaikowski, Schubert, Kreisler, Paganini, and Sarasate.
>
> December 22, 1925

The memories of some of those in attendance lead one to assume that more went unstated than said. Sigmund's playing was predictably fluid and impeccable. And the sound of his 1752 Guadagnini—he had received it as a gift from a group of Viennese philanthropists before the war—was sweet, but rather cramped and tiny. His visage, already beginning to be odd, was not enhanced by his reserve and tightness, both of which were accentuated by the strangeness of the environment. The audience left, unimpressed, even disappointed, by a program that promised much, was so brilliant, yet was only on the surface and without much dynamic range. There were a few recitals in various cities. The loneliness of this young man, who heretofore had been nestled in the protecting arms of his father and mother, was extreme. He had no experience to help him overcome his solitude.

Upon the recommendation of several musicians who had known him in Vienna and because of his credentials as one of Sevčik's star pupils, the New York College of Music offered him a teaching position, which brought him back into a more sympathic environment, New York City. And it was here by dint of dogged pride that he persevered for the bulk of his years in America, making fewer and fewer appearances, teaching the Sevčik method, until he could return to Vienna in 1931 with at least the semblance of having fulfilled a task as independently as his younger brother had been doing since 1917.

The years 1931–1933 were tempestuous and aggravating years for the Feuermanns. The parents were deeply frightened about the fate of Sigmund, now that their most optimistic dreams of a Kreisler, Elman, or Heifetz in their home seemed to be evaporating. The possibility now existed that their son would have no concert career. They would have been content for him merely to be active in Viennese musical life. There were so many ways to make one's mark. The long and distinguished career of Arnold Rosé was an example of a fine violinist who did not have the temperament to be a concert artist of the first rank, yet his contribution to the musical life of Vienna was enormous. But Sigmund seemed to be avoiding practically all contact with the musical world around him. Besides teaching he would occasionally play with orchestral groups or a few solos at special concerts. But by and large he had taken himself out of the mainstream of competition in the profession.

With each month of Sigmund's increasing withdrawal during these years, came a staccato of successes in Berlin through Munio. The frightening contrast between the brothers began to distill its own meaning. As the attempts to move Sigmund off dead center waned, a gradual realization and acceptance of the malaise of the violinist settled into the minds of the Viennese community.

Very simply, the impetus that had thrust him forward as a young prodigy, a creation of the will of his parents, eventually throttled his development. Added to the ineluctable determination and presence of the parental ambitions had been the rigid methodology of Sevčik. There had been no relenting even as Sigmund entered adolescence. Then, more tours squired by the dominating Maier or else encapsulation in the apartment on Weimarstrasse, hours of practicing and virtual isolation from normal friendships. The normal adolescent surges, which bubble so insistently into the consciousness, were given no outlet, either in activities or attitudes.

An adolescent, as the psychologist Erik Erikson has pointed out, finds his own personality by throwing off the childhood ties with the parental superego. In order to find a new identity he must reject the old parental images. He must secure the legitimacy of his fantasies of himself and the intimacies of his age-mates. In Sigmund's case, not even touring (which might have given him a small measure of autonomy and opportunity for exploration as he matured) was possible, owing to restrictions imposed by World War I.

The terrible consequences for his own genera! personal development were greatly magnified in the cumulative stultification of his maturation as an interpretive artist. Sigmund was never able to explore in a leisurely and personal way the relationship between the natural emotional eruptions of maturation, the by now almost instinctive technical facility that lay under his fingers, and the buried personal musical voice that might have given life to his performances. The lack of integration of these elements in Sigmund's personality provides an almost classical exemplification of the prodigy shipwrecked on the shoals of puberty.

But the price was even greater. One does not merely thrust aside those cognitive, emotional, and individual elements which are the birthright of every human being. The compulsions, phobias, and dependencies that characterized Sigmund in his twenties, perhaps made doubly painful by his increasingly bizarre appearance and the growing rejection by the musical public of his violin playing, stunted his personal and mental development.

When Munio would return to Vienna for concerts or a holiday, both parents, but especially Maier, would lie in wait for him and quietly but with hysterical intensity ask him to help them jar Sigmund out of his lethargy. Munio made some half-hearted attempts to urge his older brother to do more concert work, but in general he was ineffective. The brothers never communicated as personal friends. In addition there was an invisible barrier between the two, one that often exists between siblings of the same sex. The younger must not criticize or correct the older—it would be unseemly. Munio found it painful even to contemplate pushing Sigmund in any way. And Sigmund was certainly not attuned to listening to advice.

As the months wore on into years, the relationships at home became more and more strained. Maier was getting older, complaining of illnesses, and becoming more and more dependent upon the children, especially Munio, for a modicum of support. He irritated Munio by his incessant complaints of intestinal difficulties and his need to go off to the various spas to try the waters.

On the other hand, Munio now lived in another and far more cosmopolitan world than the rest of the family. He hobnobbed with the wealthy; the very fact of his success rankled his father and made his mother uneasy. They had put all their life and energy into the prodigal genius of Sigmund. And here, almost without their nurturing, their unattended one had blossomed into the great artist while the oldest son languished. There were increasingly bitter arguments when Munio was home, a constant din of bickering in which the cellist more and more saw the dual presence of father and older brother, the latter for the most part saying little, as the key to their mututal malaise.

On one occasion he stormed out of the apartment, cello and suitcase in hand, to a hotel where he would stay for the night to compose himself before his Sunday morning solo performance with the Vienna Philharmonic. It was his feeling, and Sophie would later agree with him, that Maier often stirred up these tempests so that Munio would not be capable of doing his best. A father's bitterness and chagrin over the fate of the other son lay heavy on Maier's soul.

Munio tried to avoid his home when he visited Vienna. Rosa, now married to Adolph Hoenigsberg, lived close by and Munio often stayed there. But the smells of Rachel's kitchen, the *Flüden,* the hot chocolate drew him back too often for his own emotional well-being. Also, there was Sophie. He felt especially close to her. She was bearing the brunt of the deteriorating home situation. Their tours together had made Munio sensitive to her abilities; he instinctively feared for her artistic future if she stayed much longer at home in Vienna.

After 1933, Munio rarely came back to Vienna. He, along with many others outside Austria, felt the dangers to be acute; but he was hopeful, having lived through other periods of stress. In the summer of 1934 he left for the world tour that occupied him until the spring of 1935. A few short visits, mainly to introduce Eva to his parents before their marriage in October, 1935, after which he left for a second world tour, broke up his sense of continuous association with those at home. Munio was increasingly a stranger. In late 1936 he was given permission to reside and do a minimal amount of teaching in Zurich. But this was in the main a concession to Eva, who did not want to leave her family and the world that still existed in relative peace in Germany. But it was apparent by then that America was where Munio's future lay and he was there for most of every musical season.

It is interesting to note that in the fall of 1934, simultaneously with Munio's embarking on his world tour, Sigmund ventured out in a tentative attempt to renew his career. Management and publicity were arranged, a few concerts were contracted for. It did not come to much, the domestic political situation was too unstable, and Sigmund was now loth to venture far from home.

Munio was in New York awaiting the birth in Zurich of his daughter, Monica, in February of 1938 when Austria tottered; he was playing in Indianapolis in March when the Nazis finally moved in. For a few months all was quiet. Munio knew that eventually everyone, his parents in Austria, the Reifenbergs now in Zurich, would have to be removed. The summer of 1938 was an especially busy one. He had a large class of students in Zurich, and various plans for the fall season in America, including an appearance with Toscanini and the NBC Symphony in the Don Quixote of Strauss. They had caused a sensation the previous May in London with the B.B.C. Feuermann had finally had his long-awaited triumph in England, at the very moment that he was thinking of abandoning Europe.

In fact he was in Lago Maggiore with Toscanini, not only discussing plans for his fall radio collaborations with the latter but also to consult with the Maestro concerning his plans for life in America. Toscanini rebuffed him completely when Munio broached the possibility of taking the first chair of the NBC orchestra. In the conductor's mind there was no question but that he should concertize. To Feuermann, with a wife and child to support, considering the high American standard of living, the economic factors loomed large and menacing. Feuermann was disingenuous enough about his status to report this conversation to several of his students. He lost no status whatsoever in their eyes as player or teacher by this consideration of an orchestral position.

He had concluded his serious conversations with Toscanini and was taking a last swim when he received an urgent summons from the Maestro. A news report had been forwarded. It stated that Sigmund had become involved with the Nazis. The story turned out to be a horrible and pathetic one. Sigmund, along with other Viennese Jews, had been accosted by groups of Austrian Nazis. He had been forced to get down on his hands and knees to scrub the sidewalk with a hand brush, using a caustic acid that had peeled the skin off his hands. Released, he returned home and medical aid was summoned. It was thought that there would be no permanent damage to his hands.

Munio was now galvanized into action. He had a premonition that here, too, the entire edifice would soon collapse. He wrote pleading letters to Huberman as well as to a number of persons with connections in embassies, in the hope that one of them might grant visas to the members of his family. The ever-reliable Huberman finally was able to obtain visas for them for Palestine (his Philharmonic Orchestra had already been established there). The frenetic efforts were successful and the three harried and almost possessionless Feuermanns arrived in Zurich early in September. Fortunately, Sigmund had been able to rescue his precious Guadagnini.

Communication between Munio and Huberman that summer was filled with a variety of plans for musicians who now saw Palestine as a second refuge, America now being beyond their reach. Michael Taube was one whom Feuermann helped to get into Palestine at this time, and who subsequently had a distinguished career as conductor and pianist in that land. Sigmund, who had on occasion conducted at the New York College of Music, even asked that Munio suggest his name to Huberman as conductor or concertmaster.

Although Munio advised America for his family, they were adamant about Palestine. Sophie had married and was on her way to America, but Rosa was already in Palestine with Adolph Hoenigsberg. Hoenigsberg had been personally selected by Toscanini as his first trumpet for the Palestine Symphony. The parents had a feeling of strangeness with regard to the America of Munio. By now their previously hidden resentments had evolved into an overt sense of inferiority, of being left behind in a march of events that had carried their younger son to his new position in world music. They were probably excess baggage.

There is an additional note of irony in this search for refuge. The news about Sigmund's terrible humiliation had gotten back to New York. It happened that there was an official of the New York College of Music in Austria at that time. He was instructed by telegraph to find Sigmund Feuermann and help him get out with a promise of a position in the school. They had been very fond of him. Though Sigmund was not by any means a great interpretive coach, he had a fine understanding of the basic necessities of violin technique, having literally absorbed Sevčik's teachings. In the existing state of chaos in Vienna, the two men never met and a real opportunity to establish the family in the United States was lost.

It probably ought to be noted that Munio himself thought that Palestine was an appropriate refuge for his parents. He did not know how he would fare in the United States. And he knew that once more he would bear the responsibility for at least Oma's welfare. Thus were he relieved of the obligations of his own family his burden would be that much lighter.

Early November, 1938, saw Munio, his wife, and child already ensconced in an apartment in New York City, and he took out his first citizenship papers. Further residence in Europe was now out of the question. Two months later, in January, 1939, Sigmund and his parents finally arrived in Tel Aviv, exhausted but with renewed hope for the future. An interesting transformation now came over Sigmund. He had led his aging parents into this new world. Maier was sixty-seven and Rachel, still strong and vigorous, was now sixty-three. They had lived in Vienna for almost thirty years. Inevitably they leaned on his somewhat greater experience and youth. Their very survival depended upon how he would react in this new society. And Sigmund did take hold. This was certainly not a milieu for an international concert career. Munio had played here briefly with Sophie two years earlier, but had not been able to return in spite of a series of tortuous communications with Huberman. Recompense was just not available in these times, compared with Europe, much less America.

But Sigmund began to offer himself out to play either solo or in ensemble, and to teach. In fact, he married. She was an ex-seamstress from Vienna, bland and reticent, just as he was, also searching for someone with whom to ease the loneliness of resettlement. Shortly, he was rewarded for his modest professional enterprise with an excellent offer to teach violin at the American University in Beirut. Maier and Rachel were elated. Considering the great competitiveness in Palestine—given the paucity of opportunity—this was indeed a distinguished position, a recognition of a name that had not yet lost its luster.

In the fall of 1941 Sigmund and his wife left Tel Aviv for Beirut. He was to contine in this position of teacher of violin, sometime chamber chamber music coach and conductor, for four years. This was to be the great moment of his maturity. The lessons he had so arduously learned in New York, how to live somewhat autonomously, together with the experience and impetus that grew out of his burst of energy on coming to Palestine, finally bore fruit. He could now stand on his own feet and come to some terms with the world in a stable and mature way.

Nevertheless the price had long been paid. Notwithstanding his recently acquired capacity for independence, he had by now become a prisoner of odd, bizarre tendencies that had hampered his development. Students saw him as a quiet, sweet, self-effacing man who never ceased to awe his students with his technical wizardry as well as his unbelievable memory and knowledge of the entire string repertoire. But while they were respectful of his instrumental prowess, his peculiarities made them unable to take him seriously as a person.

They would occasionally have a lesson in his apartment and partake of his hospitality. Memories of the personality of Mrs. Sigmund Feuermann are all indistinct. She is recalled as a small, blond woman who rarely spoke or smiled. She literally melted into the woodwork. Sigmund himself was not loquacious. One student once appeared with violin and tennis racquet, which both amused Sigmund and piqued his interest. With real and ingenuous disbelief he listened carefully to the student's explanation of his love for the sport. To a Jew from the ghettos of eastern Europe, this was another world, one incommensurate with the violin. And yet he knew of Munio's love for the game, acquired in Cologne. It was still foreign to him.

He became animated only as he recalled experiences in Vienna. Occasionally he would giggle knowingly about the legendary bohemian antics of his idol Kreisler, when the latter was a young man in Vienna.

It was hard for the students to reconcile the enormous competence embodied in this pedagogue's knowledge of the violin, its techniques and literature, with his person. His fingerings were unerring. His pedagogical approach was almost pure Sevčik but without the heavy, aggressive pressures of the legendary Czech. His conducting of an ensemble was straightforward and musicianly. At the student level of performance there was as yet no great demand for interpretation or personality.

Yet in almost every prosaic activity in which he engaged there was always some odd behavior, at times almost a compulsive series of symbolic actions, in the way he walked around the room during a lesson, or when he would precipitately pack up his Guadagnini and lay it on a top shelf, where it would be secured from danger. In short he was what many call "fey." Since there was little competition in Beirut in those war years, Sigmund flourished. He was not only appreciated for the name Feuermann, which by now was world-famous, but for the fact that few violinists who had passed through that city could play as well as he. And as a teacher he was at least steady.

The war ended in 1945, and this phase of Sigmund's life fell apart. The stirrings of Jewish nationalism in Palestine as well as Arab nationalism in Lebanon made his tenure insecure. His marriage, which was fragile at best, also began to dissolve and alas, one day, instead of returning in triumph to Tel Aviv, as he had often done on his vacations, he came home that summer a man without a position. The parents, more aged and alone, were far more crushed by this event than Sigmund. He took it, at least on the surface, in his stride.

Father and son were now, in this last year of the elder Feuermann's life, always together. The old man, now nearing seventy-five, seemed to slip perceptibly downhill as the months went by. He and Sigmund could be seen together at every concert, Maier sitting, as usual, stiff and unsmiling, and Sigmund, at times overly animated, sometimes almost preoccupied and uninterested.

At a Philharmonic concert in which the Dvořák Cello Concerto was being performed, an unusual thing happened. Father and son were there, sitting in the middle of the orchestra section, almost as if the seats had been assigned to them. With the concluding chords of the concerto, Sigmund was seen hurrying out of his seat. As the applause began he walked rapidly towards the stage. The soloist, cellist Albert Catell, was bowing as Sigmund came to the edge of the stage and waved his hands at him, to the general astonishment of the audience, who of course, could not hear him. But the cellist remembers the high-pitched voice calling out to him with great enthusiasm, "You played it just like my brother, just like my brother." Munio had now been dead over three years. It was one of the few times that Sigmund was ever heard to mention his younger brother, especially with regard to Munio's instrumental achievements.

The end came for Maier early in 1946. Many were convinced that it was a death caused by heartbreak over what had befallen his eldest son. During that awful week of Munio's death back in May, 1942, a steady stream of friends had come to pay their respects to the parents. Even given the unexpected and calamitous death of their younger son, the parents had barely spoken about Munio. The unfulfilled potentialities of Sigmund, or the lack of recognition of his greatness, still seemed to perturb and preoccupy them more. It was an open sore in their lives, which never healed. Sigmund's departure from the Beirut American University was Maier's final disappointment. It crushed what had been a unique and indomitable, if perverse, spirit.

Sigmund was fixed enough in his patterns of life to go on with the semblance of a musical career. Status and success seemed to concern him less and less. He played in the Kol Israel Radio Orchestra, taught a little, and even on occasion played a solo recital or appeared with an orchestra. There were few violinists in Israel at that time who could come near him in his command of the concerto repertoire. But invitations to solo were rarely proffered twice. His playing was "dissociated." It was not even that he played the music straight without interpretation or that, as some put it, "he practiced on stage." The playing did not seem to touch him personally in any appropriate way. Its rote qualities had taken on a peculiar surface character. It had created a twilight life of its own. Whether it was Bee-thoven or Tchaikovsky, idiosyncrasies appeared that might be expected were someone from another culture to play the music, yet giving all due regard to the values of the written symbols. It was reminiscent of the way European or Oriental dance bands, in bygone days, played American jazz.

The musicians of Kol Israel, typical of all musicians, took particular delight in mocking this poor man behind his back. He was after all a great man and still retained some of the poise and dignity that had been nurtured in him from his earlier concert career. His peculiar devotion to the Guadagnini and the fact that he never left it alone for an instant, even bundling it into its case to take it along to the washroom, provided fodder for countless hilarious jokes, which even visitors were forced to share with the musicians.

Sometimes out of genuine curiosity, sometimes in mock interest, Sig-mund would be explicitly asked about the source of his odd visage. He would reply off-handedly that it was a defect of the birth process caused by a poorly executed forceps delivery.

It was impossible to know whether Sigmund was aware of these cruel taunts or how they affected him. Quietly and unobtrusively, never giving harm to anyone, he made his living by playing the violin, supported his aging mother, and drifted into oblivion.

7

WORLD TOUR

Feuermann and his accompanist, Fritz Kitzinger, had just completed their debut concert at the Gungin Kaikan in Tokyo. It was the evening of October 4, 1934. Even the insistent applause of the 200 enthusiasts in the audience could not neutralize the emptiness of the 1,800 other seats in the auditorium. The musicians were perplexed. Backstage, manager Strock was moaning audibly. Faced with an impending financial disaster, he was not to be assuaged by the cellist's diffidence.

Strock, a shrewd and shriveled old Russian Jew, was the local representative of the International Artists Organization of Paris. He and a certain Straus, the general manager of Nipponophone (Columbia's lucrative Japanese affiliate) and a German Jew, made a unique tandem, a real intrusion of the Occident into the east. Strock had made good use of Feuermann's earlier recordings in Germany. But he was worried by the scholarly image of the German musician. The Japanese could not comprehend the concepts "virtuoso musician" and "professor" in a single meaningful image. That relationship was not part of their own world of meanings.

The manager had been worried by Feuermann's professional reputation and appearance. He had created considerable publicity to counter this impression. But apparently to no avail. "Yet," and he waved several clippings in Feuermann's face in evident bewilderment, "apparently the audiences liked you in Shanghai, even if the critics didn't." They were letters in rebuttal to several qualified critical reviews. "The trouble was that it was as hot as hell in that theatre," Feuermann commented. "Not one of the harmonics in the *Zapateado* sounded. Next time," he winked at Strock, "don't have me play in Shanghai in September. Bring me here first, maybe the people will want me more then." "Hmpf," replied the manager, "the professor business may be good in Java, Singapore, or China—for the Europeans. But here it will hurt you. Yet, you do play well . . ."

The evening of October 5th, the second recital, was another story. Both word-of-mouth reports and the critical encomiums conspired to pack the hall. The audiences cheered continuously and Strock smiled benignly and fanned himself with the Shanghai rebuttals.

For the next few days, Strock was a torrent of energy. Several concerts were added to Feuermann's Tokyo schedule. Photographs were taken, publicity releases prepared. Strock and Straus even started the machinery for the immediate production of several special Japanese shoit pieces to be recorded for this new market situation. He repeatedly emphasized to the bewildered, excited, and exhausted young cellist that he should not expect any great largesse as the product of his apparent success. "First," he expostulated, "you must open up a territory for your art. You exploit your newness, sell yourself, even cheaply, so that people will get to know you. Then when you come again, you will reap the rewards of your earlier seeding." This seemed so eminently logical to Feuermann that he accepted it and would himself repeat the principle to other novices as a law of concertizing, even when it did not necessarily hold true in practice.

In the two-and-a-half weeks during which he was to concertize in Japan, Feuermann gave a total of nine concerts in Tokyo, and a half dozen concerts in such cities as Nagoya, Osaka, and Kyoto. He was besieged by a host of young cellists and, as usual, obliged; he squeezed a number of master classes into his schedule.

His major appearance in Japan was to be on October 17th in Hibaya Hall (seating capacity 2,800) with a symphony orchestra led by Viscount Konoye. He was to perform the Dvořák Concerto. Tickets had long been sold out and the Japanese Broadcasting Corporation had arranged to have the concert broadcast, as Feuermann's fame had evoked considerable public interest. Strock had hoped that the recordings Straus had planned for Feuermann would be ready to cut by the 10th. Unfortunately the composer-arranger Yamada had been unable to complete the four arrangements until the evening of the 14th.

The session was set for the morning of the 15th. This would not allow for the production and distribution of the records for the day of the concert, even with the Westerner's eagerness and Japanese efficiency. Yet Strock had prepared for any eventuality and thus with all due fanfare October 14th saw the release throughout Japan of elaborate publicity announcing the upcoming tour schedule, the available Parlophone recordings, and the imminent release of the special Japanese discs. Featured in the publicity was one of several photos the local photographer had taken showing Feuermann's round face in the most Japanese manner possible—a tribute to the ingenuity of both manager and photographer.

The four Japanese songs that Feuermann and Kitzinger recorded on the morning of the 15th were pleasant enough pieces, rather European in structure with a plaintively evocative oriental nuance. Released on October 25th, just prior to Feuermann's departure from Japan, they sold as well as Strock had predicted.

The concert in Tokyo's Hibaya Hall was a great success; there were many encores. But it was outside the auditorium that most of the excitement took place. Although the concert was broadcast in order to provide maximum coverage, there were still many who would not be able to hear it. At that time only a small number of people had radios. Thus it had been announced that loudspeakers would be mounted in key places. In several instances the crowds grew so large that the Tokyo police had to rope off the streets from traffic. Again, speakers had been set up outside shops that sold records—a land-office business in Feuermann recordings was had that night. Later Feuermann, as was the Japanese custom, would be asked to autograph these records. It became a wearying routine.

From October 29 to November 8, Feuermann concertized on the China mainland—Darien, Tientsin, Peking, and Shanghai. In Tientsin, the headline in the *Deutsche Chinesische Nachtrichten* enunciated, "A cello sings in Tientsin." Following his recital in the Shanghai Lyceum Theatre on November 6, the reviewer recanted his prior lukewarm review and acknowledged that the objectors to his earlier critique had been correct. Indeed, the German cellist was unique; the playing such a departure from the usual expectations with regard to cello playing that one needed acclimatizing to Feuermann's accomplishments.

On Feuermann's returning to Japan preparatory to his November 16th embarkation from Yokahama, Strock had a final surprise in store. The new records had been selling so well that he had engaged him for a final farewell concert in the Asahi Kaikan Hall in Osaka, playing the Haydn Cello Concerto, Joseph Laska conducting. It was a fairly large hall and Osaka had received Feuermann very warmly before. This special event, Strock enunciated, would be the capstone to Feuermann's tour. The cellist, extremely weary—exhilarated to the point of exhaustion—meekly submitted to the old impresario's greater wisdom and appeared at the hall at the appointed hour.

But economic disaster was to be their fate. The turnout was unbelievably small, perhaps a fifth of the auditorium filled. The publicity had been opulent as usual. "What happened, what happened?" moaned Strock to the conductor at the intermission. The conductor, a European, merely shrugged unconcernedly and beckoned his soloist to precede him onstage amidst a ripple of applause.

In musical terms the program had not gone badly. As Feuermann reappeared backstage, eager to change his clothes and leave, Strock was still pacing back and forth, this time accompanied by an equally old and wizened Japanese, the manager of the hall. The oriental was attempting to fathom the concern of Strock. The latter was hardly coherent. Both his ego and his purse were hurting. Finally, as Feuermann, Kitzinger, and

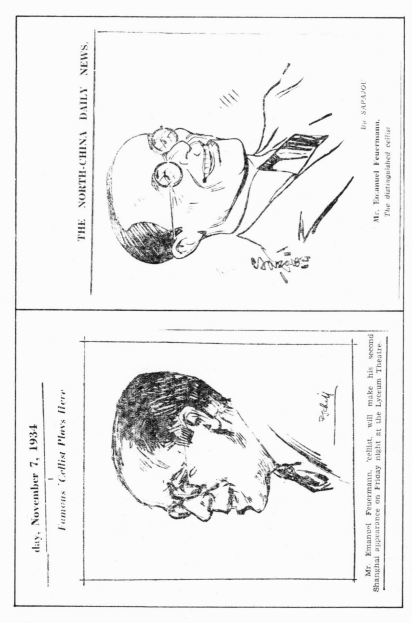

Two cartoons of Feuermann in China during his first world tour, 1934.
Note in one a resemblance to a contemporary Russian cellist.

Laska looked on from a distance, the old Japanese paused, a faint glint of comprehension in his face. He had grasped the problem and could render a solution. "You see, Mr. Strock, you do not yet understand the Japanese people. They did not come to this concert because they did not understand its purpose. They had already said farewell to Mr. Feuermann the last time he was here."

Now, aboard ship bound for Vancouver, Feuermann finally had some time to digest his impressions. It helped immensely to write to Eva. The entire sequence of events, from the day off Colombo, Ceylon, when he was one of the few to weather a storm without seasickness; his suntan victory over his rivals aboard ship as they neared Singapore; he even had to chuckle again at his now old trick of using a personalized parody of Yiddish to impress the Dutch in Batavia with his knowledge of their language. Theo van der Pas was the only one to find him out. It went without saying that the Orient, still relatively untouched by Western influences, impressed him deeply. Those images would never be forgotten, but Eva alone would share them.

The most important experience went far beyond his enormous shock at the insatiable musical appetite of the Japanese or his reception everywhere. He was gaining a new awareness of himself. He wrote to Eva about it shortly after it happened. He was traveling back to Shanghai from Peking on the Shanghai Express, passing through endless miles of farmland with endless numbers of peasants in an as yet oblivious universe. Only then did he realize how free he had become of Germany, indeed of Europe with its sickness. What had begun as an almost imposed voyage or a tour to forget and to build new career possibilities, was becoming a means for self-discovery. Up to now he had been rooted in a static vision of a career or place in high society, exemplified in his coveting of the Hochschule professorship. His art had stagnated in consequence. Now he had discovered that his place was almost anywhere, as long as he had his cello and his music. No doubt Huberman was correct: Germany would lose more than he. He, along with so many other Jews, was destined to wander.

Feuermann arrived in Victoria, British Columbia on November 27 and a concert was scheduled in Vancouver for the next day. There was little time even to take in the air of North America. After the concert Feuermann, Kitzinger, and a young Japanese cellist whom they brought along were almost immediately aboard the Canadian Pacific Railway for Winnipeg, where a concert was scheduled for December 3. However, he would have a week in Chicago, where his student Daniel Saidenberg, now a cellist in the Chicago Symphony, had offered his apartment to Feuermann. In Chicago he would have to prepare for two appearances with the symphony in the Lalo and the Dvořák concertos. Saidenberg found his

teacher by now inured to the terrific pace. When he discovered just prior
to the first appearance on December 6 that Feuermann's bow had just half
the necessary hair on it (the rest had broken off in the course of the tour)
he inquired with astonishment how Feuermann could play that way.
Feuermann replied laconically that it was a good way to test himself.
However, if there was a good man in town, he would have no objection to
having the bow rehaired.

If he took the Chicago interlude lightly, it was because the ultimate test,
New York, was now close at hand. That was all he had heard, practically,
since he left London. The real test would come, in either Carnegie Hall,
Town Hall, or both. And as he neared this ultimate destination, the
warnings became increasingly loud. The pervasive anxiety amazed, intimidated, and intrigued him, depending on his mood at the moment.

His relative success in Chicago was absorbed without comment in his
letters to Eva. He played in Montreal on the 13th and arrived in New York
on the 15th. Each letter to Eva concluded with the phrase, "I hope they
will like me in New York. . . . . I hope for success. . . ." In many of the
letters he practiced his English, which already showed remarkable facility.

New York was all that he had expected and more. It contrasted sharply
with "sleepy London." For himself, he preferred London. Yet one had to
wonder if earning a livelihood would ever be possible there. In spite of the
depression in the States and the frightening freneticism of the New York
musicians, who looked upon every new arrival from the Continent as a
threat, New York and the States had the potential which was becoming
ever more questionable in Europe. Joseph Szigeti commented to him
ominously that "every recital in New York is like your original debut." Yet
the weeks there were not all grim. There were so many old faces from
Vienna, Berlin, and London.

He was especially delighted to find Schnabel and Huberman. They had
plans for a trio and this possibility conjured up great opportunity.
Schnabel's greeting was as effusive as ever. Feuermann's face was
wreathed in the kisses of the tiny keyboard master. He talked just as
much; if anything the old wit was sharper. Schnabel's ego had been
transferred intact into the new world. Feuermann commented in his
letters that it was a glorious thing.

One evening they played and babbled into the wee hours of the morning. As the cellist described it they scratched, beat, and shouted at their
instruments until Feuermann's in his excitement broke the "C" string on
the Montagnana, a feat that only another cellist would appreciate. What a
great time!

The only thing that saddened him was the large number of negative
opinions of Huberman's playing. But this was apparently characteristic of
the musical climate in this city—intense competition to the point of de-
structiveness. How it contrasted with Europe, where music was so much

more a part of the normal run of life. There were many things that
bothered Feuermann, which he wanted to comment upon. But the concerts were still in the future and he was a guest, so, "I kept my opinions to
myself, even if they are correct."

One example of the utter and unfeeling capriciousness of that musical
elect, the critics, was especially cruel. It concerned his friend, Bruno
Walter. Walter had many characteristics with which Feuermann was to
find fault. Feuermann at times had teased him unmercifully. Though
they had somewhat differing musical sentiments and outlooks, Feuermann did understand the point of this difference. And, as a matter of fact,
he accepted and respected Walter for it.

Since Feuermann would debut with the Philharmonic on January 2,
1935, one of the first concerts he attended was a Walter performance of
Das Lied von der Erde with that same orchestra. Not only did Feuermann
admire the orchestra but he was overwhelmed with the beauty with which
Walter invested the Mahler work. The reviews the next day were unfa-
vorable. The critics seemed to have missed the essence of what Walter was
trying to communicate. Feuermann was disappointed. It did not augur
well for himself. He now wondered, considering the attitude of the
reviewers towards Walter, whether it had been such a good idea to
persuade the orchestra to take him on for the New York debut.

He had had quite a time in London the previous spring in arranging
this concert. Initially Walter, who was having his own difficulties in
making the transition to America, was loth to take on this unknown
German cellist, even if they were friends. After all, what with Casals and
the glamorous Russian, Piatigorsky, was there indeed room for another
cellist? And then, preliminary scheduling had already placed a well-
known violinist for January 2. Feuermann had disdainfully shrugged
when he heard the name. "Change it, he can play another time."
Walter asked him what he would play. Feuermann said, the "Dvořák."
Walter threw up his hands. "We can't have two Dvořáks. The New World
is definitely settled for that concert." Feuermann barked "The New
World? Who wants to hear that now?" Walter finally ended the debate.
"We will see," he said. "It's in the hands of the managers anyway." In the
meantime it was Mrs. Walter who was reapproached and who tried to
persuade the conductor to make a small sacrifice for the sake of the old
days. However, it was the Haydn D Major that Feuermann would have to
play.

Christmas week before the Philharmonic concert was a good week. On
the 26th he played for Mrs. Roosevelt and a women's group in Washington. Grete Stueckgold, the soprano, was also on the program. *The Washington Post* noted that Feuermann was in the class of Casals and Felix
Salmond. On the 27th he played for Bagby's Waldorf Astoria morning

soirée. Bagby and the audience liked him. The Montagnana was responding to the American climate nicely.

The Philharmonic was a national institution. And well it should be, Feuermann thought, as he heard Walter put it through the Roussel G Minor Symphony, which opened the program (no Dvořák on this program). It was a great orchestra, better than those in Europe, and more exciting. Even the Chicago was a fine orchestra, perhaps equal to those in Berlin and Vienna.

Feuermann felt that the Haydn had gone well. A great crowd had descended upon him after the concert and he was surrounded by programs to sign. Perhaps the image of signing records in Japan flitted through his mind. It contrasted with the more tangible Japanese way of obtaining a memento of the musical experience. Walter had disappeared momentarily into his dressing room after patting Munio briefly on the back in congratulation. A few moments later he came back into the crowded artists' room to see how the young cellist was faring. Feuermann was talking and gesticulating in obvious delight as he alternately shook hands and signed programs. He looked up, saw Walter standing near the door, and with a twinkle, waved his hand at him and called out mischievously, "Walter, I need you no more," and turned to autograph the next program.

The reaction of the reviewers to the concert was interesting. They certainly recognized all the factors Feuermann now took pains to integrate into his post-German level of performance. The technique was, as usual, clear, precise, and forceful. Interpretively there existed the same classic restraint as in earlier years. Yet there was in addition a certain molding quality, joined with an effort to sound beautiful, that had advanced his playing from what it had been barely two years earlier. Thus it was not essentially new Feuermann, even though the artist was aware that he was moving in a newer and better direction—a more mature integration of what he heard with his inner ear.

The reviews of Francis Perkins in the *Herald Tribune* and W. J. Henderson in the *New York Sun* were quite favorable. However Olin Downes, while devoting much space to the G Minor Symphony of Albert Roussel and Berlioz' *Harold in Italy* (played by Michel Piastro), before going on to the other matters, briefly passed over Feuermann's performance with this comment: "Mr. Feuermann played the Haydn Concerto in D Major with a sonorous tone, with amply sufficient technique, but not in distinguished style, not with the grace, the transparency, the classic proportion that the music implies. It would be interesting to hear Mr. Feuermann in other works. His reputation justifies expectation of more distinctive qualities than he displayed last night, though the audience greeted him cordially and called him back repeatedly after he had played."

The review by Samuel Chotzinoff in the *New York Post* especially en-
raged Feuermann. Chotzinoff, too, devoted most of the review to the
other works on the program. Then in a final paragraph he commented,
"The concert served to introduce to New York the celebrated Russian
violoncellist, Mr. Emanuel Feuermann, who played Haydn's Concerto in
D Major. Mr. Feuermann's European reputation had preceded him here
and many of our local cellists were on hand to judge for themselves. I liked
Mr. Feuermann very much for his cool and accomplished technique, his
firm but not extraordinary tone, his musicianly but not imaginative phrasing. He is a distinct addition to an already large circle of good cellists. But
he is as yet, no Feuermann."

Publicly, Feuermann was able to contain his own personal bitterness; he
expressed himself only in his letters back home. Let NBC and the others
deal with Chotzinoff themselves. Surely Chotzinoff had seen his biography from the NBC publicity releases. Feuermann had been educated in
Vienna. He was a professor in Cologne and Berlin. He had recorded
much in Germany. Why then did Chotzinoff label him as Russian and take
special note of his European background? Was he projecting onto
Feuermann some of his own feelings about his origin? There was something about the "impudent Jewish tone" of the review, he wrote to Eva,
that perhaps suggested the worst kind of anti-Semite—the Jewish anti-
Semite.

The ten days he spent in New York awaiting his Town Hall recital on
January 13 were gruelling. He was constantly with people he enjoyed.
Everything he heard, however, seemed to confirm the incompatibility of
this milieu with an environment in which he could successfully pursue his
career. His one departure, for a recital in Quebec City on January 8, gave
him an opportunity to write about the relative peace and beauty of this city
and that "I am not right for New York." If only he could get away sooner.
But no, he was scheduled to leave on February 16. There would be a
whole month of touring after Town Hall.

On the morning of January 14, there was another and completely
different Feuermann. He was high—ebullient with the conquest of the
night before. Barely half of Town Hall had been filled. But in addition to
the usual group of reviewers, the audience was almost exclusively populated by cellists and other string players—many of them prominent ones.
They had also been in Carnegie Hall the Wednesday earlier. Now they
applauded and cheered. For the earlier concert the critics had attempted
to hold the line, to be judicious. What the reviewers now experienced
must have seemed ominous. There was a pervasive excitement and anticipation, much fraternal greeting and, on several occasions, curious
though discreet glances toward the incomprehensible critics in question.
There was a declaration—indeed an intimidating affirmation—by the
roaring audience after the initial Valentini Sonata. The complete review

by Olin Downes speaks for itself. But being of a stern and independent nature, Downes, as should be noted, allowed himself a final reservation.

New York Times: **January 14, 1935**

FEUERMANN HEARD IN CELLO PROGRAM

Sonatas of Valentini, Brahms
and Schubert Included at
Town Hall Recital

BACH SUITE IN C PLAYED

Many Colleagues Join in Hailing
Musician, Who Receives High
Critical Praise

By OLIN DOWNES

It is safe to say that no cellist who was at large last night in New York City failed to attend Emanuel Feuermann's recital in the Town Hall. There they sat, some with folded arms and beetling brows. They listened; they cogitated; earnest conversations were held in corners of the foyer during intermission. Mr. Feuermann had met and survived the ordeal by fire—not merely the judgment of newspaper reviewers but the more severe examination of his colleagues.

They had reason to be attentive. They heard cello playing which in some respects was absolutely phenomenal. The gratification of the specialists was shared by the entire audience. Mr. Feuermann, after his last group, had to play numerous encores, and there was an impressive demonstration.

When he played the Haydn concerto recently with the Philharmonic-Symphony orchestra, there was not opportunity to estimate the extent of his technical mastery. This was shown last night in the sonata of the early eighteenth-century composer, Giuseppe Valentini, whose violin and 'cello sonatas have not been widely known, and whose musical legacy has been for the greater part in the form of concerted pieces of chamber music; in the rather weak and redundant sonata in A minor of Schubert; the unaccompanied C major suite of Bach, and a group of final pieces which enraptured the audience. Last night's program asked almost everything a cellist could give, and if everything was not given, enough was provided, with a degree of authority and resource, to make a sensation.

Difficulties do not exist for Mr. Feuermann, even difficulties that would give celebrated virtuosi pause. It would be hard to imagine a cleaner or more substantial technic, which can place every resource of the instrument at the interpreter's command. And there is, of course, more than technic. There is a big tone, finely sustained in singing passages, and warm. There is palpable sincerity, earnestness, musicianship attained as the result of exacting study.

As soon as Mr. Feuermann had played two dozen measures the audience belonged to him. This was in spite of the fact that a peg slipped just as he was beginning, which might have upset him. But the mind of a musician, as well as his hands, were at work; his power was felt immediately. The Valentini sonata affords opportunities for various aspects of the interpreter's art, which must here be expressive as well as brilliant. When this performance was completed there was a crash of applause, for it was evident that the concert stage of this country is the richer by the proved capacities of an artist whose fame had preceded him.

The Schubert sonata, second on the program, is weak and repetitious work, and palls before it has run its course, in spite of the beauty of many of the ideas. Though the performance was admirable, it had neither the richness nor the distinction of the work that preceded it.

The audience waited to see what would happen with Bach. In the playing of Bach's music this writer found Mr. Feuermann disappointing. Some there be who claim that the C major sonata is dull music in any event—that Bach nodded a little when he wrote this composition for the low-pitched stringed instrument. But we have heard cellists with far less technic than Feuermann make the C major sonata fascinating and significant. The phrases were performed accurately and well, but they had little distinction, either of curve or of tone quality. The power of this music must lie in the interest of its line and the grandness of its phrases. As played last night, it was a workmanlike job, but not a great one, or one that added anything to the evening.

The Brahms F major sonata was given a fiery reading, with the collaboration of Fritz Kitzinger as pianist. Mr. Kitzinger's temperament and pianistic accomplishments were ample, but the balance of tone was not always good, for his feelings were inclined to run away with him. The last group of pieces, which we could not hear, were, according to authoritative report, one of the major triumphs of the evening. They asked a sensuous tone and more virtuosity, and the encores included, if you please, the Sarasate 'Zapateado' for violin, transposed for cello.

In the retrospect of yesterday evening it is evident that only a part of Mr. Feuermann's gift was shown when he played the Haydn concerto on an occasion already mentioned. That performance was highly competent, but not distinguished, and not precisely of the aristocratic quality of the classic masterpiece. It is questionable whether Mr. Feuermann would not have had a greater success in a concerto of quite another sort. But the reservation felt after his interpretation of Haydn still holds: the acme of refinement and style does not appear to be his. His qualities are obvious, rather than subtle. They will insure him success, which is amply deserved, even if he, being human, has his limitations as interpreter.

Even more remarkable is Samuel Chotzinoff's critique, in which he not only reversed his biographical error but consented to "eat his words."

New York Post, **January 14, 1935**
from *Words and Music* (a column)
Review: Samuel Chotzinoff

Last night at the Town Hall Mr. Emanuel Feuermann, the Austrian cellist, appeared in recital. His very European program accounted for a sonata in E major by Valentini, a sonata in A minor by Schubert, Bach's unaccompanied C major Suite, Brahms's F major sonata for cello and piano and a group of pieces by Dvořák, Chopin, Senaille and Popper. Mr. Fritz Kitzinger was the assisting pianist.

When Mr. Feuermann made his New York debut, a week or so ago with the Philharmonic-Symphony in the Haydn concerto, I found his considerable talents gratifying but not astounding. Now I find myself forced, in the light of his achievements at last night's concert, to revise this first impression. Surely Mr. Feuermann must have been under constraint of one kind or another at his debut, for his playing last night justified the great reputation which had preceded him to this country.

There are pleasanter things for a reviewer to do than to eat his own words. Yet, what else can I do but say that as a virtuoso on his instrument Mr. Feuermann seems to me miles ahead of his colleagues. I have heard more sensuous tones on the cello but never so amazing a technique. The bowing in spiccato and staccato, the masterfully dexterous left hand would be astonishing even in a virtuoso of the violin. Indeed, Mr. Feuermann plays the cello like a great violinist. In addition he can summon passion that is sincere and a style that reflects a patrician musical personality. I feel better, now that this report is off my chest.

Only hours after the reviews were out, Feuermann started receiving frantic calls from NBC Concerts that they were trying to arrange another date in Town Hall for a farewell New York concert. They wanted him to have a program ready when he returned from the final leg of his United States tour. The entire sequence was a rerun of Japan, but as yet without a hall. New York was completely booked at this time of year. Finally, success. Town Hall was available February 15, the night before he embarked. He wrote to Eva that same day, wondering who it was that they were able to push aside in order to obtain the hall on that short notice. How differently NBC handled him here in the States. Ibbs and Tillet, his London managers, were so sleepy. Could it have been poor management that had prevented him from storming the English musical world?

The short final tour as well as the final concert in Town Hall were sell-outs, great successes. NBC had already prepared the ground for his next American tour, starting in December of 1935, which would be part of a new world tour to include South America and the Orient.

The entire series of events had puzzled him, the almost-reticent welcome he had received in each of his "landfalls," to be followed by an effusive, almost hysterical acceptance. He never resolved it in his mind as being other than the peculiarities of both reviewers and audiences—each tempered by personal and cultural idiosyncrasies.

It was hard to decide about New York. He spent most of the trip across the Atlantic pondering the difference in perspective that New York had given him, both before and after the Town Hall recital. If only England would be warmer to him, Eva and he could have the best of the two worlds.

Eventually he would conquer England. This was to take place in 1938, on the eve of his abandonment of Europe for America. It was a concert with Arturo Toscanini and the B.B.C. symphony during a May festival performance of Strauss' *Don Quixote*. This remarkable performance finally jolted the English into realizing what they were losing. The English slowness may be attributed to their lack of a tradition of string musicians and thus their relative insensitivity to the finer nuances of achievement in the *genre*. With regard to the other audiences and especially the American critics, there is a different explanation.

As with any quantum jump in an art form, half the battle of acclimatization lies in understanding the meaning of the change. In Austria and Germany Feuermann had been presented as a *Wunderkind* as well as a revolutionary in cello performance. The former paved the way for the accommodations to the latter. Although it should be said that, once Feuermann matured, it took constant exposure in recital before the critics accepted him for what he had achieved and before he was finally brought to Berlin.

The critics in England, the United States, and elsewhere had already accommodated themselves to the earlier revolution of Casals. There was no one in Feuermann's generation to prepare them for the fact that more was to come. Certainly Piatigorsky, who had already made his mark in America, made it in terms of his own great romantic image, lush sound, and a manner to enhance the public image. Piatigorsky alone of that generation had the gifts to go beyond Casals. But these he squandered.

Another notable factor is that, from the time of World War I, America had been besieged by a flurry of great violinists, each seemingly building on the achievements of the others. From Kreisler and Elman to Milstein and Heifetz, a continuum of achievement was established and the esthetic and auditory ground was gradually prepared. It was an almost logical building toward the peak ultimately realized in the playing of Jascha Heifetz. And the Russian violinist realized fully the rewards that came of his extraordinary preeminence.

What made Feuermann's impact more diffused and difficult to appreciate was what we have noted earlier concerning Casals. In spite of real (at least in retrospect) technical deficiencies, Casal's musical strength was such that he turned them into assets. Thus it was hard to disentangle his interpretive nuances from his technical accommodations, for what Casals did technically was always musically integral.

The thirty-two-year-old Feuermann came to the American stage with an extraordinarily brilliant technique. He needed none of the interpretive "crutches" of lesser cellists, none of the sliding, whining, and grunting that disguised the music in a "mist of profundity." The critics' immediate, visceral reaction—for they were human—was to label the cellist's achievements superficial and flashy.

It is interesting to note how quickly they were corrected; for the professional cellists knew better. Taking the cue from other, more progressive instrumental techniques (piano and violin), they had been pushing toward the ultimate goal of overcoming the raw bulk and distances of the cello. They were attempting to subject the cello to the same artistic canons as the other instruments.

Many of them knew of Feuermann's earlier recordings. Some had heard the Philharmonic concert. Most others, in spite of the poor reviews, which kept the public away and caused Town Hall to be half-empty, came to hear what the musicians' underground had already rumored: cello playing the like of which had never been experienced. During the Town Hall intermission, musicians gathered into groups animatedly discussing the significance of what they had heard. The lobby lights had to be blinked repeatedly to get them back in their seats. The first half of the recital had provided too much excitement to hurry it over. When the recital was finally concluded the audience refused to let Feuermann leave the stage. The American cellists in the audience had heard the instrument played that Sunday evening as they had hoped to hear it played only in their most wishful dreams.

8

STRADIVARIUS

Back home once more in London, all was quiet by comparison in Feuermann's life. Ibbs and Tillet were still reiterating the need to build up slowly, to accustom the English audiences to his presence. They would eventually appreciate and accept him. It was at moments like this that he thought about the calm security, the sinecure amidst the fun and stimulation of Berlin. In retrospect New York had a quality of excitement and tension, yet it was vastly different from Berlin and Germany.

There were concerts to be given this spring in Italy and Switzerland. The news of his success in the States had had a modest impact on his tour schedule, if not in England. He had however received a warm welcome in that old establishment institution, Hill Brothers. At Hill's he had returned to have his Montagnana refurbished and his bows rehaired and adjusted. The brothers Hill, typically reserved Englishmen, had always been, in prior visits, correct if not warm. Perhaps Feuermann's direct and pointed comments did not strike them as sympathetic. Or perhaps Feuermann's attitude of both suspicion and competition showed itself—he was still Maier Feuermann's son.

This time they greeted him like a long-lost brother who had finally proved himself and now returned home. Feuermann on his part was dependent upon their expert knowledge and handling of his instrument. His livelihood necessitated its health and like most instrumentalists he was somewhat over-anxious about its condition. Thus he was both surprised and gratified by their attitude. Except for his beloved students, the Hills gave him the best reception he got all that spring in England.

He was already looking forward to the fall. Most of the performing and teaching (Switzerland, St. Gilgen master classes) would be over and he would be able to take Eva away from Germany, even if it meant her leaving Cologne. After so many years of bachelorhood and wandering, Feuermann was looking forward to the time when they could wander together. However he did have to return to Cologne towards the end of

April. The tremendous expenditure of energies of this and the previous tour had taken its toll. He would require a hernia operation. Fortunately the renowned Dr. Rosenow would be in charge. And though he knew the procedure was not dangerous, Feuermann admitted forthrightly that he feared the pain the whole process would cause.

There were unexpected complications, but Rosenow's intuitive skill and his breadth of knowledge prevented serious consequences. By early May, Feuermann was better. The summer was spent teaching and relaxing.

When he had first come to Cologne years before, Eva would ride on the broad shoulders of her "Uncle Munio." She worshiped him then as a distant hero, an idol of whom many glorious achievements were expected. Later he was an older brother, a counselor to a family that, in spite of wealth and power, was undergoing great internal stress, without a male head and guide, except for this young, optimistic adoptee of theirs. As Eva matured, and with Oma's consent, Feuermann's deep and emotional involvement with this family had begun to take on more serious dimensions. The young girl had become a symbol to him of the romance and love that, in his long professional journey, had as yet eluded him. As the European world around him went to pieces, Feuermann's dream of a wife, a family, a home was increasingly focused on that very environment which in years past had meant stability and permanence.

And thus in late October, with the clouds darkening over Germany, Munio came back to Cologne for the last time to marry and take his bride away from their past. This fall of 1935 was an ecstatic time for him. So optimistic was Feuermann that he even ventured to travel back to Vienna to introduce his twenty-one-year-old fiancée to his family. He usually avoided Vienna as much as he could. Both Sigmund and his father grated on his nerves. Yet that first evening after their arrival, his mother and Sophie offering a resplendent banquet, the atmosphere was unusually amicable and relaxed in spite of the typically stiff and tense Maier.

Maier was well aware of the good fortune of the Reifenbergs, but could not know of the delicate impermanence of this wealth in Nazi Germany. Perhaps he was both intimidated by Munio's success and at the same time already distant from it. Maier would never suspect Munio's own naïve incredulity at his great good fortune. To all the old friends both before and after their marriage, Feuermann would burst out, "How is it possible that Eva would marry me, a kid from Galicia?" Eva was the beauteous symbol of a world that he could never fully accept as his own.

One incident at the dinner impressed both Eva and Munio. Knowing the traditional Jewish hostility towards intermarriage, it was with some trepidation that Munio volunteered the information that Paul Reifenberg had baptized his children in the Lutheran faith. And that though they were Jews by blood, they were all officially Christians. This was perhaps a doubly sensitive issue. Rachel listened quietly, awaiting Maier's cue. The father thought for a moment, perhaps contemplating the prospect of non-Jewish grandchildren (the mother being the key to the child's religion) and then waved his hand offhandedly. "It doesn't matter," he said quietly. "Perhaps it is good . . . . good."

In later years when Feuermann would look in on his daughter Monica and contemplate the holocaust overtaking the world, he must have thought back to Maier's words. In a world where to be a Jew had been so painful, perhaps it was a good idea finally to assimilate, to go beyond the limitations of the Jewish world. And perhaps through assimilation one could avoid through one's children the heavy stigma of persecution.

No matter the love-hate relationship with his own faith and his quickness to abuse and satirize it, still Feuermann, as with most Jews, would always defend it with both speed and ferocity. One recalls Feuermann's almost monotonous reiteration of his repugnance for Bloch's *Schelomo*, how he hated to study it, it would not "enter his head." Yet when he did play it, the piece came alive with deep poetry and passion and not a little of the Hebraic spirit.

Exuberant, optimistic, with a veneer of typically Viennese gaiety, Feuermann was an emotional and impetuous person underneath. The surface characteristics did much to buffer the urgency of the deeper bent and, importantly, keep it to its creative musical function. But the thrust for innovation and change was real this fall. Constant nagging had finally persuaded his very talented student from the Berlin days, Mosa Havivi, to find himself a good cello. And since he now had a warm spot for Hill's, he dragged Mosa off to the New Bond Street building of the firm to pick out an instrument. After several visits, Havivi found the right cello—at a price he probably could not afford—which he very much needed for his own burgeoning career.

On one of these visits, Feuermann ran into his old Tecchler cello. It was being looked over by a well-off amateur lady cellist by the name of Thelma Yellin, later, when she was in Palestine as the wife of the British high commissioner, to be called Lady Bentwick. Hill lost no time. He brought Feuermann into the room in which the instrument was being auditioned. When the formal introductions were duly completed, Hill, seeing this as a marvelous opportunity to close the deal on an instrument that should have been sold three years earlier (when Feuermann traded it in), pointedly let the distinguished lady know that this instrument had been a big element in Feuermann's early recording and professional career.

Evidently Feuermann was not listening to the dealer's cues, for he burst out in his typical way, "You are buying that cello: It's too big. I wanted to get rid of it for a long time. . . ." Notwithstanding that enthusiastic "en-

Engaged to Eva Reifenberg, 1935.

dorsement," Lady Bentwick purchased the Tecchler. The lure of playing on a Feuermann cello was irresistible.

The cello had an interesting subsequent history. Several years later, the original Budapest Quartet, Emil Hauser, first violin, was touring Palestine. The extremely dry weather caused the glue to crack on the Testore of the cellist Mueller. The belly of the instrument opened up in a way that would have taken several days to repair. In the meantime the Tecchler of Lady Bentwick was solicited and the quartet drove off to a concert in Haifa. On the way the car was in an accident. No serious personal injuries were sustained, but the cello was smashed. So extreme was the damage to this great instrument that it arrived back at Hill's in a sack. The work of reconstruction was painstakingly long and necessitated great care. Lady Bentwick would have no more of the instrument and it was eventually sold to Rudolph Wurlitzer in New York. Later the owner of this instrument was the former first cellist of the New York Philharmonic, Laszlo Varga, and, still later, David Miller, in Toronto.

Shortly after his marriage, Munio was back in London again for a concert with Sophie. He made a special point to go with her to Hill's. During one of the earlier visits with Havivi, Alfred Hill had taken out a cello which intrigued both men, but which was far beyond the younger man's purse. It was a Strad and Feuermann liked it. But what with all the preparations for the wedding, etc., it never entered his head that he should, or could, consider acquiring it. Now, in his enthusiasm about his new life and international prospects, this intriguing possibility could be looked into. The Montagnana was beautiful and rich. In retrospect it did lack some of the power of the Tecchler, though he was thankful that in those years of advancing senility (age thirty-three) he did not have to expend the energy to manipulate the Montagnana day after day on tour.

The Strad was different, as he demonstrated to Sophie. It was small, 29½ inches in length as compared to the 30-31 inches of the larger instruments he had owned. Yet there was something about its construction that made it far more brilliant than the Montagnana. Perhaps the Strad did not have the throbbing mellowness of the Venetian beauty. There was a bell-like lightness to its tenor voice, but it seemed to carry. And though it apparently had been lying around Hill's for several years, the instrument responded easily. Sophie concurred. Perhaps it would be more correct to say that she disliked the Montagnana, which typified to her the usual cellistic canons of sound—heavy and clumsy. She remembered the beautiful Amati that Munio played on in Vienna. That Kux instrument was the Feuermann family favorite.

Hill suggested that he take it to his London apartment for a day or two to try out in privacy—Feuermann had an upcoming performance with Sir Thomas Beecham and the Hallé Orchestra in the *Don Quixote* and the Schönberg-Monn Concerto. It might be a good test for the instrument.

But first Feuermann and Hill had to discuss the Strad in more detail. Hill would be willing to take the Montagnana in trade at its full price of £3500 ($17,500). The Strad was priced at £5000 ($25,000). But since Feuermann had been doing business with the English company, the price would be reduced £500 and the total exchange would cost Feuermann £1000 ($5,000). Terms could of course be arranged.

The cello was a beautiful, almost unmarked instrument and had had no major repair. It had a thick chestnut-red varnish, slightly worn at the left shoulder, and gave slight indication (as in the purfling) of Stradivarius' advanced age when he made it in 1730–31 (age eighty-six or eighty-seven). In answer to Feuermann's question of its relatively small size, Hill opined that cellos of the latest period in Stradivarius' life were probably made for lady players. The instruments made before 1700 were almost small double basses and usually had to be altered. Feuermann had once tried out a very large and beautiful Strad but had found it too awkward. His Tecchler had seemed wonderfully appropriate in size by contrast.

The cello itself had had an undistinguished history. It was first known in Paris in the 1860s. At this time it was owned by a Parisian amateur, a M. de Barrau, who apparently obtained it from the famous luthier and dealer Vuillaume. A few years later it came into the possession of the well-known French cellist Franchomme (b. Lille 1808, d. Paris 1884). At that time Franchomme owned the great Duport Strad (1711, named after the early nineteenth-century virtuoso cellist). He had purchased the cello in question for his son, who showed great talent. Unfortunately the boy died and Franchomme sold the cello through the firm of Gand and Bernardel to Ernest De Munck. This was about 1869–70. This gentleman was the son of another famous cellist, Francois De Munck. However he did have another modest claim to fame. Ernest was married to Carlotta Patti, sister of the famous Adelina. Together Carlotta and Ernest toured as a cello-voice team, both in Europe and the United States, settling eventually in London, where Ernest was principal cello teacher at the Guildhall School of Music. Shortly before he died in 1915, the instrument was sold to a student, a Mr. Herriot, from whom Hill obtained it. (Later Hill would write to Feuermann that De Munck sold it to a student named Gardner.) In the Hill book on Stradivarius, the cello is alternately described as the De Munck or Gardner Strad.

A bit of good luck intervened in these negotiations in the form of a proffered contract by English Columbia to record the Haydn D Major with Sir Malcolm Sargent. Feuermann decided at the last moment to substitute the Haydn for the Schönberg-Monn with Beecham and the Hallé and to use the Strad. It worked beautifully. Feuermann and Beecham got along famously. Beecham even proposed, too casually the cellist thought, an extended tour together. The reviews were favorable, considering Casals had played in London the same day, although Casals' reviews were far more reverential. Ibbs and Tillet had been quick enough to get a notification of the new cello into the reviewers' hands before the concert. The papers marveled at the easy transition. The contracts for the recording were signed the next day, November 25, 1935, and the recording session set for a day later. Feuermann had to be off for Paris and Italy before returning on December 16th to meet Eva and leave for the world tour.

Columbia had planned a one-day affair. Perhaps the morning would be sufficient, since the orchestral part was simple and Feuermann knew the piece inside and out. The usual Feuermann entourage of students was on hand at the studio, thus providing eyewitness for a story that went the circuit of English musical lore for several years. Sargent was stiff, typically English, and quietly insistent on taking his conductorial prerogatives.

Feuermann and the orchestra members were already in their places when Sargent came to the podium. The engineers were still setting up. There would naturally be time before the rehearsal ended and the recording began in earnest. The setting was casual, except perhaps for Sargent's businesslike attitude.

The orchestra, a pick-up group of professional London musicians, began playing the long introduction. At Sargent's cue to Feuermann to begin, there was silence. Sargent glanced questioningly at Feuermann's passive expression. He went back several phrases, began, and then—still no Feuermann. "Anything wrong, Mr. Feuermann?" ". . . Aren't you going to tune the orchestra?" Quickly a wailing oboe "A," then the rest of the group half-heartedly sounding in. Again the introduction . . . no Feuermann. "Well . . ." "They are not in tune . . . here." He blared out an "A" on his cello. The oboe and the rest quickly entered. Going back a few phrases, the conductor and orchestra began again.

Feuermann remained adamant and silent. Sargent was out of breath, a little angry at his German prima donna, and generally nonplused. What to do? Finally, from Feuermann, "have the violins play a D Major scale." No move from Sargent. The young upstart . . . Sargent was barely aware of Feuermann's reputation and at the same time protective of his own and the orchestra's dignity. Again Feuermann took the initiative and started playing a scale. By this time the Columbia producers and technicians were wildly gesticulating to Sargent to comply and get it over with. The whole affair was beginning to cost them production monies. Sargent said, "Everyone," and lowered his baton. The musicians did not respond. They had been insulted. Who did that impudent *"Bosch"* think he was? Finally a distant fluttering as a nonimplicated flute began the scale. Then the concertmaster. Finally a few others joined in, until most of the other unenthusiastic musicians were playing the scale. They knew that unless the recording session was completed they would not be paid. Also, they would want to be rehired. Columbia was not doing this recording for their benefit.

A moment later Feuermann picked himself up and said, "Well, Mr. Sargent, why don't you leave them here to practice up a bit more. Let's have some lunch first." With that he left the studio. As he entered the artists' room to put the Strad in its case, one of his students, Jane Cowan, accosted him. "What are you doing?" she whispered fearfully. "Sargent is very important. He is titled. You will be ostracized here." Feuermann made a disdainful gesture and then pointed wistfully and painfully towards the studio. Perhaps he had in his mind the memory of the Chicago Symphony or the New York Philharmonic, maybe even Beecham and the Hallé of the day before. How could Columbia have done this—a second-rate orchestra, perfunctory conducting. Yet, it did have to be finished today.

When Sargent appeared, a moment later, obviously ruffled and disconsolate, Feuermann greeted him with renewed ebullience. "Well, sir . . . your highness . . . lord . . . where shall we eat!"

The ultimate results of the recording were predictable. The orchestra sounds terribly ragged, almost like an improvisation. Feuermann's cello playing is classical in shape, extremely fluent technically and limpid in sound. The Strad had responded on all strings. The Haydn interpretation represented only the first phase of a new dimension in his playing and the Strad seemed to make it come forth with unbelievable ease and naturalness.

Still, at this stage of his career, newly married, without a secure musical base, Feuermann was hesitant to spend five thousand dollars on a new instrument. First, he did not have the money and second, he was afraid to make another mistake, as he now felt he had with the Montagnana.

There was time to think. Several concert commitments in France and Italy had to be fulfilled before he left for America. He returned the Strad to Hill, took back the Venetian cello and was off to the Continent to play and mull over his decision. A number of things bothered him about the negotiations. Hill had had the instrument for at least eight years. Why had he not shown him the Strad when he traded in the Tecchler? Hill knew he was looking for a smaller instrument. Also, he had heard so many bizarre stories of peculiar transmutations of instruments, great instruments of minor makers being rebaptized to fetch the enormous prices that only a name could qualify for. Was any business establishment, even one as reputable as Hill's, immune from this temptation? After all, an instrument guaranteed by Hill would never be questioned. They could create its venerable pedigree by fiat.

The story about Franchomme's buying a Strad for his young son was odd. Did not Franchomme own the Duport Strad to bequeath to the boy?

The instrument was first acquired from Vuillaume, that famous French genius of instrument making and dealing, who himself copied the masters with unbelievable fidelity and who had a reputation for sometimes dubious practices. It is said he imitated Paganini's great Guarneri so well that the violinist was at first fooled. Fritz Kreisler had Mischa Elman play on a Strad and then two del Jesu Guarneris that he owned. Elman found them equally beautiful. One of the Guarneris was this same Vuillaume copy.

Someone had also told Feuermann that the famous "Baudiot" Strad cello (1725) had a well-known copy by Vuillaume following it around. This added to the mystery of the Strad. Franchomme's daughter, who had inherited it, presumably claimed the cello as a Strad. She sold it through Gand and Bernardel to De Munck and not through Vuillaume, who was still alive then. Why would she not sell it back to Vuillaume? Since that time no great cellist had owned it or used it. Hill seemed inconsistent about the last person to own it.

Then there was the label, which was written "1710," oddly close to Franchomme's Duport (1711). Hill said that the label had been altered, as had most of Strad's cello labels, and that it was really one of the master's last instruments (1730–31). It was too small to be of that earlier "Duport" period.

In all, a mystery. Perhaps Feuermann felt a covert antagonism to the dealer. Possibly it was the deliciously high price exacted for the Montagnana, obtained in a day when Feuermann had the money and rosier expectations.* He should have been more restrained. Or perhaps it was Hill's paternalistic advice to the newlywed to "have a good marriage, by being reasonable." "That is, I am right?" was Feuermann's added interpretation.

Enough. The short Italian tour convinced him that he must try out the Strad over a more extended period. Hill's quickly replied to his letter. They would give him a year's trial, as with the Montagnana, which they would pick up, while delivering the Strad on board ship. In short they were as eager as Feuermann, or more so, to consummate the deal.

From December 1935 to March 1936, Feuermann concertized once more throughout the United States. The cello responded well, the audiences and the reviews were excellent. From April to June, Japan and the Orient were again to be conquered, only this time the scenario was confounded by the ever-inscrutable Japanese. The reviews were even

---

*Feuermann had a right to wonder, since in Hill's 1902 volume on Stradivarius, the cello is listed amongst a final group of celli made after the "Golden" period that ended in 1726. These celli, all made after 1730, were, with one mysterious exception, smaller instruments, e.g., 29½ inches rather than the 29⅞ or 29¹⁵/₁₆ of the "Golden" period (approximately 1704–1726). Hill surmises that they may have been partially designed by the Stradivarius sons, [and erroneously,] with Carlo Bergonzi's help. Not only might the De Munck cello not be the *last* completely made by Stradivarius himself, it may not even have been made for a lady player. Rather it could have been a final Stradivarius experiment!

more glorious than before. Witness the following critique by Motoo Otaguro in the *Asahi Shimbun* of April 25, 1936, which was entitled "I hear the king of the cellists, Feuermann. . . ."

> After a year and a half Feuermann has returned to Tokyo. The first cello performance was held on 23 April in Hibiya Hall. The program: Händel's Adagio and Allegro; Locatelli's Sonata; Brahms' Sonata; Beethoven's Variations; as well as Bruch, etc.
>
> Those who heard Feuermann for the first time in a year and a half say that he is still king of the cellists. His playing gives not the slightest indication of difficulty of technique. His masterful handling of technique lets us enjoy the music in its fullest substance. Moreover, he has a greater instrument this time. When I heard Feuermann earlier, the deep tones did not seem so sonorous to me. This time I could not confirm that [statement]; I have heard that Feuermann now owns a Stradivarius, and perhaps it was also due to his previous instrument. Sometimes his wonderful tones sound like the violin, at other times like the organ. His tone is perfectly clear and fine, broad and strong. Now (since Casals has grown old) we say that such a cellist as Feuermann is unique in the world.
>
> To write about Feuermann's accomplished technique is to fall short of the goal. However I must mention that Feuermann bowed extremely fast notes like little, fresh fish [sic]—for example, in the Sonata by Locatelli, "Allegro Assai." We can only say two words: divine accomplishment. We can only call it: magic. Now the splendid virtuoso Feuermann has a superb instrument; he has become the best virtuoso. He who wants to hear *real* music absolutely must hear Feuermann.

Unfortunately, the audiences were sparse and Strock was quite disappointed. The experience of showing Eva the wonders of this strange part of the world was enough to compensate Feuermann for the poor financial return. The explanation was that Feuermann had probably returned too soon to expect the "truly honored guest" treatment.

The summer months were spent, appropriately, in South America, during the winter musical season. Yet, since the tropics did not often lose their humid hold on the climate, even in winter, Feuermann felt the first twinges of bursitis in his right shoulder, and the Strad came unglued several times. Even Wolfgang Rebner, his new, sensitive, and accomplished accompanist, who had almost conquered his nervousness in the Orient, had several recurring bouts of "excitement" during concerts in Buenos Aires and Rio. The fall was completed in the United States (cello repaired by the master, Sacconi) and concluded with a farewell concert in New York on December 16 that "even satisfied Downes."

On board ship destined for Southampton, Feuermann had the time to rethink the year and his possible future with the cello. All doubts about the instrument had vanished. Even its incapacity to remain glued in humid climates did not concern him. Sacconi had had ample time to look it over and gave no signs of questioning its ancestry. Above all, Feuermann could feel something new in his playing, a freedom he could only attribute to the Strad.

In October while in New York, he had received permission to live in Switzerland and give master classes in Zurich, now to be his home. Even though the United States gave more promise of permanence, Eva's desire to remain in Europe would coincide with the teaching advantages there. For the moment he gave up a short and fitful romance with California and the chairmanship of the UCLA string department, which had been suggested to him during his stay there. The cult that was growing up around Schönberg both fascinated and repelled him. Yet the climate, the beautiful pure air, the flowers, the perpetual spring were unlike those of any other place he had ever visited. Even at full capacity, Carnegie Hall could not compete with Los Angeles. At least not in December.

In London, Feuermann put his plan into effect. He really did not take it seriously as a possibility, but he felt he must try it. The cello was returned to Hill and the Montagnana reclaimed. Neither Hill brother said a word. The arrangement had been for a year's trial. Apparently no concession was going to be made.

Feuermann left for Paris and a series of concerts in France and the Continent. In Paris, he spent several days working the Montagnana back into shape. Still no communication from Hill. As the evening of his inaugural concert approached, Feuermann gave in. He could hold out no longer. Diran Alexanian, the only cellist he really respected as a scholar of the instrument, was to be there. The Montagnana could no longer be his instrument. He could hear himself only on the Strad. He wired Hill to have it delivered to him in Paris.

This accomplished, Alfred Hill began to exercise his new advantage, demanding by return mail the special oak case that belonged to the Montagnana as well as payment of a delivery fee for the Strad. He finally relented in allowing Feuermann to pay the additional sum of money for the Strad in three widely-spaced payments, the cello to become fully his own in March of 1939, two years later.

We have no information about the present whereabouts of the Feuermann Montagnana. But there is an intriguing story of its history subsequent to its return to Hill's in London. For about three years the cello remained unsold. However early in the spring of 1940 it was sent to Paris. Apparently a purchaser had been located there in spite of the war. At that moment, however, the Germans broke through the French defenses and Paris and its environs were besieged and taken. The Montagnana disappeared. Since it had been sent by rail from Calais, and since the railroads had been viciously bombed by the German Stukas, it was assumed that it, too, had become a victim of war.

In 1945, as part of the general rehabilitation of France, the railroad yards outside of Paris were cleared up, burned-out freight cars hauled away, track replaced. In a remote corner of the yards, one isolated freight car, heretofore unnoticed and untouched, was inventoried. In it the Montagnana was discovered unharmed and in pristine condition, protected by the insulation in the car and the relative mildness of Parisian weather. It was one of those few miracles, a grateful restoration of a magnificent creation to a wounded civilization.

Feuermann had possession of the Strad for almost six years. He was increasingly amazed at its responsiveness, the manner in which it rose to its new musical challenges, how it even led him to pursue new possibilities.

In the years before 1936 he had striven for two goals representing, whether separately or together, aspects of the means for success—technical prowess and interpretive excellence. The almost-compulsive striving for these ends rendered the actual performance an anticlimax. Indeed, as is the case with so many instrumental artists, there existed an almost hostile attitude towards performance and audience and, of course, critic.

When the ultimate hurdles had been overcome and it became evident that his goals had been achieved and recognized, even in New York, Feuermann gradually became aware that his future lay more in external circumstance than in his own achievement. Even Casals, as much as Feuermann feared the end of the Catalonian's retirement and his active competition, did not loom as such an awesome figure. In many ways he knew himself to be the better.

In October of 1937 he would listen with Sophie and George Szell in Prague to the preliminary releases of the old master's Dvořák recording and wistfully wish that he could relax more so that he, too, could bring out the nuances Casals was so skilled in expressing. But as his private life became ever more public, as he had less and less time to live in the inner world every creative artist needs, the Strad substituted its hidden musical resources. It was malleable and gave him plenty of time to work a phrase. The Strad played so easily and limpidly, yet there were reserves, at times almost too much for its own inner beauty, as in the Stokowski recording of the *Schelomo*.

The cello was a perfect wife, since it helped him see himself and test himself, set new challenges. The instrument gradually "became" Feuermann, an alter ego. Through it he now became willing to give of himself; he was less disposed to hide his emotions. As it was, he would write to Eva while on tour to relate a factor he did not fully understand. The mixture of awe, respect, and coldness in his audiences had disappeared. "Perhaps," he would note, "it is because I enjoy playing more. It is fun and the audience senses it."

How is it that an almost symbiotic relationship can develop between a player and an instrument that might have been made two hundred years earlier? It is rare that one great instrument will speak equally well to more than one great instrumentalist. Fritz Kreisler must have made a small fortune purchasing, then selling, his various "ex-Kreisler" masterpieces. He was rare in that he was both promiscuous and equally successful in his various affairs with a score of great violins. On the other hand old Casals had been faithful for well over a half century to his battered but beautiful Gofriller. Piatigorsky finally found his Batta Strad (1714). We know the hold that the Guarneri del Jesu "Cannon" (1742) had on Paganini. It was the key to his wizardry and his consequent magical hold on the audiences. Eventually it was retired to a glass case in the Genoa town hall. Only two men have since played on it: Sivori, Paganini's only student, and Bronislaw Huberman.

There have been many such love affairs between a musician and his instrument. They represent an indelible molding or intertwining of personalities, a relationship that is difficult to disentangle or dissolve in subsequent assignations. Perhaps this is the reason many a great instrument has been inexplicably rejected by an artist. Certainly the realization of the possibilities of the De Munck Strad in Feuermann's hands after two hundred and five years of dormancy was unique.

9

TO AMERICA

Essex House was not the worst place to do one's waiting. An ample room in which one could meet people, practice, and live modestly for short periods of time cost Feuermann only thirty-five dollars per week. This was in February, 1938. For almost a week he had been in a state of virtual immobilization. True, his boon companion Gerald Warburg was pleasant enough, but the events presumably taking place so many thousands of miles away in Zurich where Eva awaited the momentary birth of their first child and the father's attendant anxieties were almost impossible to endure.

They spent most of the vigil in the ample lobbies of the hotel, where there were many pleasant encounters. Feuermann's cello repertoire series of four concerts with Leon Barzin and the National Orchestral Association began February 5. The first two concerts had been great successes. The reviews more than made up for a half-empty Carnegie Hall. "Too much cello for one evening, even with Feuermann," one of the managers had commented. For the first, Feuermann had played the K. P. E. Bach and the Haydn concertos, and Bloch's *Schelomo*. The reviews had been great and he had not even minded the "detestable" *Schelomo*, so beautifully had Barzin conducted. In fact the rest of the series looked as if it might be sold out, so that he could report favorably on what had been an important career gamble.

On the afternoon in question Gasparo Cassado and Andre Segovia had wandered by, deeply engaged in a heated discussion, Latin style. Cassado, who had seemed on the defensive, spotted Feuermann and Warburg and, with relief, tried to break off the debate. At the moment, Feuermann was feeling very good about his own professional status and in spite of his anxiety about Eva was more than anxious to renew his friendship with the Spanish cellist. Cassado, for his part, seemed to be attempting to disentangle himself from Segovia. He protested to Feuermann, with a gesture in Segovia's direction, that he had barely touched the cello in the three days since his trio concert had been given, and the next was still weeks away. The distraught guitarist had apparently been unable to rest or study because of incessant cello practicing from an adjacent room. He had an important recital in a day or so and the delicate guitar was no competition for the brawny cello. He would not accept Cassado's disclaimer.

Feuermann was about to comment, but broke off and motioned to his friends the need to depart. He could barely restrain his laughter, since it was he who was the culprit. He had been practicing literally morning, noon, and night for his concert series, for it included thirteen major works for his instrument. As he headed out the doors of the Essex House towards the NBC Concerts office, he saw Segovia renew his attack on the hapless Cassado.

At NBC he hurried to take a cablegram that one of the secretaries was waving at him. It was a girl and Eva was fine. They had agreed to name her Monica. Szymon Goldberg, who was also picking up mail, proposed a drink and they all adjourned to a restaurant. It was as if a new horizon had opened up for the cellist. America seemed more inviting than ever.

Siegfried Hearst of the concert bureau had urged him to switch his main base of operation to the United States and to concertize and teach only part of the year in Europe. In the long run, Hearst argued, America held out more promise. Feuermann was now more inclined to this view than before. When Eva and he had returned to England early in 1937 for a tour of the British Isles, he had been met with relative coolness. Not only were the audiences middling, but Ibbs and Tillet rarely placed notices in the newspapers to announce his forthcoming appearances. Build up slowly, he had been urged, take your time, British audiences need to be coaxed gradually. But then they are faithful. They cited the case of Piatigorsky to him as proof of their wisdom. Piatigorsky had attempted to take England by "bravura storm" the year before and had wound up the present season with only one recital.

France and Italy were available for concertizing, but the money was poor. The only compensation for his French tour, an artistic success of special distinction, aided by his finally reclaimed Strad, was the long and glowing review of Diran Alexanian, who had finally come around to recognizing him. But more than that, Alexanian in his review noted, with an insight commanded by all too few cellists or reviewers, that Feuermann's playing had truly evolved over the years to a new level of artistic maturity.

The Cello—Feuermann

When I met Feuermann about twelve years ago, he had come to us from Germany, enveloped with the reputation of a technician with no fear of the cello, something like a devil-may-care driver who tried now and again on a Florida beach to break his own racing record. . . . Actually [his playing] was more agreeable and aesthetic . . . one would admire Feuermann as a cellistic meteor, without taking into account his tenderness (evident despite a curtain of irony which modestly envelops him) nor his fear of bad taste which made him way back then defer the adoption of a highly inflected style. This prudence was the basis of my great admiration for him.

Later I was strongly deceived. [His playing] brought me face to face with a Feuermann whose taste seemed to flaunt a contempt for all that I had hoped from his extraordinary faculties. As for the technical aspect . . . it seemed to me like an indisputable regression. With a certain bitterness I followed the reactions of the audience, always ready to set the value of a performance at the level of the performer's reputation. What made me saddest was to think that the delirious ignorance of a mass of admirers was risking the annihilation of the conscience and the need for perfection of an artist in whom I believed.

But the great day of vindication is here. The recital on March 17, 1937 gave me considerable proof that Feuermann certainly was what I thought: a man of mature talent, of impeccable technique, of a subtle sense of music. I have not often savored such a treat. A whole evening without a wrong note, without a disturbance in the logic of expression, without superfluousness; a whole evening when I was not for the record bored, when I desired nothing but what was presented.

Thus in May of 1937, when Columbia wrote him in Zurich about the plans for a new series of records, Feuermann was especially enthusiastic. Myra Hess had consented to play the Beethoven A Major, op. 69 Sonata with him. Gerald Moore had been secured for the musically less-demanding Schubert *Arpeggione*. This arrangement was a far cry from the disastrous orchestra that Columbia had conjured up two years earlier for the Haydn concerto.

Feuermann drove nonstop from Zurich to Calais (350 miles) that June day. He wanted to be away from Zurich and his students as little as possible. There was no doubt in his mind that if Europe had to be his home, Zurich was the most enjoyable place to plead genteel poverty. Myra Hess was waiting and almost immediately they began their brief rehearsal prelude to the record cutting. To his utter embarrassment, Feuermann flopped. One error after another broke the rhythm of their warm-up. Miss Hess was a paragon of patience, never questioning the difficulties that this supreme virtuoso was having. Feuermann finally gave it up. While he was certainly not ancient at thirty-four, he was not the Berlin youngster who could flip off feats like this with almost weekly regularity, at a less-conspicuous musical loss.

The next day the rehearsal and recordings of the Beethoven, the Schubert, and the Weber Andante and Variations went well. Subtle advances in his style are represented in these recordings. In the Beethoven, one notes, as in the earlier Haydn, the remarkable stylistic control. The

Stradivarius cello is perhaps more supple, beautifully able to reflect the restraint that Feuermann intends, yet giving smoothly and richly. It is a wonderful collaboration.

The Schubert shows the Feuermann vibrato in its newer function as a medium of expressivity. In a sense it represents Feuermann's answer to those critics who complained of his stodginess and formalism. He would not relent and commit the traditional romantic tricks of "plushing up" the music. Within the classic design of Schubert's music a refined, rapidly undulating vibrato, combined with restrained yet beautiful slides, are his only concession to emotion. One can hear the uncanny shimmer with which he invests all his moving notes. No note is ever dead, no matter how fast it is played. Authorities have noted that later on in actual performance Feuermann would consent to be freer in his phrasing and rhythm. But in June of 1937 he was not yet ready to put these feelings on discs.

Eva and Munio returned to Zurich late at night. The cellist insisted on driving to the *pension* where his students were garrisoned. He gave lessons twice a week. He would remind them of their appointments and announce his return. Feuermann would also need them for afternoon tennis. He blared his auto horn in front of the house until a light showed in John Shinebourne's room and a face peered out. Content, Feuermann roared off, home.

Feuermann was still sincerely questioning where he should base himself as late as winter, 1938. With the exception of sister Rosa and her husband Adolph Hoenigsberg, who were in Palestine (he was playing in Huberman's orchestra), Feuermann's own family was still in Vienna. As much as he disliked returning to Vienna he had still, until recently, considered the Weimarstrasse address of his parents as his home. Most of Eva's relatives still lived in Germany, despite the dark events that occurred daily.

As far as his own career was concerned, America seemed like a land of future possibilities, not present reality. He had applied for an entrance visa for Eva and himself in the event the situation in Germany deteriorated. He would constantly reassure Eva in his letters that war would not come, at least not in the foreseeable future. But he remembered a fearful childhood of war-incurred privations, even if she was too young to recall them. Feuermann had no real sense of assurance that it could not happen again.

The United States was exciting in 1938. In between the concerts of his series with Barzin and the National Orchestral Association, he had several engagements in Texas and Indiana, as well as in the east. He could understand the universal European involvement with music. But here, in the wildest sections of this vast country, music seemed as much a passion as in New York or Philadelphia.

Corpus Christi was an example. He was met in Houston by a young singer named Joseph Burger who had driven the two hundred fifty miles to transport him back and forth to save Feuermann the bus trip. This meant a total trip of one thousand miles for this music lover. Corpus Christi, then a town of forty-two thousand, was in the midst of a small boom. (Oil had been discovered in the area several years earlier.)

Amidst the boots and cowboy hats nine hundred people held subscriptions to the concert series. The climate seemed tropical to Feuermann, like Central America. His cello sounded like an oboe. He had, in this season of 1937–38, only seven concerts on tour. Yet, it was a happy and exciting time. This was his first season on his own, so to speak, for it was contracted without the hoopla of a world tour to attract the various concert managements. Even if the compensation did not equal his growing fame, the portents for the future certainly seemed good. Piatigorsky, Cassado, et al. were behind him. Only Casals was a challenge, and he was getting old. His involvement in the Spanish Civil War made his transposition to the United States doubtful.

The question was, could a cellist ever command the audiences of a Heifetz? Frequent comparisons to the violinist pleased him, but could they ever get him a contract for forty thousand dollars to make a film as Heifetz had had? Certainly the rumors that the Menuhins had invested in publicity, in records and concerts for their son's career indicated expectations of a substantial nature. This contrasted with the sober outlook for both Artur Schnabel, who had as few concerts as Feuermann himself, and Erica Morini, despite the great success of her American debut.

Schnabel, however, was not daunted, so why should he be? The pianist stubbornly retained his "Hochschule" repertoire, remained charming, and talked a mile a minute. Schnabel's good humor even extended to Feuermann, in spite of the latter's constant, semisarcastic referral to him as the "Rebe" (Rabbi). Their plans for a series of trio recordings, which Feuermann had been urging for several years, now seemed feasible. Both Huberman and Schnabel considered their young upstart cellist of sufficient status. Feuermann on his part now had some doubts about his colleagues. He was feeling his oats. Recordings would certainly help his present situation, though, so he was far from throwing cold water on the plans.

It may seem odd from a perspective of forty years that an artist considered on a par with Heifetz, Milstein, and Casals would have to calculate with such care where he could best make a living, at the same time harmonizing these needs with cultural background, lifestyle, and musical development. It should be remembered—and this was often reiterated to Feuermann by those who did remember—that even the great Casals in earlier years had often played to half-empty halls. This was the fate of being a cellist in a day when the glamor of the instrument was only half-appreciated.

Feuermann would often nag at Hearst of NBC Concerts as to why they could not do better than seven or eight concerts a year on tour (he was booked for eight in 1938–39). Hearst would only shrug his shoulders and say, "You may be a great virtuoso, but you are only a cellist." Feuermann would reply in despair to Eva, "Why don't they consider me as an artist? Does it matter what instrument I play?" One day his lawyer, Al Blume, called him up, puffing with pride and joy. He had the reviews from one of Feuermann's New York appearances. The reviewer had noted that Feuermann's appearance had been greeted with far greater enthusiasm by the tough New York audience—more curtain calls and encores—than even Heifetz. Feuermann's laconic reply was that he would appreciate "less roaring and more dollars."

The musician was not being particularly mercenary. In this period, 1936 to 1938, when he was gradually being accepted into the musical elect, his great concern was a combination of career advancement, a steady home life with Eva, and the means by which to secure these ends. Heretofore he had not considered his dethronement from Berlin especially tragic economically. He was alone and carefree, and personal material things except for his cello and a car meant nothing.

Now he had mounting responsibilities. First, a wife and a child. Soon a mother-in-law bereft of her munificent lifestyle; parents and a brother fleeing their Vienna home to Palestine. Finally, at the end of 1938, Sophie and her husband Harry Braun arrived in the United States, penniless. Feuermann wanted to help them out, too, perhaps by using Sophie as an accompanist, in spite of other contractual arrangements with his concert management.

His letters during this period are full of calculations, not only with regard to the bare minimum economic needs but also how he could improve their life to make it at least an approximation of the old. There is even some chagrin that an artist with a reputation should have to scrape away (literally) at making a living. In one letter to Eva he calculates that the loss of Germany meant a loss of 60 percent of his concerts. The one-third that remained in Britain, France, Italy, and the rest of Europe might be increased if he were to accept every minor engagement and really worked at it. This would mean only a bare living. For the rest, a world or American tour would be necessary. This would mean being separated from Eva for almost half the year, especially painful since the baby had come.

A future where one could hope to settle down and live a normal family life and study one's art in a sequestered, calm atmosphere was apparently not possible. It is understandable that, during that traumatic summer of 1938, he had cause to inquire of Toscanini as to the possibility of a first chair in the NBC Symphony Orchestra.

The 40 percent that he calculated from concertizing in America loomed larger in his mind. Certainly the number of students seeking to study with him in America was equal to the number of students he had in Europe.

The Mannes School had recently inquired about Feuermann's giving a lecture course on the cello. Various recitals, such as with the New Friends of Music or the National Orchestral Association, Bagby's Waldorf Astoria musicales, added small but important fees. There was an invitation from the General Motors Hour to solo, and he had several other radio or film opportunities (he later played for Bing Crosby and Bob Burns) that paid excellent fees. On several occasions he had played chamber music with Adolph Busch, Jascha Heifetz, Milstein, and others. There were recording opportunities here that might even be better than Huberman-Schnabel.

Even more important, there were few musicians left in Europe. Men like Heifetz, Rudolf Serkin, Joseph Szigeti, and Artur Rubinstein were now Americans. The competition was unbelievably spectacular. Being near the top helped. It caused one to strive for the best. Several times Feuermann rationalized this state of affairs: "Too much money is nonsense—to strive, have a name, to care, to fight—that gives a stimulus. But too much stimulus has the opposite effect."

March of 1938 had some twists for Feuermann's life. On one hand, it concluded the cycle with the National Orchestral Association, a cycle that was met with wonderment on the part of the music critics and the public. It was an unusual and heroic feat that was musically legitimate as well. The worst afternoon had been the second concert, February 19, the same day as Monica's birth. Feuermann played the Boccherini B$\flat$, the Schumann A minor, the fiendishly difficult Schönberg-Monn, and the Tschaikovsky *Rococo Variations*. At the conclusion of the Schönberg, he felt dead—a limp rag. How he completed the variations, which he had never liked, he did not remember. But even this visceral performance seemed to have pleased the critics.

The other event in March took place while he was on his way west to play with Fabian Sevitsky and the Indianapolis Symphony. The news wires reported the *Anschluss* in Austria and Hitler's takeover. He was desperate about his family, yet helpless to do anything. More than that, all the hopes he had built up about Europe, in the relative calm of the last few years, evaporated. He wrote back to Zurich, "This week is the worst in my life—to see the calm of the Midwest at the same time as one sees the foundation of one's family collapsing—is terrible."

The performance in Indianapolis was a disaster. He had no respect for the conductor, and thus gave him the "Feuermann treatment," forcing him practically to dance on the podium to stay with the soloist. His student, Saidenberg, was dismayed, when he heard the report back in New York. He protested, "How are you ever going to build up a career if you don't cater to these people? They have the power of life or death for your career." Feuermann knew very well that this was true. "I can't help myself," was his muttered half-apology. A few weeks later the engage-

ment with Indianapolis was renewed for the next year. When he met
Saidenberg, he waved the telegram in front of his face merrily. "See," he
grinned.

In late April he was back in Zurich. The takeover in Austria had thus far
been relatively bloodless and communication had been maintained with
his parents. The happiness he had in seeing his infant daughter and wife
once more, the enthusiasm of his students, and a truly fantastic success in
London on May 23 with Toscanini and the B.B.C. symphony in the *Don
Quixote* of Strauss perked up his hopes for Europe. The critics for once
were simply delighted. He had never gotten such a response before. And
just as encouraging, the engagements for his February, 1939, return to
England were numerous.

However, it all came too late. He remembered how a year earlier he had
encountered the conductor Knappertsbusch on a train bound for Vienna.
Knappertsbusch was one of those acceptable to the Nazi regime and had
stayed behind to benefit from the exodus of non-Aryan musicians. As
much as Feuermann had hated such "acceptable" artists, especially when
they did not speak up in defense of their colleagues, he had to test his
liberation from the past by approaching Knappertsbusch.

The conductor was at first reticent, but finally broke down in a torrent
of words. It was pathetic. He did not attempt to justify his present status.
He merely shrugged his shoulders to implicate his human frailties. On the
other hand he tried to ingratiate himself with the cellist. "You are first,
Munio, first in the world. There is no one who now competes with you."
He pleaded for a joint performance in Vienna with the Philharmonic
during one of the cellist's trips there. Feuermann was noncommittal. He
could not lend himself to such a betrayal of his brethren. In fact, he had
earlier turned down an invitation by William Steinberg, still conductor in
Frankfurt (possibly an all-Jewish Orchestra) in 1936. Still using a German
passport, at least to pass through Germany, he had seen Berlin for the last
time on a gray, rainy spring morning in 1937. It seemed to have taken on
the coloration of Nazidom.

He and Eva now awaited their U.S. entrance visas. When they did
arrive, it was in the midst of the horror with Sigmund in Vienna. It was too
late even to try to get the elder Feuermanns to America. Munio was
waiting in Zurich for Washington to act on his behalf; Oma was now in
England. Only Huberman was available. Huberman, a fading violinist to
some, a god to many others, loyal, administratively able, seemed to be
their last hope in a crumbling world.

Feuermann wrote to him in desperation, hoping that he could get the
family a quick entrance to Palestine. Sigmund would need a job, if not as a
conductor or concertmaster, as Munio had suggested, no doubt at the
prodding of his brother, then perhaps as a section violinist.

Huberman completed his miracle and the Feuermanns were whisked out of Vienna in September. In early October the Emanuel Feuermanns left for New York. In November they took out their first citizenship papers.

Stradivarius Cello

10

MASTERY

While the problem of the appearance and nature of genius in general will probably always remain a psychological mystery, it nevertheless invites curiosity and demands scrutiny. To the outsider it is exciting to see genius suddenly burst forth, seemingly without preparation. The public delights in hearing about miracles and the "odd" people who have perpetrated them. But in reality it is unusual for genius to appear suddenly. Usually and more fascinatingly it appears so gradually that we are hardly aware of its coming. Then when it is in full flower we have great difficulty in understanding and accepting its mundane and familiar presence.

There is in all likelihood a premonition or warning that it is in the bud. Good luck in the process of maturation and growth and its inner necessity will overcome the inevitable external vicissitudes. Genius will persist in its development while lesser talents will stagnate and decay. Thus it flowers and asserts itself in full form. It must yet be recognized by the prescient, its existence enunciated. After all, the genius still competes as a mortal. His vision tears loose the anchor of fixed expectations and skepticism. Too often the recognition that indeed a new mark has been set has to await his departure from the scene.

So it was with Emanuel Feuermann. Although the full fruition of his talent was not to be granted, the final few years of his life brought forth the first stage in his maturity. At the least it was a substantial sample of the potential impact of his art. Still it was the result of years of gestation. A prodigal talent in his teens, he had been nourished from childhood by unique family circumstances. In early maturity, he achieved a niche amongst his peers that represented the acme of achievement in his art. Later, his expulsion from the Hochschule proved to be an unexpectedly benign stroke of fate. Too much security, fun, and comfort in this sine-cure at too early a stage in his development could have meant the foreshortening of his development.

For four years he suffered the fate of a wandering Jew and musician in search of a haven in a disintegrating world. He had no choice but to travel, perform, and mature—to expend his energies without any fixed pattern of life or mind, to concentrate solely on his art. In the process he had acquired his Stradivarius.

His unflagging drive, his congenital optimism reaffirmed that he was still Maier Feuermann's son. Maier may have by now emotionally disowned him. The old man had pinned all his hopes on the elder boy, Sigmund, in the beginning the true prodigy. Now that Sigmund had faltered, Munio's success seemed to be only a perverse flouting of parental authority. And indeed loyalty necessitated, in Maier's oft-repeated words, "You have to stick to the weaker one."

The home Feuermann found in the United States in the fall of 1938 brought his search to an end and allowed him to begin to glean more fully the product of his long hegira. It was not really a simple task, since America added its own peculiar complications. His responsibilities grew enormously. There was a beautiful young wife and an infant daughter to settle and support. His aging parents on their way to Palestine could not be sloughed off from afar. A mother-in-law now awaited entry into the United States. She would need comfort and support, moral if not financial.

It was not all onerous. The American style of cultural life made the concert artist a quasi-entrepreneur. There was less of the nestling closeness of Europe. While less intimate, less nurturing, it was perhaps more exciting as it made one feel more of a citizen, an equal in life too. The weeks and months went by with a dazzling mix of activities. The innumerable negotiations for all sorts of engagements, travel, publicity, records, radio, students. Later, managing Oma Reifenberg's financial affairs would add its own fascinating dimension. America was certainly not lucrative as yet for Feuermann. But the possibilities demanded the necessary exploratory effort.

These complications did not necessarily have the deleterious effect one might expect on his art. Feuermann did not react to the temptations that a mass audience might have provided. His playing did not become shallow or routine. The vision he carried with him was composed of half-achieved and as yet unrealized perceptions. The latter seemed now to be composed of natural possibilities, without the inhibiting agonies of an unknown future staring him in the face. He needed the concentration, the effort to achieve the ease, malleability, and freedom he had been searching for.

In earlier years there had been complaints about the small sound that issued from his monstrous Tecchler as well as the throaty Montagnana. There was little of the lushness that audiences expected from cellists. Feuermann himself seemed to play stiffly and formally. His interpretations were professionally correct. Feuermann refused to resort to "Kitsch," even at the price of not ingratiating himself with audiences. He wanted to be an artist in the old and highest sense. Rather lose popularity in the short run but gain the credit of colleagues and those critics whose knowledge one could respect. Whatever one did had to come from within. And for many years that fluid, relaxed persuasiveness that comes from spontaneous confidence was simply not part of his personality.

It did not matter now if he had one bad night. "I was lousy tonight—too excited," he once commented to a friend. Next time he would be better; he had learned something. And sure enough his vibrato became freer, subject to the subtlest shadings. Each finger was emancipated from the other to create independently its own texture. His breathing relaxed, even if his cheeks puckered with tension. The setting and poising for shifts no longer needed to be hurried. There seemed much more time to move around the cello once the internal rhythms were calmed and subjected to the mind. The bow held rigidly and powerfully between forefinger and thumb bent to his will.

While he never played flawlessly—he lived dangerously on the cello— the small mishaps were an inconsequential price to pay for the pristine clarity of attacks and the total congruence between intention and realization. His friend Heifetz, the one string player to approach most closely Feuermann's technical abilities (Kreisler was his ideal for sound and style), gained his demonic physical control and passionate spontaneity at the price of a limited, if sensual, tonal range. Heifetz would not tolerate the few imperfections that Feuermann knew were the price of being mortal.

When NBC Artists offered to sign him to an exclusive management contract, one of the lures was that the company would assign Franz Rupp to be his accompanist. Rupp was in the class of Gerald Moore, a brilliant and seasoned pianist, who for a number of years played with Kreisler and recorded the Beethoven sonatas with the violinist. Rupp was to be the most experienced of the pianists to play regularly with Feuermann. In addition he was an ebullient and engaging person. They had a fine, a more nearly equal working arrangement (especially in terms of kidding each other) than Feuermann had had with the other pianists, Sophie Feuermann excepted. Munio considered Sophie to be in a special class. Of that we shall speak briefly later.

Rupp stayed with Feuermann for most of his American years. However for the season 1941–42, Sol Hurok offered Rupp a splendid contract to accompany Marian Anderson, who had recently made a dramatic impact on the concert public. NBC could not match it. Feuermann was simply not getting enough concerts to come anywhere near Miss Anderson. Albert Hirsch, also a fine pianist, was Feuermann's last accompanist. Feuermann always took a certain amount of fatherly pride in giving his accompanists—they made pitifully little—an opportunity to get the requisite experience to further their careers.

Publicity photo for N.B.C. Concert Service, 1938.

Those years with Rupp, traveling about the country for an average of a dozen recital engagements per year, were the years of fulfillment. Each concert, because there were few in number, meant a great deal to the cellist and he prepared for them with a calm seriousness. He would often study the music away from the cello—on the train, or in the hotel. At other times he would take along possible additions to his repertoire and go over the music mentally. He was fascinated with history, musical and other; he enjoyed it in an amateur way. Occasionally he had along a volume of Grove's dictionary or a copy of Burckhardt's *The Civilization of the Renaissance in Italy.*

He and Rupp would arrive in a new town and settle into a hotel. Feuermann would take out the cello for a few minutes of careful warm up—scales, arpeggios, the opening phrases of a Beethoven sonata, perhaps one of the works on the program at half-speed, and of course the bow, spicato, staccato scales. Rupp would often come to the room to fetch him for lunch. He could never believe it was possible for a cello to issue such crystalline, diamondlike sounds. If he had been angry about a Feuermann remark, it evaporated as he watched the cellist spin out those sounds with such zest, yet refinement. The instrument was never attacked—raped, as other cellists were wont to do in their attempts to gain control. There was love, and no one could be angry with a man possessed of such a spirit.

Feuermann always scouted out the dimensions of each town until he found a movie. Movies calmed his nerves and put his mind off the performance for a few hours. After the concert there was invariably a frenetic flurry in their dressing room as Rupp and Feuermann attempted to reorder the chaos prior to the entrance of the well-wishers. The cellist probably could have used a traveling housekeeper.

Feuermann, like everyone else, had many faces. To the public, his visitors in the artist room, he was charming, wise-cracking, and gay—in short, European and *galant.* This was not merely a professional facade meant to stimulate reengagements. He enjoyed meeting and being with new people. On the job with fellow musicians there was another side. He never put himself on another level—as, for instance, above them. This feeling of naturalness he put to use in working off enormous amounts of pent-up energy. The Feuermann anecdotes are legion. Whenever he played with orchestra, he left memories that persisted indelibly for a generation: he would sometimes come out before the conductor and hide in the back of the cello section while the conductor went through agonies worrying where the soloist was as he warmed up the orchestra. At other times he would arrange a stunt with the conductor, whereby the cellist would make a spot on the fingerboard with a piece of chalk. During the rehearsal his left hand would suddenly become "disabled" and the conductor would swoop to the rescue, depressing the string, while cellist, his left hand dangling helplessly, would bow fortissimo to the shouted delight of the musicians.

At the recording session with the Philadelphia Orchestra for *Don Quixote*, a passage where Feuermann was to enter on a high *F*, joined by the trombones a fraction later, did not work. When this happened twice and even Eugene Ormandy was unsure how to proceed, Feuermann called out in a mock-pleading voice, "Please give me a piece of chalk so I can mark where the note is." The tension was dissolved and the recording went forward.

The series with the National Orchestral Association was especially rife with Feuermann tricks. During one rehearsal the orchestra was playing the introduction to one of the concerti, perhaps the Haydn. Feuermann was presumably backstage preparing to come forth. When he did, it was at the appropriate entrance. He walked forward, cello tucked between jaw and left shoulder, playing his solo entrance, etc.

In the early years of their marriage it was difficult for Eva to reconcile the public and private poles of his personality and she would protest some of his antics. She did not want people to think he was a clown. Feuermann would wave her protests away. "What does it matter what they think, we know who we are."

The breakthrough Feuermann realized in these culminating years of his life is difficult to describe. At the time he was regularly concertizing it would seem the air was filled with literally a host of great string instrumentalists. The zenith of this art form was being approached and it was difficult then to disentangle from the various esthetic canons, where taste and personal expectations left off and a new canon of artistry began.

Our ears are not enough. Critical understanding, indeed cognition, is necessary. But this could come fully only with time, when our old favorites have passed on and we can rise beyond sentimentality and personal identification and finally examine where the art form has gone.

The peaks of Feuermann and Heifetz have not been approached. On the other hand, their example has lifted the general state of the art to an unbelievably high level. The irony of those years is that the cellist was making artistic history to, often, half-empty auditoriums. Those who loved his art, however, were fanatically loyal and have persisted in spite of the turn of events that have given Pablo Casals so great a longevity and have elevated him to the position of a cultural hero. To Feuermann, Casals was ever the old man whom he was in process of dethroning. To be sure, Feuermann never publicly described their relationship in those terms.

The memories of this diminishing and devoted segment of music lovers and professionals have, inevitably, faded. A new generation is born and new critical problems arise unique to no other area of endeavor. How can one communicate the achievements of a Feuermann or any of the other half dozen or so immortals of this century?

The statistical achievements of great sports figures cannot be extrapolated into art. Even musical composition cannot stand without the performer. True, a trained musician can read a score and translate the symbols into static sound images. Or else, with even a mediocre recreation of the music one can, with the score at least, approximate a modicum of auditory understanding of a Beethoven or Brahms. But in the end great music can only live again through the performer, the interpreter, the living link between past and present.

Thus it is that giants of performance in the eighteenth and nineteenth centuries, in consummating the musical intentions of composers of their own era, stimulated the advance of instrumental art into ours, yet themselves subsequently faded into the historical background. When they were both great performers and composers, it is the latter skill that has taken on historical importance.

In the nineteenth century, Paganini truly revolutionized the art of violin playing and in turn influenced the course of musical composition for generations. He certainly was one of the most important musical figures of his time. The music he left behind was fiendishly demanding, unique for his day. Today, virtually all violinists in major symphony orchestras can toss off his caprices. But the creative genius of Paganini is certainly far broader than just the music he left behind. The possibilities that Paganini saw in that little box of wood were given life in the enormous expressive and technical advances in music written for stringed instruments since then. Yet all that remains of his presence, besides his compositions, are a few handbills announcing his concerts, the only testimony to his conquest of Europe in those early decades of the last century.

While we must regret the gap that separates us from other performers such as cellist Duport, pianist Liszt, and violinist Joseph Joachim, we must be thankful that there is a recorded link, as deficient as it may be, that allows us to follow the evolution of Feuermann's art through to its final florescence between 1938 and 1942.

A series of major commercial and live performances captured on records give evidence of this maturity. In chronological order they are:

(1) R. Strauss: *Don Quixote,* Toscanini and the NBC Symphony, live radio broadcast, October 22, 1938.
(2) Reger: *Suite for Cello Alone,* Columbia Records (London), February 1939.
(3) Brahms: *Double Concerto,* with Jascha Heifetz, Ormandy and the Philadelphia Orchestra (Victor Records), December, 1939.
(4) Reicha and Dvořák concertos, National Orchestral Association with L. Barzin (live amateur recording), January 28, 1940.

(5) Strauss: *Don Quixote,* Ormandy, with the Philadelphia Orchestra (Victor), early March 1940.

(6) Bloch: *Schelomo,* Stokowski and the Philadelphia Orchestra (Victor), late March 1940.

(7) D'Albert: *Concerto,* Barzin and the National Orchestral Association (live amateur recording), April 27, 1940.

(8) Trios (three piano and two string) with Heifetz, Rubinstein, Primrose (Victor), August and September, 1941.

(9) Bloch: *Schelomo,* Dvořák: *Rondo, Waldesruhe,* Barzin and the National Orchestral Association (live amateur recording), November 10, 1941.

Note: The Mendelssohn *Sonata* with Rupp (late 1939) and Beethoven *Duo* with Primrose (August, 1941) were both rejected by Feuermann (Victor may have had doubts about technical standards of the Mendelssohn). They were brought out only after his death.

The *Don Quixote* performance with Toscanini was an attempt by Feuermann to repeat his belated success in London, before the American radio public. Feuermann had some trepidation about Toscanini, hoping the Maestro would be gentle with him, now that he was on home ground with his own orchestra. The prior May, Toscanini had replaced the trumpet player of the B.B.C. Symphony with a clarinetist for a performance of the second Brandenburg Concerto. Toscanini was not getting what he wanted in terms of free sound in the upper registers of the trumpet. This had caused a stir, the British critics going out of their way to rationalize the change and assuage the slight to the reputation of the well-known trumpeter, Ernest Hall.

The New York critics were also quite happy with the NBC *Don Quixote.* It was a typically exciting and sharply etched Toscanini performance. Lawrence Gilman was especially ecstatic at the collaboration of cellist and orchestra. Feuermann had a personally easy time with the old Italian, who had taken a liking to him in spite of the latter's youthful slump in Berlin.

But the Maestro's respect for the cellist did not cause him to relax his grip on the pacing of the piece. Feuermann had difficulty breathing life into the character of the knight of soulful countenance. From the evidence as given in a "retouched" broadcast by NBC, which still does not compensate for the deficiencies of studio 8A and the poor placing of the mikes, the performance is one of the least impressive by Feuermann. Some of Toscanini's effects are wondrous, the orchestral imitation of a flock of bleating sheep in one of the scenes being unbelievably real. The drive of the piece is typical of the Maestro. It is, however, not evocative of the more poetic qualities of the tone poem.

Feuermann sounds pushed throughout. His own nerves, since this was his debut as a novice American, did not allow him to relax, given the constant push of the conductor. There are several small flubs as well as a uniformly harsh sound. The sound (if it is not retouched excessively) is as atypical of Feuermann as we are to experience. It is suggestive of what the Strad might offer in lesser hands.

The Reger unaccompanied suite represents one of several recordings that Feuermann made in order to complete his obligations to Columbia (Japanese Nipponophone, Straus). While Columbia practically forced him to record the encore pieces, he returned the favor by holding out for the austere and unsalable Reger piece, which had been a particular favorite of his from the days in Leipzig. Reger had taught there shortly before Feuermann's arrival. The Reger *Suite* is important in that it is the closest performance that we have to the style of the Bach suites, which Feuermann never recorded.

The problem of Bach is interesting because it brings to the fore Feuermann's ambivalent feelings towards Casals. The young cellist had always said that those things that he had studied himself, i.e., that he had not learned as a consequence of a great performance by another cellist or teacher, were played better by him. The endemic sense of inferiority he had absorbed early in life and which he always strove to overcome was especially potent with regard to Casals and the Bach suites. Feuermann was perennially intimidated by the reputation of the great Catalan. And always, his natural respect for the history of music and traditions of his own instrument made him more respectful than perhaps would ordinarily have been the case had there not been such a great difference in tradition between the two men.

It was the niceties of Casals' playing, born of years of maturity and a relaxed attitude towards the concert platform and the recording microphones, that particularly impressed Feuermann, even though in the Dvořák he could see his own superiority both in terms of his old recording and his current manner of playing the piece. Casals' Bach recordings were another matter. They were masterly in the sense of understanding; and yet in another aspect, they deviated from his own conception of appropriateness, both technically and interpretively. He wrote an admiring letter to Casals about them. Casals wrote back appreciatively from Prades. Feuermann was jubilant.

Yet, at other times when he would admit to the senior cellist's greatness, he would puzzle about the peculiar aura Casals allowed to build up about his person. To Feuermann, such a foible was incomprehensible. Why would a great man need to allow it?

Once, after playing a recital in Britain and unhappy with the way a Bach suite turned out, he commented to his student John Shinebourne, "Maybe I'll leave Bach to the old man." On another occasion, after listening to one of Casals' recordings of the Bach, he commented to Sophie, "As much as I admire what he does with it, I just can't play it that way—it doesn't seem right." But he did not have the strength at that point to play the suites in a way compatible with his own less romantic, rhapsodic, or personalistic canons. Gradually, in the later years, Bach appeared less and less on his recital programs. He was apparently biding his time.

The Reger is an impressive piece of music. In its postromantic evocation of Bach's contrapuntal style, Reger's suite lacks a clear and evolving melodic line; instead, it is episodic, yet intriguing. In Feuermann's hands, it is powerful on all counts. It is sober, rich in sound, romantic, yet not idiosyncratic. A fitting farewell to Columbia records.

It should be stated here that Feuermann's appreciation of Casals' musicianship ought not blur the fact that he appreciated it not in some absolute sense, rather because it represented someone else's achievements. Feuermann's later style builds its own special nuances into the interpretation, which makes it unmistakably Feuermann's own. It belies the claim that thought and feeling are incompatible.

The Brahms Double Concerto, contracted in December, 1939, brought together Feuermann and the instrumentalist whom Feuermann respected far and away beyond any other, Jascha Heifetz. It may be conjectured that it was Heifetz's freedom and passion on his instrument, undertaken with complete technical impeccability, that had alerted Feuermann

Recording the Brahms Double Concerto with Heifetz, 1939.

to such possibilities, much as Sigmund many years earlier had stimulated Munio to imitate on the cello what his older brother did on the violin. Heifetz and Feuermann had collaborated before the recording in numerous evenings of chamber music in New York City and in the violinist's Connecticut home.

Eugene Ormandy gave both instrumentalists their freedom. The performance is brilliant and full-bodied, definitely a meeting of minds on the part of all. A slight objection might be taken to Heifetz' especially ardent pushing of the pace in some of the more technical sections. It is a classical performance that will always be in the repertoire—two giants and a great symphony orchestra.

Shortly after the recording of the Brahms, Feuermann made his first appearance with the National Orchestral Association—conducted by his friend Leon Barzin—since the historic cello cycle of 1938. On January 28, 1940, he appeared in Carnegie Hall to play the Reicha and Dvořák concerti. (Reicha was an obscure eighteenth-century composer who wrote somewhat in the style of Haydn.) Feuermann was to play twice more with that orchestra before his death.

At that time, the president of the nonprofit association which sponsored this training orchestra for the most talented young symphonic instrumentalists in the country was Mary Flagler Cary, the daughter of a wealthy oil associate of John D. Rockefeller, Mrs. Cary had a sense of history, for she employed a service to record all the works played at NOA concerts. This began in the fall of 1939, and the three 1940–41 Feuermann appearances were taken down. They were resurrected by the author in 1968 from the NOA archives. Leon Barzin kindly provided the initial lead as to their existence.

In spite of the poor technical qualities of the recordings, they are extremely valuable in one crucial way. They confirm all that we have believed concerning vintage Feuermann as represented in his recorded appearances. The live playing is unbelievably beautiful and secure, and evidences the fact that the practice of making several "takes" for commercial recordings could have added but little to Feuermann's recordings.

Further the NOA records reveal interesting and significant insights into the cellist's personality. This is his relationship with conductors. Feuermann seemed to play best when the conductor was himself a malleable, not a formidable, figure. The cellist certainly had no fear of any conductor. What intimidated him were those one or two men of whose powers he was in awe, i.e., Toscanini and Stokowski. On the other hand Nikisch, Furtwängler, Walter, Mengelberg, Beecham were also great conductors with whom he played. However, he subjected all of them to his humor and pranks.

With both Toscanini and Stokowski, he could not remain himself. They forced him into a mold and thus limited the fullest expression of his own genius. Toscanini we have already discussed. Stokowski will be mentioned below.

We should not by any means infer that Feuermann respected less the abilities of the others. He thought Barzin was a brilliant conductor, far better than most and perhaps, had he been given wider opportunities, on a par with the greatest. Barzin knew how to handle Feuermann musically as few other conductors did. On the other hand Barzin had noted that Feuermann's body always told him what the soloist was going to do well in advance of his actions.

The Dvořák of January 28, 1940, and the D'Albert of April 27, 1940, are great achievements. The Reicha is also lovely, but of secondary musical interest. There can be no doubt of the enormous development of the cellist in the Dvořák performance, a full ten years after the Berlin recording with friend Taube. It has all the technical brilliance, but in addition is now softened and molded. The phrasing is carefully shaped, never severed abruptly from sequence to sequence. The D'Albert, a beautiful work undeservedly ignored in the repertoire, contains the most ardent and pellucid playing of the series. D'Albert was a friend of Julius Klengel and perhaps composed it for him. Feuermann's performance is haunting.

The Bloch *Schelomo,* Feuermann recorded twice, the first time with Stokowski in late March of 1940 and the last time on November 10, 1941, with Barzin and the NOA. This latter performance is Feuermann's last on records. Feuermann had first heard Stokowski and the Philadelphia Orchestra in 1936. At that time he had written, "I never believed that a human being could bully out of the passive resistance of an orchestra such sounds—it dances—sings—I heard what I only dreamed of."

Stokowski and Feuermann collaborated in a Chinese Relief concert in March, 1940. So well had it gone that at the suggestion of Stokowski, Victor proffered a recording contract. Here again the powerful personality of the conductor propels the soloist. In truth there is notably less tension or restriction than is shown in the Toscanini *Don Quixote.* There is here a better blending of intentions. Stokowski's vision of *Schelomo* is passionate, intense, and dramatic. Feuermann responded to this conception and gave a completely impassioned rendition. If there are any reservations it is that the Strad was forced beyond its richest capabilities. The sound is sometimes strident, but certainly not as in the Toscanini, where Feuermann never seemed to loosen up. The orchestra's sound, of course, is voluptuous and powerful. This must have been as much a stimulus as the conducting itself.

Barzin's interpretation almost two years later (November 10, 1941) is, on the other hand, quieter, more contemplative, and introspective. Yet it is perhaps more beautiful if one gets behind the veil of an *extremely* poor recording sound. Conceivably this interpretation was more Feuermann's own view of the piece. He obviously set his own pace here. The fact that he was able to come through so well in two so different perspectives of this piece again raises doubts about his expressed dislike for its "whining Jewishness," a quality which he constantly deplored. He would not even accept compliments for the Stokowski recording—"You like it?" One has the feeling that Feuermann protested too much about his distaste for its ethnic qualities. Both performances belie distaste.

The Dvořák *Waldesruhe* and *Rondo* preceded the Bloch on the program. The *Rondo* had been filmed with Teddy Saidenberg at the piano during the summer of 1941. It is not quite so impeccable in concert as it was under the tensions of film-making, but is still beautifully done. The *Waldesruhe* is extraordinarily gentle in conception and realization. It is a piece Feuermann discovered in the Edwin Fleisher collection in his wide-ranging search for new music. As such it was his own, and perhaps stands as a musical epitaph.

We have not yet discussed Ormandy's *Don Quixote*. It is special because it contains the most amazing single passage in all of Feuermann's recorded work. In listening to this passage one gets as close as possible to Feuermann's realization of the expressive potentiality of his instrument.

Feuermann arrived in Philadelphia the night before the recording session (early March, 1940) in time to hear a performance of the Strauss work, but with another cellist as soloist. Immediately after the concert Feuermann rushed into Ormandy's dressing room to consult with him about the interpretation. They went over the music from score for about two hours. The next day the recording session was begun with only a brief warm-up to adjust and set the microphones. There were no interruptions except for that one incident mentioned earlier.

Ormandy provided the cellist with a perfect background for his evocation of the personality of the demented Knight. The passage in question is the recitative where the exhausted Quixote, fresh from his disastrous joust with the windmills, maintains an evening vigil and dreams of his beloved Dulcinea. This reverie for cello solo with a soft string accompaniment is a free, rhapsodic evocation of the knight's passionate affirmation of his devotion to his imaginary idol.

In an early recording with Strauss himself conducting and Enrico Mainardi as soloist, the passage is played straight. One wonders if Strauss envisioned its possibilities. Other and later performances by various cellists are little improvement. Feuermann plays the cello as if it were a tiny *pochette* (pocket violin). His radiant cello literally bends to his phrasing.

There is a sense of totality to this recording. Samuel Lifschey is perhaps more Sancho Panza—awkward, clumsy, and foolish—than was Carleton Cooley of the NBC Symphony. The various sections of the music are not as striking orchestrally as in the Toscanini version. But the conception is more of an entity, even more personality because the main characters of the music stand out from the background rather than the reverse. Quixote's death scene is certainly more subtly accomplished by Feuermann and Ormandy. Feuermann fingers a descending scale instead of sliding, to mark the Knight's demise. On hearing a performance of this piece with Feuermann as soloist, Artur Rubinstein has confessed, he wept at its conclusion. He had never heard the part played with such beauty and compassion and could now respect the composer's intentions.

Again, Ormandy was one of those conductors under whom Feuermann enjoyed playing but who certainly never awed him. Ormandy, a former violinist, could never really bring the cellist under control. Once he asked Feuermann to call him by his last name, perhaps in order to gain the respect of the musicians, long used to the authoritarianism of Stokowski. When, during rehearsal, Ormandy referred to the cellist as Muni, Feuermann replied seriously, "Mr. Feuermann, if you please."

Another time Feuermann tried to push Ormandy into scheduling the Toch and Mozart-Szell cello concerti. This led to a bitter series of letters when Ormandy attempted to gain for himself the traditional conductorial prerogatives of choice of program, especially when a rival conductor's work was involved.

Feuermann had two disappointments with regard to conductors. He was never invited to play with Mitropoulos and the Minneapolis Symphony. He wrote a card to his devoted student Claus Adam (later with the Juilliard Quartet), who had graduated from the NOA several years earlier and was at that time first cellist of the Minneapolis orchestra, asking him to inquire discreetly as to why Mitropoulos had not yet engaged him. Above all, he reiterated, be diplomatic. Perhaps Mitropoulos would like the first performance of the Toch Concerto, either in New York or Minneapolis.

While the desire for an engagement with Mitropoulos and the Minneapolis Orchestra was born of a respect for the Greek conductor, his being ignored by Koussevitsky, to his dismay, was a result of both the musician and the institution. When he played with the Boston Symphony it was invariably Richard Burgin who conducted.

He hoped he had finally broken the ice with his engagement by the Boston for the fall of 1939. So eager was he when news of the engagement arrived in Zurich that he risked a break with Schnabel and Huberman, who had planned their (ultimately unfulfilled) trio recordings for this period. The conductor turned out to be Burgin. Koussevitsky favored his fellow Russian, Piatigorsky. Perhaps there was a bit of traditional Jewish prejudice of the Litvak for the Litvak (Baltic and North Russian Jews) and against the Galizianer (Southwest Russian and Polish Jews). It was Koussevitsky who secured the world premiere of Hindemith's Cello Concerto for Piatigorsky and the Boston Symphony. Feuermann had tried hard to get his old friend to let him have first crack at it. But he understood that the politics of the situation required the debut to go to the most propitious outlet.

Feuermann was thirty-five years old when he came to this country to establish residence. In three and a half years, he was too new and as yet unestablished as a fixture in American concert life as, say Kreisler or even Heifetz, to receive the recognition that his achievement warranted. Also the world was heading rapidly into a second world war and the attention of the nation was directed more towards this horrible inevitability than towards the consideration of new standards of musical greatness.

What Feuermann did was to transcend the physical limitations of the cello. But in overcoming the bulk, the distances, and the psychological fearfulness of the instrument, he did more. He took advantage of its wide range of sound, its varied palette of colors, and also its broad dynamic possibilities. In effect he showed that, overall, the cello has greater musical possibilities than the violin.

We do not claim that Feuermann brought the final word in profundity of mind or soul to his playing. We must remember that Casals made his first recordings—modest salon pieces—at age thirty-nine. Feuermann died before he was forty.

Without being too extravagant, we can say that, for at least the cello and perhaps for all stringed instruments, with Emanuel Feuermann a plateau was reached—in expressivity, beauty of sound, freedom of movement, and control of all the elements in the art of string playing. It has yet to be equaled.

11

THE FINAL YEARS

In the east, the rumblings of war were getting louder. But in California, this summer of 1941, the air was perfumed with flowers, and salt spray from the ocean sometimes wafted its pungent way towards their home. It was the Feuermanns' second summer on the West Coast. June started out full of exciting possibilities. Their rented house in Pacific Palisades was increasingly alive with the welcoming of new arrivals. Almost two dozen students had picked themselves up when Feuermann's California plans became known and formed themselves into a master class. They came from all over the country, indeed from all over the world, since some were refugees. Several were violinists and violists; most were practicing musicians who could use their summer vacation for this purpose.

Suzette Forgues, a talented young Canadian cellist, acted as housing coordinator, running a veritable agency with an efficiency that amazed the arrivees, who expected her to be a little old lady operating out of a shack with a battery of telephones. This summer would be Feuermann's best, as he would be surrounded by a large, enthusiastic group of young devotees, perfect foils for his exuberance. In addition, Eva was expecting their second child.

Finally, a great professional opportunity. The success of the Heifetz-Feuermann duo in the Brahms Double Concerto had emboldened Victor to ask Heifetz, the commercial as well as the artistic diamond in its crown, to form a series of chamber music combinations with Feuermann and others. It was to be the first step in an experiment that might yet include a large part of the repertoire. The other participants were Artur Rubinstein and William Primrose.

The master classes themselves were hectic. Feuermann would gather the students together in small groups. Various students would play, then there would be criticism, by and large by Feuermann. However, the distance between the master's playing and the students', in spite of their talent, was so huge that for many the situation was an inhibiting one.

Those who spoke another language would often speak to Feuermann in their native tongue about their technical problems, so as to avoid putting themselves on public display more than was necessary. Feuermann tried his best to translate his unique technical and physical solutions of the problems of the instrument to the special circumstance of the student. But, for Feuermann, the technical and the musical were so intertwined that he found it almost impossible to solve a technical problem for a student without bringing in a musical problem or to go after a musical problem without becoming enmeshed in a technical one.

While Feuermann was completely persuasive and insightful in the musical realm, his explanations of the physical realization were much tougher for the students to grasp. He could show them, analyze what he was doing—as in the left hand, the open palm, held fan-like, open towards the bridge, pivoting fingers meanwhile freed when not in use; the slow, measured, secure slides, the Diran Alexanian-like freedom of fingers wildly thumping on the strings; the power and control achieved on the bow through thumb and forefinger; wrist, arm, shoulder, and torso coordinating securely to achieve controlled legato and staccato bowings. For most of the students, enormously talented as they were, what he showed them in a week necessitated many months of concentrated attention in private. This more than anything else was the legacy of Feuermann's teaching: a musicianship deriving from the seasoned use of the finest technical equipment in the service of the most refined sensual delineation of the composer's ideals, combined with an awareness of how the body must respond to the demands of the instrument in order to achieve the musical goal. In short, a lifetime of work for a student usually in need of re-educating himself, from a person who had consciously disciplined himself to the task since he was fourteen years of age.

Feuermann was exuberant, hard, sarcastic, and childlike. One just could not always take his comments to either students or colleagues seriously; for example, to a student after years of study and significant progress—"das Kind wird grosser—das wunder kleiner"; to a famous colleague (Joseph Schuster) after his recital and Feuermann's very warm congratulations—Colleague: "You really mean it, Munio, thank you, thank you"; Feuermann, roaring in delighted laughter to the onlookers: "He really believes me!"

He would make no bones about his complete disgust with students who were insincere or blustery show-offs on their instrument. One advanced West Coast student who appeared for the first time at the classes slid all over the instrument. He did everything that good cellists had gradually abandoned in the last quarter of a century. Feuermann finally sent him home, saying "I won't take it, all you do is schmaltz. If you come in the morning, I can't work, if you come in the evening, I can't sleep—schmaltz!"

His students usually went through emotional phases. At first, when

Feuermann would yell at them and tear them to shreds, they would despair. Next they would wonder why it was necessary for him to get so wrought up and they would be angry with him. Finally, as they began to know and understand him, as would his other friends and acquaintances, their hostility would disappear. This was the man: a tense, superactive, nervous individual who had an unquenchable desire to see great music come out of the instrument. Even when he was asleep—Eva would notice this many a night—he would run the fingers of his left hand over the pillow as if he were playing. Yet he was completely unstuffy, friendly, and personally very giving. The cello was merely his obsession.

The ultimate defection of one of his most talented students, Bobby LaMarchina, would have been especially disturbing to Feuermann had he lived to see it. Once, he tried to fool Eva by having both Bobby and himself play passages on his cello. It was very difficult to distinguish who was playing. At that time LaMarchina was still practically a child and thus his promise was extraordinary (he soon after became a cellist with the NBC Symphony). But his father reportedly pushed him on in somewhat the same way Maier had pushed Sigmund, and eventually he gave up the instrument for conducting.

Feuermann felt disdain for musicians who found it necessary to launch out into other fields such as conducting or composition. He had no objection to their seeking power or prestige. But he believed strongly that in this day and age, when the pinnacle of one's profession was being besieged by so many talents, it was necessary to muster all one's energies in pursuit of a single goal. He was both proud of his achievement and defensive about it, perhaps even hurt that great instrumentalists invariably had to play the servant to even second-rate conductors.

On the way to his recital in New York City one time he saw a sometime student of his, Alan Shulman, who had done some composing. Feuermann called out sarcastically, "How's the great composer?" A few months later, learning that the young cellist had stopped his lessons because he couldn't afford the fifteen dollar fee—Feuermann had been fooled by Shulman's Hudson convertible, and he used his more well-off students to help subsidize his many scholarship students—he wrote the cellist-composer saying that if he had only known his situation, he would have been happy to give him a scholarship.

Far from the tumbling in the surf, the ping pong tournaments, and the general atmosphere of a Boy Scout troop that Feuermann had spontaneously stimulated away from the classes, the war in Europe had widened. Russia had now been invaded. God only knew what had become of the many relatives still in Kolomea. Still it was only an ominous backdrop. Periodically during the lessons, Feuermann would stop everything to get the news on the radio. He was interested and analytical. But the bad news only made him more tense.

Bruno Walter arrived in midsummer. George Szell would come shortly after. There was much scurrying around to find the proper cook to conjure up all the old Viennese favorites. Walter, especially hurt by the events taking place in central Europe, seemed still hopeful. Feuermann, inwardly respectful of this "truly good man," was ever ironic. At every small indication of Allied initiative—a Russian counterattack, a small bomber raid by the English over Germany—Walter would be elated. Feuermann would comment, "Is it possible that Mr. Walter is again winning the war for us?"

Feuermann was convinced that until America entered the war the result would be indecisive. He was extremely pessimistic, on the basis of his experience in Russia, of the Soviets' stemming the German tide. He had not yet imagined the stupidity of the Nazis in alienating this vast population of peasants and turning them into anti-fascist partisans. On the other hand he was correct about the eventual role of the United States and later wrote to his old sponsor Kux in Switzerland that the Japanese at Pearl Harbor had speeded what could only be an inevitability—the full confrontation of two world views and powers.

Eva had a miscarriage in early summer, which of course sobered them both. They had wanted another child badly. This event added to the mixed qualities of that summer. Feuermann wrote to Kux, now in his eighties, perhaps his only *confidant*, that amongst cellists he had nothing to fear, but that in the case of talented Piatigorsky, the only mark that the Russian had attained was that he now had a boy as well as a girl. Feuermann's family and the economic means to secure a quiet, comfortable life for them were to be the only counterpoint to his professional quest.

He rarely practiced the cello from that point on, that summer. The nails grew longer and his students worried and warned him of the impending recordings. Feuermann steeped himself in ping pong, instead. His bursitis had necessitated giving up tennis. Also he had heard that Heifetz was literally a champion of this art and gave no quarter. Alas, here Feuermann was no Heifetz. The students would tease him unmercifully, "Relax, don't anticipate, don't force, there is plenty of time—prepare your body before you move your arm—be calm." He still lost all the tournaments.

The rehearsals for the recordings began in mid-August. Since all participants lived in the area, they took turns rehearsing in their respective homes, on occasion outdoors, next to a pool, the wives serenely knitting nearby. The choice of a pianist had given Victor and the string players some concern. There were pianists such as Serkin and Schnabel, very serious and solemn artists. There were Horowitz, a thundering soloist, and Rubinstein, extremely popular, suave, romantic. Victor argued for Rubinstein, who was under contract to them. There was no doubt about his considerable musical skills and intelligence. However he was such a relaxed, debonair person that they wondered if he would fit into the intense, hardworking, and serious pattern that Heifetz and Feuermann represented. In brief—would Rubinstein practice?

Several days before the rehearsals were to begin, the cellist cut his nails and started warming up. In three days there was a distinct improvement and even Szell, in his typically acerbic manner, commented to Feuermann after they had read through their newly created Mozart-Szell Cello Concerto, "It's not how many notes you *missed*, but it's how you could even play the piece after a few days of practicing."

The Beethoven duo was recorded on August 29. It did not go well. In spite of that, Feuermann and Primrose went out to dinner together to celebrate. The cellist thought Primrose to be a sensational violist. Part of Primrose's violinlike technique could be attributed to his use of a moderate-sized viola, 16 to 16½ inches, not the 17+-inch behemoth Tecchler Hindemith always played. When the dinner was over, Feuermann grabbed the check and commented wryly, "Well, the Jew beat the Englishman—at least to the check."

The Dohnanyi *Serenade in C* (op. 10) was recorded September 8; the Mozart *Divertimento* (K. 563), September 9. A few days' additional rehearsing with pianist resulted in the Brahms trio in B (op. 8) being recorded on September 11, 12; the Beethoven, "Archduke" on September 12, 13; and the Schubert trio in B♭ (op. 99), completely on the 13th. They recorded steadily for eleven hours on that last day. The sessions were all amicable. The Dohnanyi is a simply amazing performance and for all-around effort will never be equaled. The Mozart *Divertimento,* perhaps Feuermann's favorite bit of chamber music, is strong in the violin, which predominates, perhaps naturally. Some have argued that Heifetz here searched for technical impeccability to the point that the grace of the music suffered.

There was a certain amount of tension between pianist and violinist, although the diplomatic Charles O'Connell of Victor tried to iron out all the difficulties. The pianist often complained that the violinist took every opportunity to edge the microphones covertly in his direction. On the other hand, O'Connell points out that Feuermann's low notes were often drowned out by Rubinstein's pedal. The engineers had to deaden one of the mikes near the pianist at several points. The cellist now satisfied, the recordings continued.

While the pianist liked to linger, the violinist often wanted to thrust ahead. One felt that the other was flaccid. The other felt the former to be cold. Perhaps, these differences were necessary to create the emotional pitch requisite for the creation of great music.

One incident the pianist particularly relished recalling was an evening chamber-music session on an island off the coast of California. Being played was the Schubert string quintet, including the three string artists. Rubinstein was one of an appreciative group of listeners. He stated that he was so moved, especially by Feuermann's playing of the first cello part, that he took out his wallet "to contribute everything in it to the Musicians' Emergency Fund in honor of this performance. Luckily I only had eighty dollars in the wallet. But friend Heifetz was completely amazed!"

September, 1941 was concluded with Feuermann's commercial filming of Popper's *Spinning Song* and the Dvořák *Rondo,* with Teddy Saidenberg accompanying, and their subsequent appearance on the Bob Burns Show playing a Chopin nocturne. The latter broadcast furnishes the only known recording of Feuermann's voice.

Back in New York Feuermann eagerly pursued a variety of projects. He had proposed to Carl Engel of Schirmer's that he reedit the bulk of the cello literature for that publisher. And while Engel was both friend and admirer, he knew that the potential public for such a series was limited. However, in the end, for a modest outright purchase, he commissioned Feuermann to start it off. The cellist had proposed the Brahms E minor Sonata to begin the series. If time would allow, it was to be completed by April 1942.

The rest of the fall Feuermann spent in preparation for a series of winter and spring concerts, commuting once a week to Philadelphia's Curtis Institute, where he had been appointed to their string department, preparing the Mozart-Szell Concerto for its late December inaugural in New York, and engaging in a vigorous correspondence about the trio recordings.

As it turned out, both Jascha and Artur, California residents, had pretty much agreed between themselves which of the various takes they preferred. It remained for Feuermann to be the stubborn iconoclast. It is impossible to trace the exact nature of their disagreements. Probably each musician wanted to be heard at his best without in any way subverting the whole. By mid-December the business was settled and Feuermann was anxiously awaiting the public concert debut of the trio to introduce the records, as Victor hoped to arrange this. The reviews of the earlier series of recordings (Brahms, Bloch, Strauss) were just now coming into publication and there was some optimism about a commercial success.

Financial affairs loomed ever more important in the cellist's mind. It was difficult to keep them from intruding into his artistic preoccupations. There were his recitals and concerts, still too few in number (by spring of 1942 he was booked for only twelve for 1942–43) wherein he felt an obligation to play the best and the most serious; for example, Mozart-Szell, with Daniel Saidenberg's Little Symphony; the Toch, wherever he could get it performed. There were benefit concerts of all kinds for which he volunteered; the talented scholarship students he felt obligated to accept on his own; Curtis was paying him $1,800 for the year. His total income for 1940 was $11,200, including his earlier Columbia records.

On this he had to live as the "king of cellists" must live, as well as help out his family in Palestine. The new house he was building in Rye, New York, would cost a fortune. Even though Mrs. Reifenberg was providing the down-payment, his other costs—landscaping, furniture, etc.—were mounting daily. In December, arriving in Indianapolis from Montreal for a concert, he wrote to Eva in a rare expression of complaint.

So many anxieties are piled up for me at the same time, it makes me quite sick. It doesn't enter my head that I am going to be forty years old. Such an age doesn't fit me at all. But since the age can't be changed . . . *I* have to change . . . adjust myself. . . .

The intensity of American musical life, while it had a significant, positive effect in stimulating Feuermann's maturity in performance, had a number of somewhat deleterious consequences. Naturally competitive and yet at the same time lackadaisical, even lazy about certain things, Feuermann had to fight this duality of attitudes. Those close to him were keenly aware of his ambivalence. America and the heavy responsibilities of family life had the effect of choking off the latter quality. While as ebullient as ever, Feuermann now rarely lost a chance to further his career. He was far more likely to put himself out for a young student, a junior colleague in need of a job, or for another instrumentalist, such as pianist Franz Osborne, for whom he solicited a position in practically every town he visited.

But as to those on the fringes of the concert cellist circuit, he was persuasive in getting managers to shift an engagement to himself or to arrange a program so that he would appear in a better place. Feuermann's rationalization to his friends when on occasion he was sorrowfully reprimanded, was that it wouldn't have done the person much good anyway—he was destined for orchestral or chamber music playing; the other's temporary advantage would only show up the inevitable. He was right of course. What the others did not know was that even at the pinnacle there could be no respite. He was not in *that* advantageous a position. There were no alternatives for him now but the top. Thus the perpetual entrepreneur motion, which he undertook with gusto, but also with inner dismay.

If only there were more time to relax, to unwind. On Sunday mornings, when he happened to be at home with his family, he would make a special, if late, entrance. By this time in his life at an advanced stage of baldness, he would enter the kitchen, his thinning hair parted a different way in celebration of a normal bourgeois Sunday with Eva and Monica.

The drive toward the pinnacle had been attended by the acquisition of many minor scars and a few major ones. Some could be healed, others proved permanent. One of the most unfortunate episodes, yet ultimately retrievable, was a siege of temporary friction with Bronislaw Huberman. Huberman had been in many ways a father confessor for the cellist as well as an idol and hero of Continental musicians for his work on behalf of refugee musicians and in founding the Palestine Philharmonic. He had done much for the Feuermann family and for the cellist himself.

Feuermann's rising stature following his first world tour had led Schnabel and Huberman to discuss the possibility of their joining in a piano trio, both for concerts and recordings. Feuermann was elated and

Practicing in Scarsdale
home, 1939.

Serenading daughter Monica, 1940.

eager. He was persistent in inquiring as to how plans were progressing. His earlier string trio had, of course, folded when he and Goldberg had been ejected from Germany. This new combination sounded like a possible successor to the old Cortot-Thibaud-Casals trio.

In February of 1936, he played in Town Hall with the trio at the concert of the New Friends of Music. Musically, it went well and the critics were pleased except for a comment about Huberman's excessive sliding. The experience sobered Feuermann somewhat since he realized there were real stylistic differences between the older musicians and himself. But since he was still "the kid" in their eyes and they were worldly and famous, he thought more about the positive factors of opportunity than about his reservations.

Throughout Feuermann's second tour, he kept in close touch with both musicians. Huberman was then completely involved with the Palestine Orchestra, so plans remained moribund for a time. By the time the idea was reactivated, Feuermann had already completed his marathon series with the NOA, Europe looked less and less inviting as a base of operations and, more important, there were hints of bigger things in the United States once he could free himself of the Columbia contract.

March of 1939 saw a series of misunderstandings, twistings, and avoidances between the trio string players. Huberman had arranged, apparently with Feuermann's tacit approval, for a recording contract with H.M.V., to be consummated the following September and October. At the same time, when Victor had made a definite commitment that a contract would be forthcoming, the Boston Symphony engaged Feuermann for late October, early November. It seems to have provided Feuermann with a good opportunity to extricate himself from what was an increasingly embarrassing situation, doubly so because he had disappointed Huberman in 1936 by not going to Palestine for a concert tour. And of course he felt strong obligations to Huberman because he had been instrumental in getting the Feuermann family into Palestine. Still, such favors could not be considered ransom on one's career.

Feuermann attempted to juggle the dates, ostensibly because of his desire to play under Koussevitsky. (Burgin eventually conducted.) He also attempted to free himself from the warm-up concerts: "I can hardly understand why these concerts should be of fundamental importance for the ensemble. Of course, it is not up to me to judge whether you personally need absolutely to play each trio publicly before [the recordings], but if you will allow me, I do not hold this opinion." Huberman attempted to use his seniority to press Feuermann to his purported responsibilities. An inadvertent metaphor set off an explosion and the cellist fired back on March 19, 1939: ". . . Nevertheless, there can be no mentioning of 'marching orders' and the like towards me, neither as far as dates are concerned nor as far as artistic premises are concerned."

Apparently the letter calmed both men and at last the recordings were set for early October. The political situation that spring (in Czechoslovakia) worsened and Feuermann again had to postpone a trip to Palestine, not without several cross missives from the concert authorities in Palestine and a disappointed Huberman. The youngster certainly had risen in the world and concomitantly the elders were gradually slipping back, their moment in the sun receding into history. Feuermann completed his recordings with Columbia in London that same April and shortly after gathered his family together and embarked for the United States. The war intervened in September and permanently foreclosed the possibility of the recordings planned for October.

Huberman finally arrived in the United States in late 1940, too late, as Feuermann noted objectively, to take full advantage of his fame. The violinist was no longer a young man and was old-fashioned as violinists went. Yet, in spite of their drift apart artistically, Feuermann was exhilarated by Huberman's finer performances. On their part Huberman and Schnabel never bore Feuermann any ill will. In fact Huberman, having an uncanny knack for connections in high places, was later able to use his influence in having Mrs. Reifenberg admitted from Cuba to the United States, at Feuermann's request.

Both musicians recognized in Feuermann a genius whose personal style had to be given latitude and understanding. But more, the cellist was a completely open and disingenuous person. There was no cant in his makeup. He said and did what he thought proper and if he at times went overboard in his enthusiasms, his small-boy smile and kidding "yes, I am human too" dissolved any hostility. Repeated over and over again by his friends is the comment, "his playing dissolved everyone's hurt sensibilities—you could never hold a grudge against someone who played like Munio—he was a naughty spoiled kid, but—."

The great hurt was not with friends or colleagues but within his own family. Of all the Feuermanns, only Sophie had come to the United States, with husband Harry Braun. Munio was elated that their plans would take them to the United States. Sophie was almost like a young protégé. When barely beyond her student days, Sophie had been a brilliant performer indeed. Munio had taken every opportunity to utilize her as accompanist in his recitals. Over the years they had grown together musically.

At a time when his relationship with his family was undergoing tribulations—because of Sigmund the family itself neared dissolution—Sophie and he had stood together. Because she had been at home more than anyone else, Sophie bore the brunt of the arguments, dissension, and general tension.

But much as Munio wanted to give her every opportunity to rise on her own musical merits, the fact remained that she lived in the shadow of her famous and successful brother. In truth, she was the best pianist he ever had. He would reiterate, "With Sophie, I feel so sure." If Feuermann had a complaint about her, it was that she was a perfectionist, even more so than he. In the Berlin days he would often want to relax, to take a recital in stride. Sophie never let up. She would chastise him for his casual attitude toward music with students. He would offhandedly comment on a piece of music—negatively or positively. The students would naturally accept what he said with great gravity—the great man had spoken. Sophie would later berate him, "Why don't you explain to them why you feel that way, not just to give your opinions." Certainly, he wouldn't have acted so casually several years later in the United States.

Sophie and Harry came to the United States in 1938. They were penniless. In the beginning Feuermann was happy to help Sophie out by using her as an accompanist. But very soon it became clear that the collaboration would not work. There were probably several reasons. In one's drive to push forward, one wanted to be unencumbered by the past—even by a younger sister. Perhaps he needed an accompanist in the true sense of the word, rather than a co-equal who needed attention and consideration. NBC was skeptical of the ultimate success of brother and sister teams, Menuhins and Iturbis notwithstanding. One artist in the family inevitably took away from the other. Both Sophie and he now had separate lives and separate families.

The denouement came in Ponce, Puerto Rico, on December 21, 1938, at a recital wherein Munio apparently gave his sister a workout—changing tempi, skipping sections of the music, etc. Sophie was able to keep up with him, but it was the last straw in a situation that had been deteriorating throughout the fall. She flew home. They rarely spoke to or saw each other thereafter.

Neither of these stubborn Feuermanns would give in. Munio attempted to make a conciliatory move. But when Sophie did not quickly respond, Munio would withdraw. They spoke of each other to friends and relatives, always trying to elicit a sympathetic response. Sophie felt that in Munio's hour of triumph he had abandoned her; Munio, that Sophie made unreasonable and neurotic demands upon him, which he could not meet.

The entire affair was a terrible hurt that became increasingly unbearable after Eva and Monica arrived in the United States. For now they were separated from all the rest of his family. He so much wanted his mother to see Monica. Of his father and Sigmund he had despaired. Each was now in his own private world. In March of 1940 he wrote to Director Kux in Switzerland of his life and work in the United States and of their mutual acquaintances: ". . . Sigmund has married a Fräulein Zuckerberg who is supposed to have a corset shop. He only wrote to me after I congratulated him! Before the wedding he had a falling out with the poor father, who must have suffered more than one can imagine."

The winter-spring of 1942 was, as usual, hectic. Most of his regular concerts had been concentrated in this period. The war had produced a flurry of benefit concerts, appearances at military bases, all of which he was happy to participate in. Feuermann's own obligation to the military had been satisfied by his registering for the draft and subsequent classification as 3A. The records note his height at 5' 7", weight 169 lbs.

Early in March he gave a series of concerts with the Philadelphia Orchestra in its home city as well as in New York. The program featured *Don Quixote* and the Haydn concerto. They were great performances. But the audiences were small, wartime having its effect on interest. The reviewer for *Musical America* commented as follows:

> [Feuermann] was at his best, which is to say that one could not hear more beautiful playing on any string instrument. In his characterization of Don Quixote, in Strauss's tone poem, Mr. Feuermann put all the resources of his prodigious technique to the noblest of purposes. His playing was as flexible and expressive as human speech, and the whole score was illuminated by the humanity of his interpretation. The contrast between the jovial vulgarity of Sancho Panza and the Knight, beset with his dreams and aspirations, in the third variation was magically realized, and the Knight's Vigil was a rhapsodic vision of overpowering intensity, as Mr. Feuermann embodied it. Never has his astounding range of tonal brilliance been more tellingly employed. When he was down in the cellarage, so to speak, one would have sworn that he was playing a double bass and on the upper strings he made the instrument sound like a violin.

Feuermann had arrived in Philadelphia dog-tired and not feeling at all well. The plethora of concerts, concentrated as they had been, the teaching, the house, now almost completed, with its mounting costs, had put him on edge. He complained to few people about his health. It had been mentioned casually to Jascha in California, in a note written in late November. It was noted with concern by his old friends, the Benar Heifetzes (Benar Heifetz was then first cellist with the Philadelphia Orchestra), with whom he was now staying: "He guzzled literally gallons of coffee—and of course, he smoked as usual."

Rehearsals had been suffused with the usual banter, a bit more pungent and strained on the parts of both soloist and conductor. At dinner one evening, with Ormandy and Erno Rapée (conductor of the Radio City Music Hall Orchestra) Feuermann began to tell what he thought was an hilarious joke about two East European Jews named Blau and Rapaport (Ormandy and Rapée). In spite of a number of frantic under-the-table nudges and kicks on the part of his hosts, the Heifetzes, he persisted. He was the only one to laugh; the conductors found it distinctly unfunny. They reddened perceptibly.

Ormandy, concerned about their verbal jousts, yet extremely impressed with Feuermann's performance, wrote him immediately after the concerts:

Dear Muni:

Just a line to tell you that in spite of my various wise cracks about our concerts, the experience of making music with you was one of the highlights of the season, and having conducted for you meant more to me artistically and personally than I was willing to admit while joking with you. I am looking forward to the date when we will record the Haydn Concerto and I am also looking forward to accompanying you at the special-relief concert, the date of which will probably be May 12 or 13. As soon as this is definite you will, of course, be advised. . . .

Affectionately, as ever yours
Eugene

P. S. Don't forget that you promised to send me a picture. If you send me two I may exchange both for one of Piatigorsky.

Incorrigibly,

At the end of March Feuermann finally moved into his magnificent new home in Rye, overlooking the Long Island Sound. It broke the tension and allowed him to look with a bit more optimism into the future, especially after he could take care of a hemorrhoid problem.

A side interest that had developed a particular fascination for him was a small drawing, supposedly an original made of Bach during his life, which Oma Reifenberg had acquired in Germany. He commissioned Oma's cousin, Gerhard Hertz, now a young musicology professor in Louisville, to help him authenticate and write an article about it for the *Musical Quarterly*. The correspondence was long but breezy, Feuermann even doing a critique of the young scholar's style and approach. In the end (several years later) the Bach picture was proved to be spurious, but during the winter and spring of this year, Feuermann seems to have fixed his mind and heart on proving the authenticity of this picture. It would be a great bargain were it to be so established.

Gradually the fascination with the drawing switched to gardening. On April 6, he wrote to Gerhard,

. . . I've gone into gardening and dirt, good dirt makes my mouth water. Who knows when house and home will be in a half-way acceptable condition. I surely don't have to waste any words that I am 'total broke.' Will you visit me in debtor's prison (this isn't as funny as it sounds).

How is Bach? When I carried the picture into Oma's room, her Bavarian maid Lena happened to be there. Believe it or not, on seeing the picture she asked, is that *the* Bach? . . . Over the garage we have a playroom with bed and bath. You are welcome if you want to try out these facilities for a SHORT time during the summer. You could work in the garden with me and help me spoil Monica. . . .

On May 6, 7 he was in Ann Arbor at the May festival with Thor Johnson and the Philadelphia Orchestra. On May 15 he was in Camden to speak at an "I am an American Day" program. It is said that he was there to record.

These engagements concluded, he returned to New York to prepare to enter Park East Hospital to get his operation over with. There was so much to do once he was released—no more than a week was the expectation. He had a July booking for the Ravinia Festival at Chicago, to play the Double Concerto with Joseph Szigeti and the Philadelphia Orchestra. Also, he wanted to begin work on the viola da gamba. The New Friends of Music had engaged him to give a series on Bach doing the three sonatas for gamba on the original instrument. He expected to study them during the summer between his landscaping chores.

His teaching was slowed down in May so that not too many students would be cancelled. Only a few knew about his condition. In truth he was probably embarrassed about the whole affair. Several friends remember him mentioning how irritating his father had become in his later years with his incessant whining about the need to go to various spas to help cure his intestinal maladies.

Thus, his choice of this small, private hospital run by refugee doctors was dictated by the desire for anonymity. In fact, it was to be a gynecologist friend of the family who would perform the minor surgery. Still, he was nervous about the affair; he remembered how nearly serious his earlier operation in Cologne had been.

Feuermann discouraged those friends he encountered from visiting him. To Raya Garbousova he emphasized that he would not be shaven and thus not presentable. Better visit him after he was discharged and see his new house.

Erica Morini was not at home in her Fifth Avenue apartment when he dropped by to leave her his left-over May and June gasoline ration stamps. He slipped them under her door with a brief note and left.

Several postcards were hurriedly written, including one to Claus Adam, asking him to visit when this matter was concluded. Apparently, he decided not to write to Sophie about it. It was not a matter of concern to his friends and thus she remained unaware of his plans.

The operation had been over for several days and while Munio seemed all right, a fever prevented his immediate release. Oma had taken a room at the hospital and relayed the information home to Eva, who could not leave the house (false pregnancy).

Suzette Forgues drove up to the Feuermann home prepared to take a lesson. She was shocked to hear little Monica greet her with "Daddy's in the hospital." She spoke with Eva for a few minutes about Feuermann, when the phone rang. It was Munio. Eva paled as she listened. A terrible thing was happening to him, he pleaded. His mind seemed to wander, he talked incoherently about Switzerland, strawberries, and rehearsals. ". . .

Feuermann's last photo, ten days before his death, for "I Am an American" Day, May 15, 1942.

I want cherry cake of Mamselle . . . They are letting me die of thirst. . . ."
There was shock and fright. Suzette left immediately.

Feuermann was in trouble. The pain was great, more than he could
stand. As soon as it was humanly possible, Drs. Nisson and Rosenow, who
were called immediately, arrived. (They had not participated in the original minor surgery.) An emergency operation was scheduled. "Perhaps it
was his allergy to morphine." In Cologne, seven years earlier, nicotine had
been successfully employed to relax his system and neutralize the intense
immobilizing reaction of the drug.

The exploratory operation revealed that it was too late, his system had
by now completely failed and peritonitis had set in (penicillin of course
was not in use then). Sophie was summoned. When she arrived, a weeping
and broken Oma greeted her with, "Munio stirbt." Sophie, in horror,
found him under maximum restraint. He did not recognize her.

On Monday, May 25th, it was over, barely six days. Faithful Bronislaw
Huberman had arrived that same morning with flowers for his young
friend Munio. To his consternation, he had been turned away. Siegfried
Hearst was already speaking as Raya Garbousova took the phone off the
hook. "Raya, Raya," he called out almost hysterically. He was crying, "he is
gone, gone, our Munio is gone." "Why are you saying such a thing?" she
shrieked back at him. "He is dead, Raya, dead." She broke in, "You are
crazy, what are you saying? What are you. . . ."

The newspapers reported the event as complications after a minor
operation. Doctors noted that it was a medical mishap. Others said far
grimmer things. The loss was commented on by the *New York Times* on its
editorial page. It was entitled "Music Loses an Artist." At the Universal
Funeral Chapel on Thursday, May 28, 1942, a large group of musicians,
well over 300, gathered to hear George Szell and Olin Downes speak
briefly. Toscanini tried to say a few words, but broke down after declaring
that Feuermann was like his own son.

Arthur Schnabel played *Marche Funebre* from Beethoven's Piano Sonata
Op. 26 in A♭. A string quartet made up of Erica Morini, Edwin
Bachman, Lotte Hammerschlag, and Frank Miller played Beethoven's
Harp Quartet, op. 74, and finally Erica Morini and Albert Hirsch,
Feuermann's last accompanist, played *Arioso* by Bach. The honorary pall
bearers included Arturo Toscanini, Eugene Ormandy, Efrem Zimbalist,
Rudolf Serkin, Mischa Elman, Leon Barzin, Bronislaw Huberman, Edgar
Lustgarten, Charles O'Connell, Fritz Stiedry, Emil Cooper, Alvin C.
Blume, Siegfried Hearst, Joseph Berberich, Leo Hoffman, Sasha Jacob-
son, Nathan W. Levin, Arthur B. Percival, Paul Schiff, Artur Schnabel,
and George Szell. Burial was in Kensico Cemetery, Valhalla, New York.

At Ravinia that July, Gregor Piatigorsky, who replaced Feuermann and
Szigeti, dedicated a Boccherini *Adagio* to his departed rival. The reviewer

noted that the Russian cellist's performance signified his accession to the mantle formerly worn by Feuermann. At the concerts of the New Friends, the series for 1942–43 was dedicated to Feuermann's memory. The National Orchestral Association arranged for a musical program the following November to be dedicated to Feuermann's memory, with Joseph Szigeti performing the Beethoven Violin Concerto.

The students, for the most part artists in their own right, turned to their own resources. Feuermann had given them enough to work on for years. Suzette Forgues visited Toscanini shortly after her master's death. Toscanini himself was still disconsolate. The conductor told her that she must go off on her own now. "You were fortunate enough to study with the greatest—but unfortunately there is no one after him."

Jascha Heifetz could not get to the funeral. However, he sent his deepest condolences. Deeply affected in his own way, Heifetz made no move to follow up on their plans for further chamber music recordings with another cellist. For nine years, he refused to record with anyone else as cellist.

Eva was completely broken by the sudden dissolution of their world and by the disappearance of a man who in his private as well as public life radiated upon all those around him a humanness, a powerful and majestic individuality. For years she attempted to preserve his memory and work. The house was, of course, soon sold. A year later the Strad was sold to the wealthy New Jersey amateur, collector, and friend, Russell Kingman, who promptly published a brochure about the instrument. He noted that he also owned the "d'Achambeau" Gofriller (1728), had once owned the "Archinto" Strad (1689) and the "Beal" Joseph Guarnerius filius Andrea (1707). It is not known whether he ever played Feuermann's Strad in public. Eventually it returned to the hands of a noted cellist—Aldo Parisot of the Yale School of Music.

After a number of years Eva married Hans Lehnsen, a mathematician friend of the family. They continued to reside in Scarsdale. Monica, musically talented but not with a bent for the profession, played fine piano, attended Smith College, and became a teacher in New York City. Sophie continues to concertize, accompany, and teach in New York City today.

In Palestine the family was of course shocked and benumbed by this loss. Mother Feuermann, who outlived all her children except Sophie, died in 1964 at age eighty-eight. Visited by friends, she would bemoan the death of her children at such untimely ages. Sigmund and Rosa had died in 1952, at ages fifty-two and forty-eight respectively. She would comment, "My children all become famous and die young. I wish they had become shoemakers."

Sigmund was in a Tel Aviv hospital in May of 1952, dying of a brain tumor, when a series of programs was given over the Israeli Radio commemorating the tenth anniversary of the death of Emanuel. It is said that when a recording of the Schumann Cello Concerto was being broadcast over the radio (Feuermann never recorded it) Sigmund was roused from his lethargy, a wan smile drifted over his face, "Munio used to play that so beautifully. . . ." He died a few days later. Five months later, Rosa Hoenigsberg, Munio's second sister, died.

It was not until mid-1943 that a letter from Palestine reached the Hoenigsberg brothers in Sverdlovsk, U.S.S.R. War conditions were responsible for the delay. They were playing in an orchestra that traveled from one army camp to another, entertaining Soviet troops. The letter from the outside world was one of only a very few they received during the entire war, in their constant travels. Bearing as it did the unbelievable news of Munio, it seemed to dissolve for them the vision that somewhere in the world there were calm and peace—a stability to which they could one day return.

For most of us who never knew Feuermann, the recordings are all that are left. For those who knew him, his life is still an exciting memory, even after a generation. The impact of his personality is perhaps best illustrated by a story his accompanist Gerald Moore related over the B.B.C. in June of 1942:

> One winter's day some years ago, after a tour of America, his boat from New York docked at mid-day at Southhampton. With him was his new car, which he had never driven; he drove it to London where we met in the late afternoon at the recording studios; we made four records, then he jumped into the car and drove through the fog and darkness to Harwich, catching the Dutch packet-boat and giving a recital the following afternoon in Amsterdam. As Rex Palmer [Columbia Records] and I waved him off from the recording studios, we called to him, 'you'll be worn out.' 'I love it,' he said. 'I love it. . . .'

APPENDIX I

NOTES ON INTERPRETATION
by Emanuel Feuermann

Editor's Preface

These notes by Feuermann are culled from several spiral notebooks that the cellist carried with him on his concert tours around the United States between 1940 and 1942. The notes were written in German and English—mostly in the latter, as time wore on.

An attempt is made here to balance topicality with the sequential order that the notes were given by the cellist. Obviously there is some repetition. But this can be borne, especially since there are always slightly different nuances given by Feuermann to each of the topics.

Of necessity, some rewriting has been done to correct obvious errors in grammar or word choice that might obscure meaning. Occasionally a word or phrase has been added in order to maintain connection between ideas. And since these are occasional fragments written here and there, limited restructuring of paragraphs was necessary.

S.W.I

PART I
The Cello

Amongst the solo instruments, the cello is probably not the smallest, but it is the youngest. It is so young that I might even say that only in the twentieth century has the cello reached its maturity and earned the right to be considered on the same level as the piano and the violin.

When Amati and Stradivari, etc., made their famous celli, it seems that there was little expectation that they would be used as solo instruments. Rather it was thought that they would be used in accompanying, as for example, in nightly serenades. Many of these old instruments had holes in their backs—evidently so they could be hung on straps and played while a person was standing. These were the general uses of the cello at a time when the early masters of the violin, Tartini and Corelli, who had made of the violin a singularly popular instrument, had already died.

From the earliest days of the cello, there are actually lovelier instruments than fitting music. True, the Bach suites belong to this period. But they only move in the lower positions and do not allow the instrumentalist to realize the possibilities of the cello. Not for some fifty years after these suites were written do we find thumb position mentioned. It was first noted by the famous Duport at the time he was developing his school of cello playing in Paris. Only then did the cello as we know it today become accessible to the instrumentalist. This altered technique opened up hitherto hidden possibilities and beauties in cello playing, and in addition brought with it the first great compositions for cello and the first great artists on the instrument.

Developments proceeded rapidly. However if one studies these developments one can observe the composers groping their way forward. I have often considered how these changes came about in the last half of the eighteenth century. It must have been as cellists became more aware of the possibilities of their instruments, the composers in turn provided the music for these newly opened vistas. The leading cellists of this time were Duport Sr. in Paris, Kraft in Vienna, and later Duport Jr. and Romberg in Berlin. For quite a long period it appears that the usual personal relationships which existed between composers and cellists played a decisive role in the evolution of the cello. For example, Haydn, who had until that time used the cello only as an accompanying instrument, began writing passages for the cello in his symphonies and string quartets. These passages presupposed a new awareness, hence, a new influence, on the composer.

Also at that time the widely known cellist and composer, Boccherini, composed a quintet for two celli, in which he gave a carrying part to one cello and a solo part to the second cello, the latter having nothing at all in common with the traditional way of handling this instrument. In short, the "A" string had been discovered. We might also cite the case of Mozart, who unfortunately never wrote a concerto for cello. However, later in his career, the cello begins to figure very strongly in his writing. His last and perhaps loveliest quartets are called the cello quartets. This is because, in a manner that was novel for that time, the cello shares with the violin the solo role.

By the beginning of the nineteenth century, the era of experimentation had passed. The cello had succeeded in establishing itself as a solo instrument. In the cello part of Beethoven's Triple Concerto, we find amongst the most masterly, most difficult, and at the same time loveliest solo parts ever written for the cello. Thus in the comparatively short period of thirty years, the cello had advanced from its role as an accompanying instrument to a position as a solo instrument of great stature. The pioneer age had passed.

Why then did the composers of the nineteenth century treat the cello as a stepchild? That it was so treated is evident in the comparatively small number of works composed for cello by the great masters. It is difficult to give a valid answer to this legitimate question. There are many opinions on the matter, but, in my humble opinion, there is only one answer: cellists did not succeed in developing a technique which would have made it possible to eliminate the special difficulties of the instrument in order to attain a pure artistic pleasure from cello playing. I myself have heard different representatives of the last generation of the last century, who in turn were products of the previous generation, so that I can pass judgment about the great time span upon which my opinion is based. Technique was perfected only insofar as it enabled one to play quickly. The development of cello playing stood still where culture—that is art—begins. Though there were exceptions, the general trend only produced unpolished playing.

At this time most of the cellists were German, yet Germany, with few exceptions, had no *great* string players. (Joachim, for instance, for fifty years Germany's leading string player, was a Hungarian Jew.) One took it for granted that scratching, muddiness, poor phrasing, unspeakable glissandi, even poor intonation were characteristic of the cello. Many of the cellists were excellent musicians and good composers for their instruments. The trouble was that no one had shown them that the weaknesses of the instrument could be overcome and that the cello as a solo instrument, because of its wider range, could be superior even to the violin. In Vienna a story about Brahms was still circulating, though he had been dead for thirty years: after Brahms had played his first cello sonata with the then foremost cellist of Vienna, the latter complained to him, "you played so loud thatat I couuld not hear myself." Brahms replied, "you are the lucky one."

When I took lessons with the famous Julius Klengel and I deviated from the usual fingering, he thought I did it only because of my long fingers. He could not understand that I did it to improve the phrasing. When I started concertizing twenty years ago, the critics complained that I played violin on the cello, because they were accustomed to the usual way of cello playing. In a certain way, cellists were pitied for their unsuccessful efforts to compete with the violin; one expected to be bored at a cello recital. The public was only pleased with a few short solos; arrangements of a gavotte, a minuet, or an adagio, all played with a certain amount of "Schmaltz."

Cellists reached a certain level at the beginning of the development of their instrument, then stopped. Composers were certainly not inspired by what cello playing they had the chance to hear to write great works for that instrument nor did the public rush to hear cello recitals.

Finally, *the* great personality appeared on the cello horizon and through this one man the cello was established as a full-fledged member of the family of solo instruments. That man was Casals. Everyone who has heard him knows that a new period of the cello has come. He has shown that the cello can sing without "Schmaltz," that on no other instrument can phrasing be smoother; that through clever fingerings the disrupting jumps have disappeared and so have the ugly noises, up to then thought an integral part of cello playing. What Liszt was to the piano, Viotti or Paganini to the violin, Casals is for the cello. We younger cellists must be most grateful to him, for he showed *us* what can be done on the cello, showed to the public what an artistic pleasure listening to cello playing can be, and inspired most of the contemporary composers to write for our instrument.

May I take the liberty here to speak directly to my colleagues. It seems to me that quite a number of them do not recognize that cello playing has been revolutionized during their own lifetime. Many of them stick to the way they have been taught and remain, even perhaps voluntarily, untouched by the changes I have spoken of, even try to resist them. They remind me of people who still rode in horsewagons when the railway was already running. The way piano and violin are played now has undergone only minor changes in the last hundred years while cello playing has reached a corresponding level only recently. I wish that my colleagues might open their minds to this, and by doing so do their share to make our instrument as much appreciated and popular as it deserves to be.

PART II
Notes on Playing the Cello

To the Student

My dear friend,

It happened as I predicted. You came to me an established cellist. You played all the concerti and chamber music and felt confident of your ability. True, you had some difficulty with intonation and your staccato did not seem very good. In addition you expected some help in the interpretation of the bigger works of our literature. But you had the feeling that these, plus a few other minor problems, could be corrected in just a few lessons.

When your time was over and you left for home, I felt great pity for you. You seemed broken and no longer knew what was right or wrong. This did not happen all at once. When you first came to me, I told you there were others who had come expecting to be helped in a short time, but were instead given the miserable feeling that they would never be able to play again. You were like the man who takes his car to the garage for a paint job and two new spark plugs, only to be told the whole motor has to be taken out and a new electrical system put in, not only to make the car run better, but to allow her for the first time to take advantage of all her potentialities.

After seeing you leave in that desolate condition, I was more than pleased to read your letter, which shows so much appreciation, understanding, and good will. But it contains so many questions it would be difficult to answer all of them thoroughly without writing a whole book. And gradually this very idea took solid shape, until, finally, I decided to write it. I shall send you a chapter at a time as it is finished and I would appreciate your answering me right away to let me know of things that are unclear to you.

I had put you off balance and everything seemed upside down. You did not dare play a note for fear it would be wrong. You had become uncertain and self-conscious. You remember how surprised you were when, even as you tuned your cello, I made remarks about how I expected you to play in general. And how, in the course of the lessons, more or less for fun, I predicted how you would play certain phrases or how you would finger certain passages. Why should that be so mysterious to you? Consider the amount of experience I have collected over the years from teaching and giving auditions; consider that my present technique was developed in direct opposition to the way I was taught to play myself; and consider that I am seldom satisfied with my own playing and, if at all, only with parts, never with a whole performance. Then perhaps you will understand that, even if music and some of its great performers are still a mystery to me, there is nothing that can be done on the cello or any other instrument, whether it be improbable or impossible, that will ever surprise me.

However, I would be immodest if I let you believe that I was the only one who knew how badly a stringed instrument can be played. Not long ago, I heard perhaps the best living violinist play the first movement of a Viotti concerto so poorly, with every possible mistake, that, closing my eyes, I could have imagined I was listening to it at a pupil's concert in Kalamazoo.

Thoughts on Playing

I realize that in performing, as in all other things, there is a scale from the best to the worst. The question arises automatically, why is it that in all other professions there is an effort made to raise the standard and the average, while in our profession, there is not even the slightest attempt to recognize existing lacks or more especially the need for correction. Nine times out of ten when I hear cello playing, I cannot but ask myself, does cello playing mean turning off the brain and ear and the connecting muscular system? I shall go so far as to insist that, as absurd as it may sound, brain and ear muscles must have been turned off in order for generation after generation to have produced cellists whose playing is an insult to the ear. Even worse: that it is not generally so perceived that there is an even more shameful reason behind it—one expects nothing special from the average cellist and accepts unquestioningly that the difference between the few really good cellists and the mass of cellists must be so great. Besides, most people are too polite and few are interested enough to perceive the reasons for the difference.

The Demands of the Instrument

I do not believe the cello must be played poorly. I will maintain that in the not-too-distant future the standards of cellists, will be raised. I cannot stand idly by and see so much talent and energy wasted. To me every serious-minded, ambitious young cellist is a living reproach: I am talented, I want to work; is it not possible that my talents can be developed?

They say one must be born a musician. Of the cellist one can say one is perhaps born to be a cellist, but one is not born with the possibility to develop oneself fully. Sad, but true. Take your own case. You are talented, you have studied for many years, and you feel you have the right to assume that you are a good cellist. Still, I had little difficulty convincing you, intelligent as you are, that you are unaware of most of the things which go together to make a good musician and a good cellist. You asked me in the lessons and again in your letter why no one had ever taught you to look at things the way I suggest. The answer is that in years of studying with teachers of good standing you have not been led to recognize the simplest and most obvious principles, or almost any principles.

What *I* have told you is not that you did not grasp the idea in a certain piece or that you played out of tune. Rather I outlined to you your lack of knowledge of 1) how to read music, 2) how to look over a piece of music and recognize its structure and its moods, 3) the physics of your arms and their proper use, 4) difficulties of the instrument and bow and the rules and principles to overcome them, and 5) most important, how to bring these rules and principles to life and how best to apply them to the music.

It is surprising how few rules and principles there are and still more surprising how completely they change the entire style of playing. Believe it or not, my dear friend, the really outstanding string players, whether Kreisler, Casals, or Heifetz, are similar to each other in the way they use their muscular systems and handle their instruments and bows. The main differences lie in their different personalities, talents, and ideas, and only to a very small extent in their techniques, for which, again, physical differences are accountable.

Very simply, these rules are not demanded of the performer, but demanded by the instrument. Please understand this point thoroughly, because this is the basic fault of your approach. You have to know your instruments—cello and bow—and how to handle them, the demands of the music and your mental and physical abilities and weaknesses to be able to recognize your mistakes, the inadequacies in your playing and to try to correct them. Analysis, patience, and endurance are the main requirements for your development.

One small example: when a cellist plays fast détaché notes on the lower strings, you can hardly speak of the sound he produces, rather, you could call it a scratchy noise. The reason? You can only get a good sound from a string if it vibrates. Bring the string to vibration and one of the worst handicaps of the cello disappears. A very simple fact, certainly not a miracle, easy to remedy, yet still not recognized as the source of one of the ugliest and most prevalent ills of cello playing.

Let me try to explain to you what I mean by "approach." Except for groups of fast notes where a given number of notes are one single rhythmical unit, there is not a note in music that should be played without expression or articulation. It can be compared to speaking, in which every syllable has its rhythm and phrasing within a sentence, according to its desired meaning. So, every note must be played according to the intended expression within the musical phrase.

Approaching the Music

As in a written sentence the only guidelines are the single words, commas, periods, question marks, etc., so in music notation we have only the bar lines, the bowings, the pitch and length of the single notes, and expression marks (accents, crescendi, etc., play quite a special role). What meaning can there be in a story recited in a monotone? Very little. The words may be recognizable, but there will be little real sense.

Cultured people grasp meaning by silently pronouncing what they are reading. This is an automatic process. Only children and people not used to reading read with great effort and are content if they can get an approximately correct literal meaning, without troubling themselves with the real meaning.

When you played for me, I showed you how little attention you have given to this way of looking at music, to this kind of approach, the most important one for a performer that I know of. Of course, partly by chance, partly because we have more to lean on in musical notation than in language, and partly because you have a musical education outside of cello playing, and lastly because one cannot practice and play for years without achieving something, you quite often understood the meaning of the music. To my satisfaction you soon realized that if your playing was to improve, you could no longer depend upon chance. But you also noticed that the mental approach alone did not suffice. There must be as much pleasure in listening to a musical performance as there is in reading beautiful prose or poetry. For the performer who has expected this mental approach to bring him to a higher stage in playing, the difficulties and disappointments now begin. Now he knows and feels what he must play, but as soon as he sits down to play, he finds out he is not able to. Why?

Up to now I have been speaking of an approach to music (mental or abstract approach) which is applicable to all instruments. As a performer one must know one's instrument, its beauties and weaknesses; one must know how to help oneself. In order to avoid playing uncritically, one must not shy away from employing any trick to achieve purity and rhythmical exactitude. In doing so he will be able to reproduce the spirit of the music insofar as it is possible. A combination of a responsible approach towards music and complete mastery of the instrument to make possible the realization of the music is the ideal toward which I am constantly striving and which I would like to pass on to my fellow musicians. Talent for music is another thing; here we are discussing intelligence.

Talent: the Scale

As I have said before, it appears that cellists eliminate the mind and ears as soon as they turn to cello playing. That sounds very rude, but I am almost sure that a politician, a singer, or a farmer loving his métier and being serious about it—not just wanting to outshine his colleagues but being confident that the better off his neighbour is, the better off he will be—feel and think the same way about their confreres.

I daresay that it is not any more difficult to play well than to play poorly. Talent plays an important part in how well one plays, but talent alone, unless combined with intelligence, effort, and persistence, is not enough. How often do we meet people, especially in the arts, of whom we can speak as wasted talents. The real talents find their way anyhow. And by these very exceptions, one can say with good conscience that the better balanced one can keep talent and general intelligence, as well as specific intelligence, the better one will play.

Naturally, years of practice will advance a performer, and a certain amount of facility, a beautiful vibrato, and a good tone quality are accomplished by many. I am always struck by the thought of how much better most musicians (who now just get along) would play if they had been led the proper way.

Let us take one example of inadequacy in a cellist for an explanation; from the very beginning to the very end, scales play a big role in a cellist's life. For the beginner the scale is an aid in getting acquainted with notes, intervals, positions, and intonation. After this, scales still remain a daily practice. It is my custom to ask for scales when someone plays an audition for me. Cellists who play for me are usually considered accomplished, who, as for instance you did, come for some advice, for the "last touch." But not once have I heard a scale played from which I could have assumed that the player knew even in the slightest the fundamentals of the scale. What do I hear—uncertain intonation, uneven fingers, awkward string crossings and position changes. And what do I like to hear? A scale made up of clean tones, the fingers going down in such a way that the unequal strength of the fingers is hidden; a scale in which audible string crossings do not exist and in which the position is changed so quickly that the difference between a finger placed on the string and a change of position can hardly be felt; thus a row of notes of uniform strength, perfect in intonation and without disrupting, extraneous noises, these are the fundamentals of a scale, the ideal!

How does one approach this ideal? Just by playing a scale over and over again, believing everything is done if the scale is played fast and approximately in tune? No. By having such an ideal, an imaginary, perfect, bodyless scale in the mind and in the ear, every cellist can overcome the difficulties of the instrument to a surprising extent. Musical example: You remember, my dear friend, that you played the Beethoven A Major Sonata for me and that you never had thought it possible that you, a musician with the best of intentions, could be doing the worst injustice to the second theme, which consists of nothing but scales. You must also remember how much concentration it requires, how much careful watching of every note and especially careful connecting of notes to give those "scales" the beauty which lies in the evenness of their execution. I wonder if you can play them now to your satisfaction, after I succeeded in opening your ears a little, now that your demands on yourself have grown so much.

Basic Techniques

In order to understand something, more important still to improve something, one must get to the foundation and analyze it; it is necessary to discover the relationships of the single components to one another. Then it becomes understandable—in cello playing—how much has been taken for granted, when the only information passed down over the years is harmful and twisted: it consists of poor judgment, incomprehensibility, ignorance, and certainly lack of perception of what on the surface is obvious. As yet, no one has argued against me in this. Personality and different interpretations, etc., would be considered on a different plane. Three separate factors—music, instrument, and interpretation—play a fateful role. One can discuss the interpretation of the music as well as the amount of freedom allowed to the interpreter.

However, one cannot merely discuss the peculiarities of an instrument or man's physical structure. Just as for example one can pronounce the letter "m" by closing the lips and following a set physical procedure, so by observing and following the known immutable rules, one can draw a clear tone, play purely, produce a crescendo, etc. As obvious and superfluous as it may seem to mention it, it is my opinion that the basic ill of poor playing lies in the absolute disregard of natural laws.

The cello presents a performer with great opposition. This is true of most of the lower-register instruments. There are general physical rules, and for the instrument and bow specific rules, which one must learn and follow if one wants to go beyond the mere skills of music to stretch the capabilities of the instrument.

A. Cello

1. Contact between the player and the cello is on the strings.
2. A clear tone can be produced only when the strings are vibrating fully.
3. The string can only be brought into full motion when it is stopped as completely by the finger as by the nut.
4. As soon as the bow is drawn over the string everything that the fingers do on the strings will sound. Then it is necessary that the fingers follow one another cleanly, evenly and quickly.
5. The intervals are set and become narrower at the top.
6. The tension of the string is greatest toward the bridge; therefore the string will sound *piano* near the fingerboard. The nearer the bow comes to the bridge, the stronger the sound will be.

7. The timbre of the pizzicato changes according to the amount of space between the point where the finger plucks the string and the bridge. It is harsher near the bridge and softer further away from it. The ugly noise that usually accompanies the pizzicato on the lower strings occurs because the string is plucked from beneath (with the finger *between* the fingerboard and string), and therefore the string hits the fingerboard when plucked.

B. Bow

1. Only the hair should touch the string; even with the greatest pressure of the fingers on the bow, the stick should touch only the hair and not the string.
2. The bow is lighter toward the tip; therefore, for the bow to sound evenly from tip to frog, one must compensate by increasing the pressure toward the tip.
3. The bow must be drawn parallel to the end of the fingerboard if one wishes to avoid the unpleasant sounds that accompany crooked bowing.
4. Every alteration in the surface area of the hair that touches the string changes the amount of tone; therefore, in order to play *piano,* only a small portion of the hair should be placed on the string, the more hair, the greater the strength.

C. The Body

The body should be so comfortable and relaxed when playing that the use of the muscles, tendons, wrists, and fingers is in no way inhibited. It is not stressed often enough that the playing of an instrument is physical work and therefore the same rules can be applied to it as to any other activity in which skill is demanded. A certain amount of timidity leads musicians to fear that they will be considered craftsmen, not artists, if they give importance to the physical aspects of playing. But this is small-minded. To conceal such realities could harm the development of the real artist. It is art and music which ennoble technique and skill and which therefore make the most talented, intelligent, and skillful musician into a true artist. It could be said that Rafael, even without hands, would have become a great artist. Yet one should not forget that Rafael had his hands. Technique is necessary in order that the genius, fantasy, spiritual power, and richness of ideas of a Rafael be allowed to rise above being just good art. And besides in the painter are combined both the creating *and* the performing artist, which in music would be the composer and the interpreter.

Interpretation

In my viewpoint, one must be very clear about the various factors within the music, which are independent of one another, and whose union is found for the first time in the accomplished performing musician: a composer must have learned an instrument, must have mastery over it in order for his compositions to be performed. Thus, genius, talent, knowledge of the musical content are not sufficient to be even remotely just [adequate] to the task of interpretation. Mastery of the instrument is necessary for this purpose.

How often, however, within the interpretation, the performer's grasp of the musical content and the performance itself, as well as musicality and technique, become separated from one another. Yet they are equally important. One must put oneself in the position of a conductor. *He* is the spiritual interpreter of the music, responsible for the phrasing, the shaping, for the blending of timbres, i.e., for fulfilling the intention of the composer. But it is the orchestra which brings his interpretation to realization. Whether a composition can better survive either the combination of good conductor with genius and poor orchestra without technique or a good orchestra with technique and a poor conductor without genius is a question that can never be answered. It is a personal matter and does not evoke a generally valid answer.

I believe, however, that the question of a musical goal can be discussed and this goal is: within the interpretation, the incorporation of the most intelligent grasp of the music; and within the performance, a sense of responsibility to the smallest detail. I believe that much mischief has been done because hardly anyone has attempted to clarify the function of interpretation. The exceptions—the great talents—come intuitively or through conscious study to results suitable for them. This question has remained almost untouched within the study of music; I daresay it is rarely mentioned. Yet it could be of great benefit for students if teachers would bring their attention to this point.

What is the function of the interpreter? Without wanting to appear to have found the only valid answer to the question, it is my opinion that the function of the performer is to become gradually acquainted with the mind of the composer and with the content of the composition, and then to fit his own personality and ability to them. Without attaching such words as "classic" or "romantic," it is still clear that what is necessary for the interpretation of a Bach Suite must be very different from that which a Tschaikovsky composition demands. Small slides, ritards, and crescendi, which match the spirit of a serenade or air and without which such a piece would lose all meaning, have no place in a Bach or Beethoven composition.

The ideal interpreter for me would be one who 1) is capable of grasping the period, the style, taste, and intention of *all* compositions which he must play, 2) possesses unlimited technique and interpretative skills, and 3) is capable of applying his technique and interpretative skills to the composition.

Such an interpreter does not exist. Even the greatest, most earnest performer will play best that music which lies closest to his nature, his character, and his general musical education, yet he will still *try* to grasp the spirit of the piece he is playing. How sad, however, is the result reached by the performers who have never concerned themselves with these questions and whose interpretative skill is a closed book. How often I have heard a "famous" artist present a Bach gavotte as if it were a composition by Offenbach, and on the other hand a piece by Brahms or Beethoven in which, true, the notes were played, but with neither content nor meaning. It could be compared to listening to a recitation of a poem in a language one does not understand. Where does that leave the sense of responsibility in interpreting? Is a composition the same as a piece of wax with no specific shape, or is it something to which an interpreter must first give shape? Or is not a composition the property of the composer, which is presented to us, the players, for its final realization, an unknown property that we must oversee with the greatest conscientiousness and love, with the addition of all our spiritual and material powers.

I do not mean to imply that the answering of this question is alone enough to make a good performer out of a poor performer. But surely concerning oneself with this problem and recognizing its overwhelming importance can be of great practical use to many. In order to convince oneself that idiosyncrasy as well as overdone individualism or a combination of both by the interpreter are not a new phenomenon, one need only study the letters of composers from Mozart up until our own time. Again and again, the same complaints arise about carelessness, misconceptions, and lack of ability. Even Leopold Mozart, father of Wolfgang, in his magnificent *Violinschule,* in 1756 complains about the irresponsible teachers and the vain players who want to be alone in the limelight and completely forget the composition. It is sad to realize that nothing has changed in the two centuries since Mozart.

I used the term "interpretation technique" earlier, and I would like to discuss it more fully. Usually the concepts of technique and musicality are played against one another—a player is characterized as a mere technician, but not musical, or else as a good musician, but without technique. Usually the latter is said in praise, as if musicality alone makes the artist, while the term "technician" is an unflattering description meant to disparage the artist. This debate about technique and musicality results in much nonsense and confusion, and what is worse, is aided through amateurism.

How simple it is for the musician who can really do precious little to display an air of authority, in that he boasts about his "musicality," but consciously demeans "technique" as something inferior, possibly even inartistic. Rating musicality above technique is tempting for many performers as well as for the public, because they can then believe that they are in the upper spheres; this justification is used by many players. Well-intentioned people believe that through such an underestimation of technique, of basic skills, they can concentrate on more fitting goals in music—the spiritual—when in reality they open wide the doors and gates for those who cannot play; they sanction the desecration of music by these bluffers.

How many good artists would be found among the amateurs and in the audience, if the only consideration were the ability to recognize and comprehend the spiritual, the metaphysical, the technique of writing in music. I myself know hundreds of nonmusicians all over the world who are completely at home—as dilettantes—with either orchestra or chamber music literature, or with the instrumental repertoire, and about whom one could maintain that they have grasped the music. Nothing is easier to answer than the question why they are not also capable of interpreting the pieces. Because they do not have the *ability* to direct a symphony or to present a concert on some instrument. It is therefore useless to praise the musician above the technician; the comparison leads to confusion from which only the fakers and bluffers benefit.

There is little interest taken in analyzing or clarifying the word "technique" when speaking of an instrumentalist. This expression is usually employed to mean facility, secure intonation, and mastery over all the different types of bowing. If this is technique, how should one designate the ability to interpret a piece of music; for interpreting does not mean simply playing through a piece quickly but, after one has grasped the spirit of a piece, the important themes, the musical line and structure, then one has the means for presenting the music as one wishes.

I would say that the word "technique" be used to express mastery over the entire mechanism. When one understands that mastery of the mechanism of an instrument makes the real artist as little as does simple comprehension of the music, I can then go farther to say that the combination of these two factors is still not sufficient. It is the link *between* mechanism and music which counts, the application of the mechanism to the music: *The technique of interpretation.*

The Scale: An Example of Interpretation Technique

When I look around myself among students, orchestra and chamber music players, and concert artists, I realize again and again the amazing fact that the interpretation technique is neither known nor developed; at all events, not enough emphasis is placed upon it. We are concerned here that the two spheres—the mechanical and the musical—not be viewed as separate entities, but that it will be recognized that artistic playing in music can only be reached through uniting the two. The simplest example: a scale. Is a scale only a technical exercise? What is practiced in a scale? What *can* and *should* be practiced in a scale?

The answer to these questions is not as easy as it might appear, at least for me, because I am of the opinion that the real purpose of practice is to change an idea into reality. Therefore, it is necessary to have some idea beforehand in order to give meaning to the practicing. For me, as for all who consider a scale as something more than a group of consecutive notes played fairly cleanly, the ideal scale would be comparable to a row of pearls of equal size and lustre. Is such a perfectly-played scale only a matter of mechanics? Or is it not rather a musical challenge which must be met if a scale is called for in a piece?

What must be practiced, watched for, and accomplished to do justice to a scale according to the very highest of musical demands?
1) Even articulation for each individual note, whether fingering, change in positions, or open strings are concerned.
2) As little difference as possible between going up the scale and going down.
3) Rhythmical independence of string and position change arranged so that, as the notes are played on a string or in a position, groups of two or three notes are formed.
4) No break in the scale because of bow changes.
5) Secure intonation.
6) Rhythm: a scale as practiced is a matter of mechanics. Within a piece of music it is a musical phrase to which one can do justice only if one has completely mastered the mechanics of playing. What that requires, I have tried to show you above.

In any case, in order to make the most of a scale, it is not enough to practice only for intonation and facility.

Practice and Teaching

One of the most interesting topics in music and the teaching of music is practice. Here as in everything lack of forethought and interest commonly dominate. The pupil receives his assignment, he returns for the lesson, the teacher points out false notes here and there, changes a few fingerings, perhaps suggests more freedom of playing or scolds because the pupil has not given enough time to his lesson, and with this it is over. Even an untalented pupil will with this customary kind of instruction make progress over the years and reach a certain degree of facility.

Counter to this way of teaching is one in which one single method dominates. One teacher constantly emphasizes "technique;" the pupil must practice long hours; above all he must practice difficult pieces, must concentrate on intonation and speed. The mechanism which is so necessary for the beauty and elegance of music is not practiced, but it must be played quickly and clearly. Its melodic qualities and its phrasing are hardly touched; and the real precision work on the instrument, which is as enduring and gratifying as the inside of a watch or as the work of a smithy, does not exist. Sevčik, the famous violin teacher, said once in my presence to a pupil, after he had completed the first movement of Mendelssohn's concerto: we can go on to the third movement, the second you will play well later on your own.

Another form of teaching, found mostly in Germany, is one in which music is considered a holy matter, so metaphysical—not of- but above-the-earth—that it would be a sacrilege even to hint at anything resembling technique within music. During the lessons the student will be constantly reminded of the seriousness, the majesty, the nobility of the artistic profession. Technique or mechanism will be regarded with contempt, with the result that after years of such instruction, the young person, who believes himself an artist, an exceptional person, is sent out into the world, often conceited and arrogant, without being capable of conveying even a vague notion, whether true or false, of art.

Then there are other methods of instruction, which emphasize various specific elements: one teacher insists on a high elbow in the right arm; the other points out that the wrist must be thrown forward when in an up-bow as the frog nears the string; and still another maintains that the fingers must be placed perpendicular to the string; while a fourth is dominated by the thought that each bow that is drawn must include a crescendo and decrescendo; the other tries to allow as much racing around on the "A" string as possible, while for still another the thumb position, as used or not used, alone represents the "soul-saving church," etc., etc.

I wanted to speak of practicing, but instead I have been preoccupied with my knowledge of teachers and pupils. How is painting taught? A master lets his pupils work in a studio and they are always under his supervision. No time is thus lost as often happens with us—for example, a pupil who misunderstands the teacher and works incorrectly on one specific thing for a week. He must then return home and unlearn what he has practiced. In the former method, the results will not be demonstrated to the teacher during the lesson, rather the teacher can witness and follow at first hand all the phases of the student's progress, his talent, his diligence, and can therefore pay more attention to the student's personality.

How different it is with us! Usually one hour a week is reserved for the lesson—and what are sixty minutes?—the student has time to play a little for the teacher, correct a little, and say: I will come again next week. It is also necessary to have time to treat the pupil as a human being, to show him the problems and a way to solution. How often does it happen to me that at the beginning of the lesson a question comes up which brings up other questions along with it. I try to explain, to demonstrate how it should be done, while others pupils who are there come in with their problems. Before you turn around, the hour is over and the pupil has not had time to play what he had prepared during the week. I am very sympathetic towards a pupil who has not only done his homework obediently, but who has concerned himself with all the thorny problems. He has a right to question this "one lesson a week" system, which hardly gives the teacher time to teach his student, let along influence and enlighten him.

My ideal is for the teacher to watch the student during practice. Where would the comparison to painting lie? How and where would it be possible to carry over the art of teaching painting to music? The teacher could work with his students in the same building; in this way students could always have their teachers as "ears" and the teacher could go from room to room, correcting pupils while they are *practicing*. This would be Utopia! Not only because of the question of room. Candidly, teachers are not always inclined to lend their ears to their pupils for any longer than thirty, forty, or sixty minutes. A significant question remains, whose answer is hardly in the affirmative: how intensively or meaningfully do the teachers themselves practice?

As I have said above, the lesson for the most part goes as follows: from one lesson to the next the student must complete a certain amount of work: perhaps a scale, an étude, and a section of some piece. If the student is diligent he will practice his lesson, that is, he will repeat what he will have to play during the lesson numerous times, so that he can play the scale, étude, and piece fairly cleanly and up to tempo. The teacher is satisfied, corrects a wrong note here and there. Possibly in the piece he will suggest a ritardando at some point (that may not even belong there), at another point he may speak about poetry (without being able to explain how poetical feelings can be translated into reality on an instrument), and the student gets a new assignment for next week, which he practices just as faithfully. Thus the lessons go throughout the year until the student reaches a point where he can play fairly cleanly and quickly, attain a beautiful tone (it is to be hoped), and gain mastery over the cello repertoire or at least be acquainted with it.

An untalented or lazy pupil practices little, gets stuck in his lesson, the teacher scolds, the pupil needs two weeks for a lesson instead of one, and reaches that final point mentioned earlier after a much longer period of study, perhaps even never.

I have played cello for thirty years. My experiences with my own teachers and reports given me by many of my pupils about the lessons they had had up until then, have convinced me that with certain positive and negative exceptions, in general, the lesson proceeds as described above. And I also know that piano and violin are taught in the same manner, but with the difference that there have been many great masters in both, and there has always existed an elite of teachers who have taught in a way which I would like to see developed on the cello.

PART III
Thoughts on Technique and Interpretation

Musical life attains its height in the great talents and in the few rare geniuses, but is sustained by the less talented, "the middle class and the masses." Therefore it is necessary to change the way of playing of the masses. As a sign of poor teaching and of difficulties common to all, most of the mistakes, those that are most fundamental, are committed in smaller or larger proportion by all players.

There is the instrumentalist who, when he sees dots over notes, forgets the music and its contents and concerns himself solely with playing the notes short. Yet there are dozens of different ways of interpreting such [a] symbol, and the performer must discern from the character of the piece which method the composer may have preferred. There can be differences of opinion about how to interpret a dot, not however about the fact that a symbol can be presented in different ways, and one must be chosen. In contrast, there are those who do not even see the symbols.

Bad: the absolute lack of rhythmical sensitivity to the rests within a phrase, i.e., short pauses. As if the length of the note received more of the player's attention than the rest.

Very bad: reading of music. . . . .

Commitment to only one method: according to one principle, the fingers of the right hand must always be held in a certain position, let us say rounded at the frog. According to another principle, the fingers are held parallel to one another. They cannot always be held so, since *forte* and *piano* demand different things of the bow hand and will require different adjustments. Some methods go so far as to urge pupils to draw out the peg to a fixed length. The drawbacks of this are the following: 1) the height of the cello has to be adapted to each player *individually* because there hardly exist two exactly equal human bodies, and the position of the cello has to fit in the player, not vice versa, and 2) one can remain independent of the peg's height by drawing the cello in or pulling it out.

In any physical activity, an individual's achievement is heightened the more his muscles are used to advantage and the more comfortable he feels. This generally acknowledged theory has not yet made its way into cello lessons. As calmly and well balanced as a cellist may sit with his cello, the moment he starts to play, a change takes place in his body; suddenly his head sits lopsided on his shoulders, one shoulder is pulled up, the elbow is stretched out in a pointed angle, and the wrist of his right hand becomes stiff, like a board, or his hand dangles about as if it were drunk and the left hand assumes a position that causes one to ask how it is possible even to strike a note, to vibrate, to move from one position to the next.

Talent

As in driving a car, so much has to be done at one time that it seems impossible that it could ever be done mechanically, without deliberating about each movement beforehand.

What is talent? Desire to make sounds? Desire to create something beautiful? Vanity? A longing for something inexpressible? The fingers? The powers of concentration? Talent is composed of many talents and is dependent on fate. One likes serious music, another likes lighter music; one likes classical, the other modern. Speaking of the purely physical aspects, one may have a better left hand, the other a better right; one may have faster fingers, yet many have difficulties with trills; staccato and spiccato are also accomplished differently by each player. The greater the talent the greater the number of these qualifications the performer will be able to accumulate. Even perfect pitch does not predestine one for music.

The really important factors are a feeling for form, perseverance and patience, thoroughness and lust for discovery. Many are destined to become musicians even when they are still too small to have anything to say about it themselves. It is often said of the great ones that they are involved in a one-sided and unrequited love.

There are specific musical attributes and also attributes that music has in common with other artistic professions. And when one looks more closely, there are but a few attributes which are peculiar to music. The relaxation of certain muscles and tendons and at the same time the stretching of others, the balancing of weight to make the most of the physical equipment, the distribution of weight on the bow, the determination of fingering, of crescendo and decrescendo, accelerando and ritardando, i.e., feeling for form. There are comparable attributes for all these in sports and in business life. For the musician alone is reserved the metaphysical province of predestination for music, which includes such physical matters as flexibility of the fingers and coordination of both hands and arms.

Personality

A composition is written, conceived, and, except for those experts who can read music, it is dead, does not exist, if it is not reproduced by a musician. The situation would be very simple if a machine could do this work; then a way would have been found over the centuries to pass on to the listener the composer's intention to a hair. Instead we have humans, who act as mediators; and since no two people are alike, the reproduction of the music depends on the respective performers.

In the beginning, the composer was also the player; it was more or less one profession. Then came a separation, and gradually the role of mere reproduction became all the more important. Since composer and reproducer are no longer the same person and since the composers whom one is interpreting have been dead for centuries, the reproducer has become independent and autonomous. In my opinion the relationship has been disarranged to such a degree that the performer has become less the mediator between composer and listener and more the handler of raw material, who gives it its final form. This development was inevitable, for we are dealing with a human being, whose natural impulse is to place his own personality in the foreground. Even Mozart complained that his music was being desecrated, but it cannot have been as bad then as in the nineteenth century, in which liberalism led to the false admiration of one's personality.

We must make it clear to ourselves that it would do great harm to Beethoven's music if each musician were allowed to maintain the essentiality of his own personality for the shaping and molding of Beethoven. This arrogant attitude does great damage to both music and public. The personality cannot be excluded, but the musician must try to live up to the composer and not bring the composer down to his level. We must take it for granted that of the two, the composer is the greater. The goal which I consider as the most important for the player is: abandon vanity, and ability, if there is any thought behind it at all, will come forth.

Mechanics, Musicality, Technique—a Tripartite Analysis

Here technique, there musicality—an ancient comparison which is senseless and has done great damage to the perfection of playing. There should be a three-part division: mechanism, musicality, and technique, which when used musically is the mechanism. It is the mechanism alone that is necessary—for the juggler, sharpshooter, or maker of fine instruments; on the other hand a "musical" person—because of his musicality, his knowledge about the music, or his love for music—is still not necessarily an artist. There are many amateurs who have more sensitivity to music than some artists. There are nonprofessional people who are experts in the field of music. I knew a French general who had the most amazing knowledge of Bach.

If there is no fitting definition for talent, there is also none for an artist. I believe that an artist is a person who has an inexplicable longing for music, who has a knowledge of the music, combined with mastery of the mechanics of his instrument. Each of these components consists of a combination of innumerable items. In the case of music, come the different styles. In the case of man, there is temperament, education, dependence on physical conditions (which only to a certain extent coalesce in the same person, resulting in better or worse players), and even a predilection for specific periods within music. A person with extroverted, that is, uninhibited temperament will not be able to render well the great passion of Mozart, his most daring ideas, his wit, longing, heroism, and beauty in as representatively idiomatic or compelling manner as might have been possible in Mozart's time. On the other hand he may be a born interpreter of Tschaikovsky.

Much nonsense is expounded because art has been misplaced in the spheres, as if nothing solid or craftsmanlike exists. How wrong this is. The great composers and interpreters were scornful of this view of art. Even a Beethoven had, even as his first works had already come out, continued studying counterpoint, and I myself have seen a manuscript of Beethoven's in which he had written counterpoint studies; and at the end he says, if I remember correctly: it could be done correctly another way as well. Leopold Mozart in his *Violinschule* scolds the musicians who use the word "artist" loosely, yet cannot even keep time.

Interpretation

The position of the interpreter is highly individual because he can very easily become identified with the composition he is performing. The audience, because of the presence of the artist and the absence of the composer, will be given an incorrect impression of the piece—and so will the artist.

What is the interpreter's actual place within music? There is no doubt that music is written to be heard, and by as many people as possible. A composer is, after all, only human and since the time that there has been a concert life the composer has been described as having never derived pure artistic satisfaction from what he has written, be he a Mozart or a Wagner. Music appears to be dead on paper, and each time it is played, it is revived. Scores are a delight for the expert, but they are not written for him, and the number of experts is small indeed. The importance of the interpreter cannot be valued too highly. The more important a position or a person is, the more depends on him. Even if the question of *interpreter* is easy to answer, the question of interpretation presents greater difficulties. The interpreter is a person, not a machine, which means that the composer only indirectly addresses his listeners. Every performer is different, and it is inevitable that no two interpreters will present a piece alike.

And now I come to the most important question for the practicing artist: is a piece composed to give the interpreter the opportunity to express himself, or should the interpreter perceive that it is his task to subordinate one's talent and ability to the composer? An interpretation, because it is performed by a person, can never be impersonal, whether intended or not. To give an example: if one examines a composition as something written in an unintelligible language and considers the interpreter a translator, should he render a literal or a free translation? In my opinion the player should try to extract from the very incomplete score what the compóser could only indicate in his writing. He should place his personality and his ability at the disposal of the composition. Every intentional emphasis of one's own personality is an offense to the composition, in which only one personality should be expressed intentionally—that of the composer.

Students, Prodigies, and Teaching

Earlier I gave several examples to prove how generally the most obvious, and at the same time most important, things are neglected. In the course of the book I shall give many more. What I regret most is not so much that the cellists do not play to my taste. Even if I have to hurt people I have to tell these cellists that they have not had the proper guidance. Very little responsibility has been shown towards either the students or the music.

Hundreds of cellists have played for me and some of them have become my students. I almost always ask two questions: why they have come to me and where do they feel they are lacking. The answers are chiefly: faulty technique and depleted repertoire. Thus the cellists who come to me have all completed their formal musical training, many of them have positions with orchestras either as first-desk solo cellists or in the section, or with quartets. They are persons one could call accomplished and expert in music.

What has always amazed me is that not a one has even come close to saying: I realize that I do not play that badly but I find it impossible to express *that* which I have in my mind; or, I have a certain idea of how the cello should sound, but I cannot achieve it alone. This has led me to the conclusion that most instrumentalists, at the stage when they are allowed to become independent by their teachers, should therefore be able to think independently. They should be clear about their instruments and their music. Yet they are not prepared for such a situation, and are therefore hardly capable of developing alone.

As sad as this may be, I can only thus explain to myself the standstill most musicians come to at a certain age and level. They feel that as soon as they leave the school or the teacher they have reached the height. But is not this the point at which the development begins?

The most blatant example is the prodigy. The prodigy is usually the performing voice of a good teacher: he is soft putty in the teacher's hands. I am of the opinion that a prodigy is not even destined for music, but that is another matter. In any case, it is a fact that most prodigies do not develop into artists, but at that moment when their own personality should make its appearance, they fail completely. Many reasons have been advanced for this and each case is different. Probably common to all is that, as long as they are under the influence of teachers or their often profit-seeking parents, they are treated as machines. No one tries to influence and develop their personal lives as musicians and people. On the contrary, in order to get the most out of the object—the prodigy—it is necessary to keep under strict control whatever appears to be the most advantageous as a *momentary* goal. But the prodigy is completely unprepared for the future as an independent, thinking human being; he is completely defenseless.

This development, which is considered normal, is similar for most musicians. I intend to write neither a theory nor a method. I do not even know if this will be a thick book or a small pamphlet. I think that the title "Words of Advice" approximates what I want to say. I might say that a method describes how something should be accomplished. There have been many methods written with the best intentions and with much success. There will be directions for how one should draw the bow, what the different keys are, and surely some progressive exercises, so that the student achieves a certain facility and precision in his intonation, and if he is talented and has a good teacher, he will play fairly well up to a certain point.

Because of my experiences with musicians on my own instrument, and with violinists and pianists as well, I would maintain that the most important point, the most important goal, has been ignored. Only thus is it understandable that good players, if there were an attempt made to explain to them the goal and the route to accomplishing it, could without much effort improve their playing to an amazing extent. I would like to say that it must first be clear *what* one wishes to reach and the *how* will play a secondary role.

Musicality and Technique

What should the goal be for a performer, that is for the interpreter of a composition, i.e., the musical expression of another person? To interpret as closely as possible the composer's intentions, at least what the player believes are his intentions. *How* can one best accomplish this goal? First one should recognize this goal as such and then control the means that are absolutely necessary for its accomplishment.

In my opinion, a war exists between technique and musicality. It brings with it only confusion, and makes a great performance virtually impossible. If one understands that by musicality is meant that one recognizes the intentions of the composer, then the other half of the term—"technique"—can be explained as possessing the real means necessary for bringing these intentions to fruition. It is clear that musicality has priority; but for that very reason one should value technique even more highly, because it alone makes it possible to do justice to a composition.

I fear that the words "virtuoso" and "technique" will be falsely understood and misused. The word "virtuoso" comes from *virtus* which means *ability* and *should* also characterize one who possesses the ability that is necessary for the interpretation of music. Virtuoso should be a title of honor, and I believe that even among the greatest names on the stage, only a few deserve it. Virtuoso includes: the greatest ability, respect for a piece of art, and the ability to fit one's personality to the art work. How many of us *have* this? How many of us *believe* we have it, and are mistaken about it? And how many *could* have it if they were guided properly during their development? The word "technique" is misused and misunderstood. I do not believe that I am mistaken when I maintain that technique means something entirely different: on a stringed instrument it usually means speed and intonation.

Proof that clarification of these terms is almost an absolute necessity is the fact that one always hears: X has a great amount of technique, but he is not a good musician, or: Y is a good chamber player, but he does not play violin, viola, or cello, as the case may be, well. What is really meant by such claims? Usually they mean something entirely different from what the words convey. If one maintains that someone has good technique, but he is not a good musician, then one must mean that the player can probably play quickly and clearly, but that he has no feeling for the music. Thus two or three or four factors are being taken into consideration which constitute only a small part of technique and. . . .

APPENDIX II

A FEUERMANN DISCOGRAPHY
by Fred Calland and Seymour W. Itzkoff

Note: Unless otherwise identified, all listings are of 78 r.p.m. recordings. The abbreviation "w/" means "paired with"; thus, in the first entry "(w/2)" means that the performance listed, Dvořák, is on one side of Odeon 0-7537/41, and that performance under 2, the Valensin, is on the other side of the same record.

1. DVOŘÁK—Concerto in B Minor for Cello and Orchestra, op. 104. (with the Berlin State Opera Orchestra, Michael Taube, cond.; 1930, Berlin)
Odeon 0-7537/41 (9SS, w/2)
Parlophone 10856/8 & 10871/2; also P9667/71 w/2)
American Columbia G.68037/41D (w/2)
American Decca 25300/4 (w/2)
lp: Parnassus 1 (w/30)
Test pressings of sides 1 and 2 of this set are in the Smith College collection. Side-by-side listening confirms that tiny flubs caused Feuermann (presumably) to reject them. The orchestral playing is equally poor as on the released sides.
Listed in Parlophone (US) release announcement of September, 1931

2. VALENSIN—Minuet, arranged by Taube (with Michael Taube, piano; 1930, Germany)
Odeon 0-7541 (1S, w/1)
Parlophone 10872 (w/1)
American Columbia G.68041D (w/1)
American Decca 25304 (w/1)

3. GIORDANI—Caro mio ben (with Michael Taube, piano; 1930, Germany)
Parlophone P 9270 (w/11)
Listed in the 1930–31 American Parlophone Catalog.

4. BRUCH—Kol Nidrei, op. 47 (1931, Germany)
Parlophone P59101 (2SS)
Parlophone P 9500
Parlophone P 9500 was released in the United States, September, 1932 (which also gives the side numbers 21649/50).

5. CHOPIN—Nocturne in E Flat, op. 9, no. 2, arranged by Popper (with Michael Taube, piano; 1930–31, Germany)
Parlophone P 9110 (w/9)
Parlophone 59095 (w/9)
American Decca 25747 (w/9)

6. FAURÉ—Après un rêve, op. 7, no. 1, arranged by Casals (pianist unidentified; 1930–31, Germany)
 White label test pressing marked MC 132, probably an unpublished Parlophone
(w/8)

7. SAINT-SAËNS—Allegro Appassionato for Cello and Piano, op. 43 (with
Michael Taube, piano; 1930–31, Germany)
 Parlophone P.E 10594 (1S)
 Parlophone P 9112-11 (20218)

8. SARASATE—Zapateado, op. 23, no. 2 (with piano accompaniment;
1930–31, Germany)
 White label test pressing marked MC 131, probably an unpublished Parlophone
(w/6)

9. SARASATE—Zigeunerweisen, op. 20, no. 1, Part I (with Michael Taube,
piano; 1930–31, Germany)
 Parlophone P59095 (w/5)
 Parlophone 9110 (w/5)
 Odeon 0-7543 (w/5)
 American Decca 25747 (w/5)

10. BACH—Air from the Orchestral Suite No. 3 (with Michael Taube, piano;
1930–31, Germany)
 Parlophone P 59063; also on Parlophone 9 (Lindstrom 6956)
 Parlophone P 1762 (w/11)
 Parlophone P 1762 was listed in release announcements of May 5, 1934, as new
recordings.

11. GOUNOD—Ave Maria, Meditation on Bach's Prelude, WTC 1 (with
Michael Taube, piano; 1930–31, Germany)
 Parlophone P 9270 (Lindstrom 6957, w/3)
 Parlophone P 1762 (w/10)
 (This may be the same performance as no. 12.)
 Listed in the American Parlophone Catalog for 1930–31.

12. GOUNOD—Ave Maria, Meditation on Bach's Prelude, WTC 1 (with
piano accompaniment; 1930, Germany)
 British Columbia C.DX 855 (w/23)

13. GRANADOS—Spanish Dance in E Minor, op. 37, no. 5 (with Michael
Taube, piano; 1930–31, Germany)
 Parlophone P.E 10838 (w/14)
 Parlophone P 9291 (w/14)
 American Decca 25085 (w/14)
 Parlophone P 9291 was listed in the American Parlophone Catalog of 1930–31.

14. SAINT-SAËNS—The Swan (with piano accompaniment; 1930–31, Germany)

Parlophone P.E 10838 (w/13)
Parlophone P 9291 (w/13)
American Decca 25085 (w/13)
Parlophone P 9291 was listed in the American Parlophone Catalog of 1930–31.

15. CHOPIN—Valse in A Minor, op. 34, no. 2, arranged by Feuermann (with Theo van der Pas, piano; 1932 or 1934, London)

British Columbia C.LB 18 (w/16)

16. SGAMBATI—Serenata (with Theo van der Pas, piano; 1932 or 1934, London)

British Columbia C.LB 18 (w/15)

17. POPPER—Rhapsodie Hongroise, op. 68 (with the Berlin Philharmonic Orchestra, Paul Kletzki, cond.; late 1932, Germany)

Telefunken T-B1235 (10″, 2SS)
Matrix ½ 1864⅔

18. DVORAK—Rondo in G Minor for Cello and Piano, op. 94 (with piano accompaniment; 1932, Germany)

Parlophone P 1797; Lindstrom 6958 (w/19)
Parlophone E 10263 (w/19)
Parlophone P 1797 was listed in the United States release announcements of May 5, 1934 as new recordings.

19. POPPER—Serenade, op. 54, no. 2 (with Michael Taube, piano; 1932, Germany)

Parlophone E 10263 (w/18)
Parlophone P 9123 (w/10)
Parlophone P 1797; Lindstrom 6959 (w/18)
Parlophone P 1797 was listed in release announcement of May 5, 1934 as new recordings.

20. SCHUMANN—Abendlied, op. 85, no. 12 (with piano and organ accompaniment; 1932 or earlier, Germany)

Odeon 0-7524
Parlophone; Lindstrom 6954 (w/21)

21. SCHUMANN—Abendlied, op. 85, no. 12 (with piano accompaniment; 1932, Germany)

Parlophone 1395-11; Lindstrom 6954 II (w/23)
Listed in release announcements of May 5, 1934, as a new recording.

22. SCHUMANN—Träumerei, op. 15, no. 7 from Scenes from Childhood (with piano and organ accompaniment; 1932 or earlier, Germany)
   Parlophone P 1395-11; Lindstrom 6955 (w/20)
   Parlophone P 1395 was listed in release announcements of May 5, 1934, as new recordings.

23. SCHUMANN—Träumerei, op. 15, no. 7 from Scenes from Childhood (with Michael Taube, piano; 1932, Germany)
   British Columbia C.DX 855 (w/12)
   (May be the same performance as no. 24.)

24. SCHUMANN—Träumerei, op. 15, no. 7 from Scenes from Childhood (with Michael Taube, piano; 1932, Germany)
   Parlophone P 9109 (w/21)
   Parlophone 59075; Lindstrom 20203 (w/21)

25. HINDEMITH—Scherzo for Viola and Cello (with Paul Hindemith, viola; from the Columbia History of Music; January, 1934, London)
   British Columbia (10″ 1S) C.DB 1789
   American Columbia DB 1305 (in Set M-361)

26. BEETHOVEN—Serenade in D, op. 8, for Violin, Viola and Cello (with Szymon Goldberg, violin and Paul Hindemith, viola; January, 1934, London)
   British Columbia C.LX 354/6 (6SS)

27. HINDEMITH—Sonata for Cello Unaccompanied, op. 25, no. 3 (January, 1934, London)
   American Columbia 69001D (2SS)

28. HINDEMITH—Trio for Violin, Viola and Cello, no. 2, 1933 (with Szymon Goldberg, violin and Paul Hindemith, viola; January, 1934, London)
   British Columbia C.LX 311/3 (6SS)
   American Columbia 68274/6D (Set M-209)

29. BEETHOVEN—Seven Variations for Cello and Piano on the Duet "Bei Männern" from Mozart's *The Magic Flute* (with Theo van der Pas, piano; July, 1934, London)
   British Columbia C.LX 331
   American Columbia 68411D
   lp: American Columbia ML 4678 (w/40 & 51)

30. BRAHMS—Sonata for Cello and Piano no. 1 in E Minor, op. 38 (with Theo van der Pas, piano; July, 1934, London)
   British Columbia C.LX 404/6 (6SS)
   American Columbia 68378/81 (Set 236)
   lp: Parnassus 1 (w/1)

31. GLUCK—Melodie from *Orphée* (with piano accompaniment, Theo van der Pas?; 1934, London)
British Columbia C.LX 405 (w/30)

32. RITAKI—*Kojyo No Tsiki,* arranged by K. Yamada (with Fritz Kitzinger, piano; October, 1934, Tokyo)
Japanese Columbia 35450 10″ (w/36)

33. VALENTINI—Allegro and Gavotte, from Sonata for Cello and Continuo in E Major, op. 8, no. 10, edited by Piatti (with Fritz Kitzinger, piano; October, 1934, Tokyo)
Japanese Columbia 5534 10″ (w/34)

34. WRIGHTON—Her Bright Smile Haunts Me Still (with Fritz Kitzinger, piano; October 1934, Tokyo)
Japanese Columbia 5534 10″ (w/33)

35. YAMADA—*Karatachi No Hana* (with Fritz Kitzinger, piano; October, 1934, Tokyo)
Japanese Columbia 35456 10″ (w/31)

36. YAMADA—*Nobara* (with Fritz Kitzinger, piano; October, 1934, Tokyo)
Japanese Columbia 35450 10″ (w/32)

37. YAMADA—*Oshoro Takashima* (with Fritz Kitzinger, piano; October, 1934, Tokyo)
Japanese Columbia 35456 10″ (w/35)

38. HAYDN—Concerto in D for Cello and Orchestra, cadenzas by Klengel (with British Orchestra, Malcolm Sargent, cond.; November 16, 1935, London)
British Columbia C.LX 472/5 (8SS)
American Columbia 68576/9D (Set M-262)
lp: American Columbia ML 4677 (w/42)

39. WEBER—Andantino, from Konzertstück in F (with Gerald Moore, piano; December, 1936, London)
British Columbia LX 643 (1S, w/40)
American Columbia 69083 (w/40)
lp: Seraphim 60117 (w/40 & 42)

40. BEETHOVEN—Sonata for Cello and Piano no. 3 in A, op. 69 (with Myra Hess, piano; June, 1937, London)
British Columbia C.LX 641/3 (5SS, w/39)
American Columbia 69081/3D (Set M-312, w/39)
lp: American Columbia ML 4678 (w/29 & 51)
lp: Seraphim 60117 (w/39 & 42)

41. CHOPIN—Nocturne in E Flat, op. 9, no. 2, arranged by Popper (with piano accompaniment; 1937?)
British Columbia C̡.LX 719 (Also as the final side of LFX 538)
(Possibly the same performance as no. 5)

42. SCHUBERT—Sonata in A Minor for "Arpeggione" and Piano (with Gerald Moore, piano; June, 1937, London)
British Columbia C.LX 717/9 (5SS, w/41)
American Columbia 69341/3 (Set M-346, Side 6 blank)
lp: Seraphim 60117 (w/39 & 40)
lp: American Columbia ML 4677 (w/38)

43. STRAUSS—Don Quixote, for Cello and Orchestra, op. 35 (with the NBC Symphony, Arturo Toscanini cond.)
Live radio broadcast, October 22, 1938

44. BACH—Adagio from the Organ Toccata in C, arranged by Alexander Siloti and Pablo Casals (with Franz Rupp, piano; 1939, New York City)
RCA Victor 10″ (Unpublished)

45. CANTELOUBE—Bourrée Auvergnate (with Franz Rupp, piano; 1939, New York City)
RCA Victor 2166-B (w/46)
lp: RCA Camden 292 (w/46, 48, 49, 52, 58, 59)

46. DAVIDOFF—At the Fountain, op. 20, no. 2 (with Franz Rupp, piano; 1939, New York City)
RCA Victor 2166-A (w/45)
lp: RCA Camden 292 (w/25, 45, 47, 48, 52, 58)

47. CHOPIN—Introduction and Polonaise for Cello and Piano in C Major, op. 3 (with Franz Rupp, piano; 1939, New York City)
RCA Victor 17610 (2SS)
lp: RCA Camden 292 (w/45, 46, 48, 52, 58, 59)

48. FAURÉ—Après un rêve, op. 7, no. 1, arranged by Casals (with Franz Rupp, piano; 1939, New York City)
RCA Camden 292 (w/45, 46, 47, 52, 59)

49. HANDEL—Cantata con strummenti: "Dank sei dir, Herr" (with Hulda Lashanska, soprano, Mischa Elman, violin, and Rudolf Serkin, piano; 1939, New York City)
RCA 15365 (w/50)

50. SCHUBERT—Litanei for All Souls Day (with Hulda Lashanska, soprano, Mischa Elman, violin, and Rudolf Serkin, piano; 1939, New York City)
RCA Victor 15365 (w/49)

51. REGER—Suite for Unaccompanied Cello, op. 131c, no. 1 in G Major (February, 1939, London)
British Columbia C.LX 817/8 (4SS)
American Columbia 69787/8 (Set X-152)
lp: American Columbia ML 4678 (w/29 & 40)

52. BEETHOVEN—Twelve Variations op. 66 for Cello and Piano on "Ein Mädchen oder Weibchen" from Mozart's *The Magic Flute* (with Franz Rupp, piano; July 31, 1939, New York City)
lp: RCA Camden CAL-292 (w/45, 47, 48, 58, 59)
RCA Victrola VIC-1476 (w/58, 59, 65)

53. ALBENIZ—Tango, op. 165, no. 2, arranged by Kreisler (with Gerald Moore, piano; August 2, 1939,* London)
British Columbia BD 1860 (w/54)
American Columbia 17158D (w/54)
*Date is from a white label test pressing in the Smith College collection.

54. CUI—Orientale, op. 50, no. 9 (with Gerald Moore, piano; August 2, 1939, London)
British Columbia C.DB 1860 (w/53)
American Columbia 17158D (w/53)

55. DRIGO—Serenade, from "Les Millions d'Harlequin" (with Gerald Moore, piano; August 2, 1939,* London)
British Columbia C.DB 1866 (w/56)
*According to the 10″ British Columbia white label test pressing in the Smith College collection.

56. RIMSKY-KORSAKOFF—Song of India, from *Sadko,* arranged by Klengel (with Gerald Moore, piano; August, 1939, London)
British Columbia C.DB 1866 (w/55)

57. BRAHMS—Concerto for Violin, Cello and Orchestra in A Minor, op. 102 (with Jascha Heifetz, violin, and the Philadelphia Orchestra, Eugene Ormandy, cond.; December, 1939, Philadelphia)
RCA Victor 18132/5 (8SS, Set M-815)
lp: RCA Victor and LCT-4 and LCT-1016

58. HANDEL—Adagio and Allegro, from Organ Concerto in G Minor, op. 4, no. 3, arranged by Feuermann (with Franz Rupp, piano; December 12 and 14, 1939, New York City)
RCA Victor 18154 (2SS)
lp: RCA Camden 292
RCA Victrola VIC-1476
released November, 1941

59. MENDELSSOHN—Sonata for Cello and Piano no. 2 in D, op. 58 (with Franz Rupp, piano; December 12 and 13, 1939, New York City)
RCA Camden CAL-292
RCA Victrola VIC-1476

60. DVOŘÁK—Concerto for Violoncello and Orchestra in B minor, op. 104
National Orchestral Association, Leon Barzin, cond.
Carnegie Hall, January 27, 1940
Private taping

61. REICHA—Concerto for Violoncello and Orchestra, op. 4, no. 1
National Orchestral Association, Leon Barzin, cond.
Carnegie Hall, January 27, 1940
Private taping

62. STRAUSS—Don Quixote, for Cello and Orchestra, op. 35 (with the Philadelphia Orchestra, Eugene Ormandy, cond.; February 24, 1940, Philadelphia)
RCA Victor 17529/33 (10SS, Set M-720)
lp: RCA Camden CAL-202
lp: RCA Victor SP-33-555 (Limited Edition, Final Variation only)

63. BLOCH—Schelomo, Hebraic Rhapsody for Cello and Orchestra (with the Philadelphia Orchestra, Leopold Stokowski, cond.; March, 1940, Philadelphia)
RCA Victor 17336/8 (5SS, Set M-698)
lp: RCA Victor LCT-14 (10″)
lp: RCA Camden CAL-254

64. D'ALBERT—Concerto for Cello and Orchestra
National Orchestral Association, Leon Barzin, cond.
Carnegie Hall, April 22, 1940
Private Taping

65. BEETHOVEN—Duo in E Flat for Viola, Cello "and a pair of spectacles" (with William Primrose, viola; August 29, 1941, Hollywood, Cal.)
RCA Victor 11-8620 (2SS)
British HMV G.DB 6225
lp: Victrola VIC-1476 (w/52, 58, 59)

66. MOZART—Divertimento in E Flat for Violin, Viola and Cello, K. 563 (with Jascha Heifetz, violin, and William Primrose, viola; September 9, 1941, Hollywood, Cal.)
RCA Victor 11-8846/9 (8SS, Set M-959)
lp: RCA Victor LCT-1150 & LVT-1014

67. BEETHOVEN—Trio for Violin, Cello and Piano no. 6 in B Flat, op. 97 "Archduke" (with Jascha Heifetz, violin, and Artur Rubinstein, piano; September 11–13, 1941, Hollywood, Cal.)
  RCA Victor 11-8477/81 (Set M-949)
  lp: RCA Victor LCT-1020
  lp: RCA Victor LM-7025 (2 discs) (w/68 & 70)

68. BRAHMS—Trio for Piano, Violin and Cello no. 1 in B Major, op. 8 (with Artur Rubinstein, piano, and Jascha Heifetz, violin; September 11–13, 1941, Hollywood, Cal.)
  RCA Victor 18513/6 (8SS, Set M-883)
  lp: RCA Victor LCT-1022 & LVT-1001
  lp: RCA Victor LM-7025 (2 discs) (w/67 & 70)

69. DOHNANYI—Serenade in C for Violin, Viola and Cello, op. 10 (with Jascha Heifetz, violin, and William Primrose, viola; September 11–13, 1941, Hollywood, Cal.)
  RCA Victor 11-8176/78 (6SS, Set M-903)
  lp: RCA Victor LVT-1017

70. SCHUBERT—Trio for Piano, Violin and Cello, no. 1 in B Flat, op. 99 (with Artur Rubinstein, piano, and Jascha Heifetz, piano; September 11–13, 1941, Hollywood, Cal.)
  RCA Victor 11-8394/7 (8SS, Set M-923)
  lp: RCA Victor LM-7025 (w/67 & 68)
  lp: RCA Victor LVT-1000

71. FALLA, MANUEL DE—Jota (with Teddy Saidenberg, piano)
  Audiodisc
  October, 1941
  NBC Los Aneles

72. CHOPIN—Nocturne, op. 9, no. 2 in E flat (with Teddy Saidenberg, piano)
  Audiodisc
  October, 1941
  NBC Los Angeles

73. POPPER—Spinning Song (with Teddy Saidenberg, piano)
  Film
  October, 1941
  Los Angeles

74. DVOŘÁK—Rondo op. 94 (with Teddy Saidenberg, piano)
Film
October, 1941
Los Angeles

75. BLOCH—Schelomo, Hebraic Rhapsody, for Cello and Orchestra
National Orchestral Association, Leon Barzin, cond.
Carnegie Hall, November 10, 1941
Private taping

76. DVOŘÁK—Rondo, op. 94
National Orchestra Association, Leon Barzin, cond.
Carnegie Hall, November 10, 1941
Private taping

77. DVOŘÁK—Waldesruhe
National Orchestral Association, Leon Barzin, cond.
Carnegie Hall, November 10, 1941
Private taping

Addendum

A researcher, Jon Samuels, has uncovered new information and further leads as to Feuermann's recording career. A number of the recordings cited above in the earlier section of the chronology have multiple recording listings. Several of these multiple listings may have been made quite early in Feuermann's career, with Parlophone in 1922 and with Fritz Ohrmann, accompanist. These are:

Anonymous: "Alt-italienisches Liebeslied" (piano)
Schumann: Abendlied (harmonium and piano)
Schumann: Träumerei (piano and harmonium)
Bach: Air (piano and harmonium)
Gounod: Ave Maria (piano and harmonium)
Dvořák: Rondo (piano)
Popper: Serenade (piano)
Cui: Cantabile (piano)

Several other recordings have been reported to exist. We list these and urge collectors to inform us if they are found.

Approximately 1926:

Michael Taube conducting Orchestra (unidentified): Popper: Hungarian Rhapsody
Haydn: Cello Concerto
Popper: Concert Polonaise

1920s, Parlophone, Dr. Frieder Weissman, piano or conductor:

Haydn: Cello Concerto, 2nd and 3rd movements (with orchestra)
Chopin: Nocturne (piano)
Sarasate: Zigeunerweisen (piano)
Schumann: Träumerei (piano)
Schumann: Abendlied (piano)

INDEX

EMANUEL FEUERMANN, VIRTUOSO
was composed in VIP Baskerville
by Bailey Typography, Inc., Nashville, Tennessee.
It was printed and bound by
Lithocrafters, Inc., of Chelsea Michigan.
Project Editors: James R. Travis and F. P. Squibb
Book design: Anna F. Jacobs
Production: Paul R. Kennedy